The Complete California Landlord's Kit

(+ CD-ROM)

John J. Talamo
Mark Warda
Attorneys at Law

SPHINX® PUBLISHING
AN IMPRINT OF SOURCEBOOKS, INC.®
NAPERVILLE, ILLINOIS
www.SphinxLegal.com

First Edition: 2006

Published by: **Sphinx® Publishing, An Imprint of Sourcebooks, Inc.®**

Naperville Office
P.O. Box 4410
Naperville, Illinois 60567-4410
630-961-3900
Fax: 630-961-2168
www.sourcebooks.com
www.sphinxlegal.com

This publication is designed to provide accurate and authoritative information in regard to the subject matter covered. It is sold with the understanding that the publisher is not engaged in rendering legal, accounting, or other professional service. If legal advice or other expert assistance is required, the services of a competent professional person should be sought.
From a Declaration of Principles Jointly Adopted by a Committee of the American Bar Association and a Committee of Publishers and Associations

This product is not a substitute for legal advice.

Disclaimer required by Texas statutes.

Library of Congress Cataloging-in-Publication Data
Talamo, John.
  The complete California landlord's kit / by John J. Talamo and Mark Warda.
 -- 1st ed.
     p. cm.
  Includes index.
  ISBN-13: 978-1-57248-543-3 (pbk. : alk. paper)
  ISBN-10: 1-57248-543-4 (pbk. : alk. paper)
  1. Landlord and tenant--California--Popular works. I. Warda, Mark. II. Title.

KFC145.Z9T353 2006
346.79404'34--dc22

                                                                    2006018568

Printed and bound in the United States of America.
SB — 10 9 8 7 6 5 4 3 2 1

Contents

How to Use the CD-ROM

Thank you for purchasing *The Complete California Landlord's Kit*. We have included every document in the book on the CD-ROM that is found near the inside back cover of the book.

You can use these forms just as you would the forms in the book. Print them out, fill them in, and use them however you need. You can also fill in the forms directly on your computer. Just identify the form you need, open it, click on the space where the information should go, and input your information. Customize each form for your particular needs. Use them over and over again.

The CD-ROM is compatible with both PC and Mac operating systems. (While it should work with either operating system, we cannot guarantee that it will work with your particular system and we cannot provide technical assistance.) To use the forms on your computer, you will need to use Microsoft Word or another word processing program that can read Word files. The CD-ROM does not contain any such program.

Insert the CD-ROM into your computer. Double-click on the icon representing the disc on your desktop or go through your hard drive to identify the drive that contains the disc and click on it.

Once opened, you will see the files contained on the CD-ROM listed as "Form #: [Form Title]." Open the file you need. You may print the form to fill it out manually at this point, or you can click on the appropriate line to fill it in using your computer.

Any time you see bracketed information [ ] on the form, you can click on it and delete the bracketed information from your final form. This information is only a reference guide to assist you in filling in the forms and should be removed from your final version. Once all your information is filled in, you can print your filled-in form.

· · · · ·

Purchasers of this book are granted a license to use the forms contained in it for their own personal use. By purchasing this book, you have also purchased a limited license to use all forms on the accompanying CD-ROM. The license limits you to personal use only and all other copyright laws must be adhered. No claim of copyright is made in any government form reproduced in the book or on the CD-ROM. You are free to modify the forms and tailor them to your specific situation.

The author and publisher have attempted to provide the most current and up-to-date information available. However, the courts, Congress, and your state's legislatures review, modify, and change laws on an ongoing basis, as well as create new laws from time to time. By the very nature of the information and due to the continual changes in our legal system, to be sure that you have the current and best information for your situation, you should consult a local attorney or research the current laws yourself.

· · · · ·

This publication is designed to provide accurate and authoritative information in regard to the subject matter covered. It is sold with the understanding that the publisher is not engaged in rendering legal, accounting, or other professional service. If legal advice or other expert assistance is required, the services of a competent professional person should be sought.

> —*From a Declaration of Principles Jointly Adopted by a Committee*
>   *of the American Bar Association and a Committee of Publishers and Associations*

This product is not a substitute for legal advice.

> —*Disclaimer required by Texas statutes*

Using Self-Help Law Books

Before using a self-help law book, you should realize the advantages and disadvantages of doing your own legal work and understand the challenges and diligence that this requires.

The Growing Trend

Rest assured that you will not be the first or only person handling your own legal matter. For example, in some states, more than 75% of the people in divorces and other cases represent themselves. Because of the high cost of legal services, this is a major trend, and many courts are struggling to make it easier for people to represent themselves. However, some courts are not happy with people who do not use attorneys and refuse to help them in any way. For some, the attitude is, "Go to the law library and figure it out for yourself."

We write and publish self-help law books to give people an alternative to the often complicated and confusing legal books found in most law libraries. We have made the explanations of the law as simple and easy to understand as possible. Of course, unlike an attorney advising an individual client, we cannot cover every conceivable possibility.

Whenever you shop for a product or service, you are faced with various levels of quality and price. In deciding what product or service to buy, you make a cost/value analysis on the basis of your willingness to pay and the quality you desire.

Cost/Value Analysis

When buying a car, you decide whether you want transportation, comfort, status, or sex appeal. Accordingly, you decide among choices such as a Neon, a Lincoln, a Rolls Royce, or a Porsche. Before making a decision, you usually weigh the merits of each option against the cost.

When you get a headache, you can take a pain reliever (such as aspirin) or visit a medical specialist for a neurological examination. Given this choice, most people, of course, take a pain reliever, since it costs only pennies; whereas a medical examination costs hundreds of dollars and takes a lot of time. This is usually a logical choice because it is rare to need anything more than a pain reliever for a headache. But in some cases, a headache may indicate a brain tumor, and failing to see a specialist right away can result in complications. Should everyone with a headache go to a specialist? Of course not, but people treating their own illnesses must realize that they are betting, on the basis of their cost/value analysis of the situation, that they are taking the most logical option.

The same cost/value analysis must be made when deciding to do one's own legal work. Many legal situations are very straightforward, requiring a simple form and no complicated analysis. Anyone with a little intelligence and a book of instructions can handle the matter without outside help.

But there is always the chance that complications are involved that only an attorney would notice. To simplify the law into a book like this, several legal cases often must be condensed into a single sentence or paragraph. Otherwise, the book would be several hundred pages long and too complicated for most people. However, this simplification necessarily leaves out many details and nuances that would apply to special or unusual situations. Also, there are many ways to interpret most legal questions. Your case may come before a judge who disagrees with the analysis of our authors.

Therefore, in deciding to use a self-help law book and to do your own legal work, you must realize that you are making a cost/value analysis. You have decided that the money you will save in doing it yourself outweighs the chance that your case will not turn out to your satisfaction. Most people handling their own simple legal matters never have a problem, but occasionally people find that it ended up costing them more to have an attorney straighten out the situation than it would have if they had hired an attorney in the beginning. Keep this in mind while handling your case, and be sure to consult an attorney if you feel you might need further guidance.

Local Rules

The next thing to remember is that a book which covers the law for the entire nation, or even for an entire state, cannot possibly include every procedural difference of every jurisdiction. Whenever possible, we provide the exact form needed; however, in some areas, each county, or even each judge, may require unique forms and procedures. In our state books, our forms usually cover the majority of counties in the state or provide examples of the type of form that will be required. In our national books, our forms are sometimes even more general in nature but are designed to give a good idea of the type of form that will be needed in most locations. Nonetheless, keep in mind that your state, county, or judge may have a requirement, or use a form, that is not included in this book.

You should not necessarily expect to be able to get all of the information and resources you need solely from within the pages of this book. This book will serve as your guide, giving you specific information whenever possible and helping you to find out what else you will need to know. This is just like if you decided to build your own backyard deck. You might purchase a book on how to build decks. However, such a book would not include the building codes and permit requirements of every city, town, county, and township in the nation; nor would it include the lumber, nails, saws, hammers, and other materials and tools you would need to actually build the deck. You would use the book as your guide, and then do some work and research involving such matters as whether you need a permit of some kind, what type and grade of wood is available in your area, whether to use hand tools or power tools, and how to use those tools.

Before using the forms in a book like this, you should check with your court clerk to see if there are any local rules of which you should be aware or local forms you will need to use. Often, such forms will require the same information as the forms in the book but are merely laid out differently or use slightly different language. They will sometimes require additional information.

Changes in the Law

Besides being subject to local rules and practices, the law is subject to change at any time. The courts and the legislatures of all fifty states are constantly revising the laws. It is possible that while you are reading this book, some aspect of the law is being changed.

In most cases, the change will be of minimal significance. A form will be redesigned, additional information will be required, or a waiting period will be extended. As a result, you might need to revise a form, file an extra form, or wait out a longer time period. These types of changes will not usually affect the outcome of your case. On the other hand, sometimes a major part of the law is changed, the entire law in a particular area is rewritten, or a case that was the basis of a central legal point is overruled. In such instances, your entire ability to pursue your case may be impaired.

Introduction

The reasons for knowing landlord/tenant law are obvious—it is why you bought this book. If a landlord does not know about the law or ignores the law, he or she can lose thousands of dollars in unpaid rent, penalties, and attorney's fees. However, a landlord who knows the law can use the procedures to simplify life and to save money. Knowledge is power, and knowing the laws governing rentals will give you the power to protect your rights and deal with problems effectively.

Laws are written to be precise, not to be easy to read. This book explains the law in simple language so that California landlords can know what is required of them and know their rights under the law. If you would like more details about a law, you can check the statutes in Appendix A, or conduct more extensive research of the California Code and the court cases as explained in the section "Doing Further Research" in Chapter 1.

No book of this type can be expected to cover every situation that may arise. Every year, the California legislature passes new laws regulating landlord/tenant relations, and the courts of the state write more opinions defining the rights of landlords and tenants. Laws change and different judges have different interpretations of what the laws mean. Only your lawyer, reviewing the unique characteristics of your situation, can give you an opinion on how the laws apply to your case. This book can, however, give you the legal framework to avoid costly mistakes.

Chapter 1 gives a clear picture of the local, state, and federal laws that control the landlord/tenant relationship. Chapter 2 deals with creating the landlord/tenant relationship. This involves finding the right tenant and creating the right agreement with that tenant.

Chapter 3 explains the proper way to handle security deposits, including the limits on the amount, when you can use the deposit, and the proper procedure for using it. Chapter 4 discusses the duties of the landlord and the tenant to properly maintain the property, and the remedies available to each if there are violations. Chapter 5 explains when a landlord is *liable* to (can be successfully sued by) a tenant, as well as the difference between actions that are intentional, actions that are careless, and when the landlord is liable even though all possible care was taken.

Chapter 6 explains what may be done when it is necessary to change the terms of a tenancy and how to do it correctly. Chapter 7 deals with the possible problems during the tenancy and Chapter 8 deals with those arising when the tenancy ends. Chapter 9 explores when and how tenancies may end. This includes the unpleasant ways, such as when a tenant leaves because the property becomes uninhabitable or when the landlord must evict the tenant for some violation of the landlord/tenant agreement. Chapter 10 details the eviction process requirements and restrictions. Chapter 11 discusses the method to collect money owed by a former tenant and advice on when it is not worth the effort.

Chapter 12 concerns the rental of storage space and how the law surrounding such properties differs from the law surrounding the rental of a residence. Chapter 13 discusses mobile home parks and the laws that apply to these rental properties. Chapter 14 reminds the landlord that the law is always changing and suggests ways to keep up with the latest information.

Appendix A sets out the statutes that pertain to landlord/tenant laws that are referred to throughout the book. Appendix B contains a flow chart showing the timing for the various procedures of an eviction, as well as the legal holidays in California.

Appendix C contains blank sample forms from the *California Association of Realtors*. The blank forms in Appendix D may be used as described in this book. Most are from the Judicial Council of California and are the required forms for court filings.

When following the procedures in this book, keep in mind that different counties have different customs and some judges have their own way of doing things. Therefore, the requirements in your area may differ somewhat from those outlined in this book. Clerks and judges' assistants cannot give you legal advice, but they can often tell you what is required in order to proceed with your case. Before filing any forms, ask if your court provides its own forms or has any special requirements.

Chapter 1:
Laws that Govern Rental Property

The rights and duties of a landlord are created by ever-changing local, state, and federal laws. These laws are not always clear and may conflict on occasion. The purpose of this chapter is to help you become familiar with the content of the law, how to research the law, and when to hire an attorney.

California Landlord/Tenant Laws

California landlord/tenant law consists of statutes passed by the legislature and legal opinions written by judges. The statutes usually address specific issues that have come up repeatedly in landlord/tenant relations. The judicial opinions interpret the statutes and decide what the law is in areas not specifically covered by statutes.

When reading the laws contained in judges' opinions, be sure to note from which court the opinion originated. If it is not from your district, it might not be binding on your case. Opinions by the Supreme Court of California apply to all courts in California, but opinions by the Courts of Appeal only apply to the districts in which they sit. Decisions made through circuit court appeals of municipal court cases are only binding in the circuit in which that court sits. Municipal court opinions are not binding in other courts, but they may be used as rationale by other municipal courts.

Other California Laws

California laws, also called *statutes,* are passed by the state's legislature. For research purposes, these statutes are grouped in categories called *codes.* Most laws relating to landlords' rights and duties are found in the California Civil Code. However, the California Health and Safety Code,

California Business and Professions Code, and other codes also contain laws affecting the landlord/tenant relationship.

Landlord Tip

Always write down and keep the name of the person you received information from at the government office. You may get contradictory information from different people in the same office.

Local Laws and Regulations

Local (city or county) laws are called *ordinances*. An example of this would be a rent control ordinance. Cities and counties also have agencies, sometimes called *departments* or *boards*, that issue rules regarding rental property. Be sure to check with both your city and county governments for any local laws and regulations that may apply to your property.

Federal Laws and Regulations

Federal laws that apply to rental of real estate include discrimination laws such as the *Civil Rights Act* and the *Americans with Disabilities Act*, and the lead-based paint rules of the Environmental Protection Agency. These federal requirements are explained in Chapter 2 of this book.

The *United States Department of Housing and Urban Development* (HUD) has a handbook that explains the rules applicable to public housing and other HUD programs. Visit **www.hud.gov** and do a search for public housing handbooks.

Doing Further Research

This book contains a summary of most of the statutes and many court cases affecting landlord/tenant laws in California. However, the law is an ever-changing body of knowledge and information that is influenced by several sources. You may want to research your situation further by reading the entire statute section or court case. To do this, you should use the code title and section number or case citation. California code citations appear as "California" followed by the code title and section number (such as *California Civil Code, Section 1951* or *California Business and Professional Code, Section 17217*). Many of California's landlord/tenant laws are included in Appendix A of this book.

As you will realize after reading this book, all of these laws and regulations can create some confusion. Not only do the different laws and rules sometimes overlap and contradict each other, but many are not well written and their exact meaning is not clear. *Cases* are actions brought in court to determine what these confusing rules mean and which ones control in the event of conflict.

Case citations include the name of the case, the volume and page of the reporter, and the court and year. For example, *Clark & Lewis v. Gardner*, 109 Cal. Rptr. 2d 192 (Cal. 1926) means that the case is found in volume 109 of the California Reporter, 2nd Series, on page 192, and that it is a 1926 case from the California Supreme Court.

This book will cover the current law regarding the most common areas concerning a landlord's rights and duties. No book can cover every possible situation. A good rule to follow when attempting legal research is to ask yourself what the consequences will be if you are wrong about the law. If they are minor, attempt the research. If they are serious, consult an attorney who specializes in the problem you are facing.

Conflicting Laws

Occasionally, you will find that the laws conflict with one another in how they apply to your situation. The following are general rules that cover typical conflicts.

- ♦ Federal law controls if it conflicts with state or local law. State law controls when it conflicts with local law. The United States Constitution controls when it conflicts with any other law or regulation.
- ♦ When the laws do not directly conflict, the stricter law controls. For example, when the federal maximum speed limit was in effect, states could not permit drivers to exceed 55 mph. However, the states could require motorists to drive at a slower speed, such as 25 mph in a school zone.

There will be another example of conflicting laws in the section about the state laws and city ordinances regarding rent control.

Fictitious Names

Some landlords conduct their rentals under a business or *fictitious* name. If you use a fictitious name that appears on your lease or rental agreement, you must register the name with the county. Check with your county about specific requirements, such as paying a small fee to the county and publishing the name in a local newspaper.

The proper county to file in is wherever your primary place of business is located. You may want to file in more than one county if your primary place of business is not in the county where the property is located.

NOTE: *Failure to file or filing in the wrong county could delay eviction.*

Rent Control

Rent control ordinances in general are being phased out across the country. California still has several cities with some form of rent control. For example, when the rental price has been decontrolled, there may still be controls such as *just cause evictions* for tenants or succeeding tenants. Do not rely on the following list for all cities where there may be some form of control. Be sure to check with the following city governments themselves if your property is located there.

Berkeley	Oakland
Beverly Hills	Palm Springs
Calabasas	Pasadena
Campbell	Richmond
East Palo Alto	San Francisco
Fremont	San Jose
Glendale	Santa Monica
Hayward	Sunnyvale
Los Angeles	Thousand Oaks
Los Gatos	West Hollywood

The right of California cities to enact rent control ordinances has not only been decided in the California courts, but was affirmed by the U.S. Supreme Court. (*Fisher v. City of Berkeley*, 475 U.S. 260 (1986).)

The problem with discussing rent control is that the laws vary by city and they are amended from time to time. To be sure of the current law as it applies to your property, you must contact the city or county where your property is located and obtain a copy of the current ordinance and regulations.

Exempt Property

Not all property is subject to rent control. State law exempts any property that had a certificate of occupancy issued after February of 1995. (California Civil Code, Section 1954.52.) The rent control ordinance may also exempt property constructed after the date of the ordinance. (Be sure you know the city's interpretation of the date of construction.) Some ordinances also exempt property that only has between one and four units, and some exempt higher-priced rental units.

What to Look For

The following are some major areas that should concern you if your property is subject to rent control. Remember that these rules vary by city and some cities frequently change their own rules.

Registration

Some cities require that the property be registered with their rent control department, which will involve paying a fee. Either the landlord or tenant may request the rent control board to notify them in writing of the proper rent for the property. The board must send the notice to both parties. Either may challenge the amount within fifteen days. The board then has sixty days to review its original decision and notify the parties. If either of the parties fails to properly object within fifteen days after the issuance of the certificate of notification, they *waive* the right to object later unless fraud was involved. (California Civil Code, Section 1947.8(c).)

Failure to register could result in fines, as well as payment of *back registration fees* and the return to the tenants of any rent increases during the time the property was not registered. State law allows the illegal increases to be phased in if the landlord did not deliberately avoid registration (check the statute and any updates to it for the procedure you must follow). (California Civil Code, Section 1947.7.)

Withholding Rent

A tenant may not *withhold* rent solely because the property is not registered. (*Floystrup v. Berkley Rent Stabilization Board*, 219 Cal. App. 3d 1309 (1990).)

Rent Increases

The amount and frequency of *rent increases* will be set out in each ordinance. This may be a percentage of the current rent or a more complicated formula.

Some ordinances do not require adherence to a maximum increase, but ask the landlord to voluntarily follow their formula or to use a *mediation* service to establish a proper rent (mediation, unlike arbitration, is not binding). Do not confuse the word *voluntary* with the word *ignore*. Remember that a tenant who cannot get help from the city may turn to the courts. Completely ignoring the guidelines may be considered *bad faith* or *unconscionable*, and may lead to legal trouble for you.

Extraordinary Rent Increases

Under certain circumstances, such as greater expenses related to the property, the rent may be increased over the ordinarily allowable amount.

Some ordinances allow the rent increase unless the tenant objects within a given time. Then, only if the tenant objects does the rent control board hold a hearing to decide on the merits of the increase. Other ordinances require the landlord to justify the increase to the rent control board before raising the rent.

If you must attend a hearing, try to observe other hearings before your own. You can then decide whether you want to hire an attorney or attempt it on your own.

Tenant's Waiver

In most cities, a tenant cannot agree to a higher-than-allowable rent in place of a hearing when the ordinance requires a hearing prior to the increase. Any such waiver agreement cannot be enforced. (*Nettles v. Van de land*, 207 Cal. App. 3d Supp. 6 (1988).)

Rent Decreases

Some ordinances allow a tenant to request *rent decreases* if the landlord is especially lax in maintenance and repairs.

Vacancy

The effect on rent control of a tenant *vacating* the property varies greatly depending on the ordinance. There are several factors to consider.

◆ If a tenant voluntarily vacates, some ordinances provide for no further rent control. Keep in mind that a landlord making the tenant's occupancy so difficult that the tenant moves out does not qualify as voluntary.

◆ Some ordinances provide that if a tenant voluntarily vacates or is evicted for nonpayment of rent, the landlord may set a new rent without restriction. However, when the next tenant moves in, the rent control laws again apply to the new rental amount regarding future increases and eviction procedures.

◆ Some ordinances control the rental amount even after a voluntary vacancy or eviction for failure to pay rent.

Costa-Hawkins Rental Housing Act

California Civil Code, Sections 1954.50-535, popularly called the *Costa-Hawkins Rental Housing Act*, provides some very limited standards for rent control. The law states that a landlord may set a new rental amount without restriction when a tenant vacates voluntarily or is evicted for nonpayment of rent. Once the new tenant moves in, the property is again subject to rent control when the local ordinance so provides.

Notice that both the state statutes and city ordinances call for a tenant to voluntarily vacate or be evicted for nonpayment of rent in order for the landlord to set a new rent. State law is silent as to the effect of a tenant being evicted for a reason other than nonpayment of rent.

If you are evicting a tenant for a reason other than nonpayment of rent, check with your local rent control board to determine its position. If you do not agree with it, find an attorney familiar with the city and its procedures. You may be able to get the city officials to change their minds without resorting to a lawsuit that you could lose.

The Act exempts certain properties from rent control, as follows.

> *California Civil Code Section 1954.52. (a) Notwithstanding any other provision of law, an owner of residential real property may establish the initial and all subsequent rental rates for a dwelling or a unit about which any of the following is true:*
>
> *(1) It has a certificate of occupancy issued after February 1, 1995.*
>
> *(2) It has already been exempt from the residential rent control ordinance of a public entity on or before February 1, 1995, pursuant to a local exemption for newly constructed units.*
>
> *(3)(A) It is alienable separate from the title to any other dwelling unit or is a subdivided interest in a subdivision, as specified in subdivision (b), (d), or (f) of Section 11004.5 of the Business and Professions Code.*

There are exceptions to this law, so read the entire section in Appendix A or check with your local government agency, especially if your unit is a condominium.

NOTE: *A landlord who violates health and safety codes may not be allowed to raise rent, even if a tenant voluntarily vacates or is evicted for nonpayment of rent. (California Civil Code, Section 1954.53 (f).)*

NOTE: *California Civil Code, Section 798.21 (a) exempts mobile homes from rent control under certain conditions.*

Evictions and Rent Control

Eviction is covered separately in Chapter 10, but the rent control ordinances also include rules that cover evictions. Again, there are different rules for different cities. The biggest difference in rent-controlled cities is that most of them require *just cause,* such as violation of the rental agreement, before a tenant can be evicted. You cannot just decide to terminate the tenancy because you want to rent to someone else.

To evict for just cause, you must first give notice to the tenant as required by law, after which the tenant usually has a *right to cure* the breach. This means that the tenant may correct whatever is causing the landlord to start the eviction. If the tenant fails to cure the breach or vacate, you must then file for eviction in court.

Notice requirements may also be different from state requirements. A tenant may, for example, have to be given notice and a time period to correct the problem or stop the offensive behavior before the actual *notice to quit* (vacate) is given.

Even though also prohibited by state law, some ordinances specifically address *retaliatory evictions* and the penalties for such evictions. Retaliatory evictions are discussed separately in Chapter 7.

The following are allowable reasons to evict.
   ◆ The landlord wishes to occupy the property or rent it to an immediate family member. Not all ordinances agree on who qualifies as a member of the landlord's *immediate* family. Also, some cities require that no similar unit owned by the landlord is available for this purpose. (Heavy fines and large judgments have resulted from landlords using this reason as a ploy to evict tenants. (*Beeman v. Burling*, 265 Cal. Rptr. 719 (1990).))
   ◆ The landlord is going to do extensive remodeling of the property. The tenant will usually be given the right to rent the property again after the remodeling, although the ordinance may allow for a rent increase.
   ◆ The landlord has received all necessary permits and is converting the rental unit to a condominium unit.
   ◆ The property is being removed from the rental market under the provisions of the Ellis Act. (California Government Code, Sections 7060 to 7060.7.)

The *Ellis Act* is a law that allows landlords to evict all tenants. It also requires that all tenants must be evicted. It is usually used to change the purpose of a building, such as converting rental units to condominiums or to a single family use. If the units are rented after the evictions, the rent cannot be raised over the amount before the evictions for five years.

In February 2006, the state court of appeals upheld a San Francisco relocation benefit ordinance requiring the landlord to pay relocation costs of $4,500 per tenant (up to $13,500 per family). Seniors and the disabled receive an additional $3,000. Although the California Supreme Court has not ruled on the case, the decision is likely to stand. Check your local city or county if you plan to use Ellis evictions. Consultation with a lawyer is recommended.

Even when eviction is allowed, relocation costs for the tenant may have to be paid by the landlord. The costs may be higher for long-term tenants.

Security Deposits and Rent Control

Some rent control ordinances have stricter controls on *security deposits* than state law requires. (Security deposits are covered in more detail in Chapter 3.) There may be a requirement that the money be deposited in an *interest-bearing account*, and that the interest be paid or credited to the tenant. Remember that all extra money collected from the tenant—whether called a deposit, fee, or last month's rent—is considered a security deposit. Failure to comply with security deposit requirements may result in the landlord paying interest to the tenant *out-of-pocket*.

> **Landlord Tip**
>
> Some cities with rent control may have requirements for security deposits that differ from state requirements.

Managers

In California, a landlord is required to provide an *on-site manager* (one who lives on the property) for a residential complex over fifteen units. (California Code of Regulations, Title 25.) Some landlords like to have a manager for fifteen or fewer units. This manager may, of course, be the landlord. The following guidelines are important if you decide to hire a manager.

◆ You must treat the manager as an *employee,* even if the manager's only payment is reduced rent. This means following all rules regarding withholding taxes and Social Security, any insurance requirements, safety requirements, and applicable immigration laws. Although reduced or free rent is common compensation, it is not recommended. It is much less confusing, especially if the employment terminates, to pay the manager with money and have the manager pay rent on the unit occupied.

◆ You must *inform the tenants* who the manager is, and how and when they may serve notices to the manager.

You should understand the role a manager will play in your building. The manager, in addition to making some repairs and generally keeping an eye on things, will be your *agent*. This means that your manager's actions may be legally attributable to you. This will be true for those actions by the manager specifically authorized by you. More importantly, you will be liable for the manager's actions not authorized by you if a court decides you *implicitly* authorized them or it appeared that you authorized them.

You may also be liable if you fail to use *reasonable care* in hiring.

Example: *You hire a manager with a conviction for assault. The manager then assaults a tenant. You could be liable—even if you did not know of the conviction—if a court thinks you did not do a sufficient background check.*

Be careful when you hire a manager. Doing the following will help limit your liability.

◆ Run all the checks you would normally run for a new tenant. In addition, look for the qualities you would want in an employee who will receive very little day-to-day supervision.

◆ Make a contract with the manager. This should set out both the manager's duties and compensation.

◆ Use a separate rental agreement if the building's office is in a separate unit and not part of the manager's residence. This will avoid confusion if the employment terminates. If you give the manager reduced or free rent as compensation, it could increase your liability and make it more difficult to get rid of a bad manager.

◆ If the building's office and manager's residence are in the same unit, a combination employment contract/lease may be used.

◆ Attempt to limit liability by letting the tenants know about anything you have not authorized.

Example: *If the manager is authorized to collect rent, let the tenants know that the manager is not authorized to accept cash or checks made out to anyone except you. This can be done in your required notice.*

◆ Give the tenants a way to reach you by mail. You do not want your first knowledge of a complaint to come from a tenant's lawyer because the tenant had trouble with your manager and could not reach you.

◆ Insure against those liabilities you cannot eliminate. Consult your insurance agent.

Management Companies

Unless you enjoy taking a very active role in your property or the cost is prohibitive, hire a *management company*. Any reliable management company will have several advantages:

◆ the on-site manager is the employee of the management company, not your employee;

◆ the company will have experience in hiring, training, and firing managers;

◆ the company will have a contract spelling out exactly what it is required and authorized to do; and,

◆ the company will have liability insurance.

You are still going to have to make sure you hire a good company. Check with other landlords who use them and with a financial rating service.

Other Laws

If you have fifteen or fewer units and do not occupy the property or have an agent on-site, you must make certain disclosures to the tenant regarding *service of process* (where you can be served for the tenant to sue you) and payment of rent. This is covered in Chapter 2 in the section called "Disclosure Requirements."

Telephone Jacks

The landlord is required to maintain all interior telephone wiring and to supply at least one workable telephone jack. (California Civil Code, Section 1941.4.)

Smoke Detectors

The landlord is required to have installed a workable smoke detector as defined by the California Health and Safety Code, Section 13113.7. The Code states that stricter local laws are valid, so check your county or city for the local standard.

Chapter 2:
Creating the Landlord/Tenant Relationship

The landlord/tenant relationship is created in two parts. First, select the right tenant, then make a lease or rental agreement that conforms to the law and is fair to both parties. Both parts are discussed in this chapter. If you follow the advice carefully, you should have a good relationship with your tenant.

Screening Prospective Tenants

The first step in avoiding legal problems with tenants is to carefully choose who will be your tenant. Taking the time to do this right is the key to being a successful landlord. As long as you do not discriminate based on categories such as race, sex, and age (see pages 15–20), you can be selective in renting your property. A tenant who has had the same apartment and job for the last five years will probably be a better risk than one who has been evicted several times.

You should get a written **TENANT APPLICATION** from all prospective tenants. (see form 1, p.185.) Be sure it allows you to contact employers, banks, and former landlords, and to run a credit check. Besides allowing you to check their past records as tenants, the information can be helpful in tracking them down if they disappear owing you rent or damages. Be sure that the form you use does not ask illegal, discriminatory questions, such as a person's nationality.

Make it clear to the prospective tenant that you intend to do a thorough *background check*. This is when you can expect to hear the problems and excuses. Although it is preferable to have the application filled out on the spot, you may give the prospective tenant the application to complete and return to you the following day. You may never hear from him or her again. The prospective tenant's reaction to the threat of a background check may even save you the trouble of actually doing the background investigation.

Fee Charges

You may charge a fee for the expense of a credit report and for your investigative work. You can annually adjust the amount based on the Consumer Price Index. (California Civil Code, Section 1950.6.) The fee allowed at the end of 2005 was $37.57. The law says you cannot charge for a credit report unless you actually get one, you cannot charge for work you do unless you *do* the work, and you cannot charge if you do not have any vacancies (i.e., the tenants will go on a waiting list). Good sense says that you do not want to seem unfair to a prospective tenant, so only charge your *actual costs*.

Credit Reports

One of the most important pieces of information available is the *credit report*. There are primarily two things to look for as warning flags. The first is obvious—the individual does not pay his or her bills. The second is more subtle—the individual pays his or her bills, but is financially overextended. If you are dealing with people who have only received credit recently, how much do they owe? Do you get the feeling that they are going to have future credit problems? If you have a large number of vacant units, you may not have the luxury of being so careful. However, if you are renting a second house and depending on the income, you may be asking for trouble by renting to them if your common sense tells you that these people do not know how to manage credit.

As of March 2006, the credit report scoring system has changed. The new system, called the Vantage Score, is being used by all three major credit bureaus. This means that the scoring system will be the same for all three companies. However, it is still a good idea to get a report from all three, since they may not all have collected the same data. The new scoring system is as follows:

A—901–990
B—801–900
C—701–800
D—601–700
F—501–600

NOTE: *While the three major credit bureaus may start using this new scoring system, you will likely still see and be familiar with the FICO scoring system, which has a low of 300 and a high score of 850.*

Court Records

You should check the *defendant index* of the court records (not just the *official records*) of your county or the last county the prospective tenant lived in to see if he or she has ever been evicted or sued. It would also be wise to check the *plaintiff index* to see if he or she has sued a landlord. In some counties, these indexes are combined.

Prior Landlords

Check with a prior landlord to see if he or she would rent to the tenant again. Do not bother checking with the present landlord, who may lie just to get rid of the tenant. Be sure the people you talk to are really landlords. Some tenants use friends who lie for them.

One thing to consider is how long the tenants have stayed at their previous addresses. If they have a history of moving every few months, they may not be desirable, even if they do pay their rent for the short period of time they stay in your property.

Tenant Investigation Companies

There are some companies that, for a fee, will investigate tenants' employment, previous landlords, court cases, and their own files of *bad tenants*. Some landlords require a nonrefundable application fee to cover such an investigation. Check your phone book under "Credit Reporting Agencies" if you decide to conduct such an investigation.

Immediate Move-In

Occasionally, tenants may apply to rent the apartment and say that they need a place to stay immediately for some reason. They may ask to move in on a *temporary basis* until you have a chance to check references. This is a very bad idea. Once they are in your property, it may take months to get them out. Be sure you check them out before you allow them to move anything into the unit.

Discrimination

Since Congress passed the *Fair Housing Act*, it has been a federal crime for a landlord to discriminate in the rental or sale of property on the basis of race, religion, sex, or national origin. In addition, California has passed its own *antidiscrimination* statute.

In 1988, the United States Congress passed an amendment to the Act that bans discrimination against both the handicapped and families with children. Except for apartment complexes that fall into the special exceptions, all rentals must now allow children in all units.

Civil Rights Act, Section 1982

The *Civil Rights Act, Section 1982* applies only where it can be proved that the person had an intent to discriminate. (42 United States Code, Section 1982 (42 U.S.C. Sec. 1982).)

Penalty

The landlord must pay *actual damages* plus unlimited *punitive damages* for violating this law.

Limitation
There are no time limits to this act.

Exemptions
There are no exemptions to this act.

Fair Housing Act

Under the *Fair Housing Act*, any policy that has a *discriminatory effect* is illegal. After a subpoena is served, failure to attend a hearing or produce records can subject you to a penalty of a fine up to $100,000 or imprisonment for up to one year, or both. (42 U.S.C. Sec. 3601(c)(1).)

Penalty
A victim of discrimination under this section can file a civil suit or a U.S. Department of Housing and Urban Development (HUD) complaint, or can request the U.S. Attorney General to prosecute. Damages can include actual losses and punitive damages of up to $1,000.

Limitation
The complaint must be brought within 180 days of violation of the Act.

Exemptions
This law does not apply to single family homes if:

- ◆ the landlord owns three or fewer homes;
- ◆ there is no more than one sale within twenty-four months;
- ◆ the person does not have an ownership interest in more than three homes at one time; and,
- ◆ no real estate agent or discriminatory advertisement is used.

It also does not apply to a property that the owner lives in if it has four or fewer units.

Coercion or Intimidation
Where coercion or intimidation is used to effectuate discrimination, there is no limit to when the action can be brought or the amount of damages that can be awarded.

Fair Housing Act 1988 Amendment—Residential

The *1988 Amendment to the Civil Rights Act* bans discrimination against the handicapped and families with children. (42 U.S.C. Sec. 3601.)

Unless a property falls into one of the exemptions, it is illegal under this law to refuse to rent to people because of age or to refuse to rent to families with children. While some landlords believe children are more likely to cause damage to property than adults, no additional security deposit can be charged for tenants with children.

The law allows a disabled person to remodel the unit to suit his or her needs, as long as it is returned to the original condition upon leaving. It also requires new buildings of four units or more to have electrical facilities and common areas accessible to the disabled.

Penalty

A landlord must pay $10,000 for the first offense, $25,000 for the second violation within five years, and up to $50,000 for three or more violations within seven years. (42 U.S.C. Sec. 3612.) There are unlimited punitive damages in private actions.

Limitation

The complaint can be brought within two years of violation of the Act for private actions.

Exemptions

This law does not apply to single family homes if:
- ◆ the landlord owns three or fewer homes;
- ◆ there is no more than one sale within twenty-four months;
- ◆ the person does not own any interest in more than three homes at one time; and,
- ◆ no real estate agent or discriminatory advertisement is used.

NOTE: *A condominium unit is not a single family home, so it is not exempt.*

The law also does not apply to property that the landlord lives in if it has four or fewer units. Additionally, there are exemptions for:
- ◆ dwellings in state and federal programs for the elderly;
- ◆ complexes that are solely used by people age 62 or older; and,
- ◆ complexes used solely by people age 55 or over, if there are substantial facilities designed for the elderly, for religious housing, and for private clubs.

Fair Housing Act 1988 Amendment—Commercial

If any commercial premises are remodeled, then the remodeling must include modifications that make the premises *accessible*. All new construction must also be made accessible.

The law does not clearly define what these terms mean and does not even explain exactly who will qualify as handicapped. Some claim that up to 40% of America's labor force may qualify as handicapped. The law includes people with emotional illnesses, AIDS, dyslexia, and past alcohol or drug addictions, as well as hearing, sight, and mobility impairments.

What is reasonable will usually depend upon the size of the business. Small businesses will not have to make major alterations to their premises if the expense would be an *undue hardship*. Even large businesses would not be required to have shelving low enough for people in wheelchairs to reach as long as there was an employee to assist the person.

There are *tax credits* available for businesses of less than thirty employees and less than one million dollars in sales that make these changes. For more information on these credits, obtain IRS forms 8826 and 3800 and their instructions at **www.irs.gov**.

Some of the changes that must be made to property to make it more accessible to the disabled are:
- ◆ installing ramps;
- ◆ widening doorways;
- ◆ making curb cuts in sidewalks;
- ◆ repositioning shelves;
- ◆ repositioning telephones;
- ◆ removing high-pile, low-density carpeting; and,
- ◆ installing a full-length bathroom mirror.

Both the landlord and the tenant can be liable if the changes are not made to the premises. Most likely, the landlord would be liable for common areas and the tenant would be liable for the area under his or her control. However, since previous leases did not address this new statute, either party could conceivably be held liable.

Penalty
The maximum penalties are $10,000 for a first violation and $50,000 for a third violation within seven years.

Exemptions
Private clubs and religious organizations are exempt from this law.

HUD Contact
For more information about the laws, contact the U.S. Department of Housing and Urban Development (HUD) at:

HUD
450 Golden Gate Avenue
San Francisco, CA 94102
415-436-6550
800-343-3442
www.hud.gov

California Laws

In addition to federal laws, California has enacted the *Fair Employment and Housing Act*, enforced by the California Department of Fair Employment and Housing.

The most comprehensive law is California Civil Code, Section 51, known as the *Unruh Act*, which prohibits discrimination on the basis of race, religion, national origin, ethnic background, gender, marital status, age, disability, sexual orientation, income from government assistance, personal traits, and families with children.

Discrimination can take place at any time during the rental process. This includes advertising, negotiating the agreement, during the tenancy (raising the rent, for example), and evicting the tenant.

A few common sense rules to follow are:
  ◆ treat all applicants and tenants alike;
  ◆ keep good records;
  ◆ run credit checks on all prospective tenants;
  ◆ require approximately the same rent and security deposit from all tenants;
  ◆ raise rents and security deposits equally;
  ◆ do not evict one tenant for something you ignored when done by another tenant; and,
  ◆ document all instances that may negatively affect a tenant (this means keeping accurate records of exactly why you refused to rent to a prospective tenant or exactly what a tenant did to deserve eviction).

California allows discrimination based on age by allowing senior citizen-only housing. California Civil Code Sections 51.3 and 51.4 set out the rules. If you plan to acquire, build, or convert to senior citizen housing, consult an attorney.

You cannot refuse to rent to a person with a dog that is used to alleviate the handicap of a blind, deaf, or otherwise handicapped person, even in a no-pet building.

You cannot refuse to rent to a person convicted of drug use or possession, because drug addiction is considered a disability. However, do not confuse this with a drug-dealing tenant. A conviction for the manufacture or sale of drugs would be a legitimate reason to refuse to rent.

NOTE: *A landlord must act to stop the drug dealing, typically by eviction, or be subject to liability.*

Local Laws

Landlords should check their city and county ordinances before adopting a discriminatory policy, such a seniors-only complex.

Agreement to Lease

What are your rights if a tenant agrees to rent your unit but then backs out? An agreement to enter into a lease may be a valid and binding contract even if a lease has not yet been signed. However, as a practical matter, it will probably not be worth the time and expense to sue someone for breaching an oral agreement to lease.

What if a prospective tenant puts a deposit on a unit, changes his or her mind, and then wants the deposit back? If you quickly find another tenant and have no financial loss, the tenant might be able to get the deposit back if the matter went to court. The law is not clear and the result would depend on all the facts of the case.

Landlord Tip

If you give a refund, make sure the tenant's check has cleared first.

To avoid a misunderstanding, you should put on the receipt of the security deposit whether the deposit is refundable.

Rental Agreements and Leases

A lease or rental agreement is a contract. A *contract*, simply put, is an agreement between two or more parties that is enforceable in court. A contract (your lease or rental agreement) may contain anything you want, as long as your tenant agrees to it. However, a contract may not have a provision that does any of the following.

- ◆ *Violates the law*—For example, you could not rent your property in violation of a rent control ordinance.
- ◆ *Is against public policy*—This is less clear, because the purpose may be legal, but not something a court would want to encourage. For example, your city has rent control voluntary guidelines. You rent your property at a substantially higher rent than the guidelines suggest. Does the court wish to encourage this behavior by enforcing the contract? Probably not.
- ◆ *Is unconscionable*—This means the court finds the provision to be so unfair that it cannot, in good conscience, enforce it. Remember this one when you get a tenant who will agree to anything—do not take advantage of such a tenant.

There are different opinions as to whether a landlord should use a *lease* with a set term, such as one year, or an open-ended *rental agreement*. Some argue that they would rather not have a lease so they can get rid of a tenant at any time. The disadvantage is that the tenant can also leave at any time, which means the unit may be vacant during the slow season.

The difference between a lease and a rental agreement is how long the tenant is *required* to stay—not how long the tenant *actually* stays. For example, you could have a lease for three weeks, or a month-to-month rental agreement that lasts for many years. The lease would be for the fixed term of three weeks, and would end at the end of the third week. Under the rental agreement, the tenant could move out at any time after giving proper notice.

Rental Agreements

In all cases, including *month-to-month tenancies*, there should be some type of written agreement between the parties. If the landlord does not want to tie up the property for a long period of time, he or she can use a **RENTAL AGREEMENT** stating that the tenancy is month-to-month. In this case, be sure to include rules and regulations that protect you. (see form 8, p.203.) A **RENTAL AGREEMENT** may include the same rights and duties for the landlord and tenant as a lease. The difference is that a rental agreement is based on the rental period (e.g., weekly or monthly). This creates two important differences from a lease.

1. Either the landlord or tenant may terminate the agreement by simply giving notice to the other. For example, a month-to-month tenancy would require a thirty-day notice.
2. The agreement may be changed by giving the same notice. Most often, this means raising the rent, although any other part of the agreement could also be changed.

Remember that different rules may apply if your property is under rent control or other government regulations such as subsidized housing. Federal laws will supersede state laws, and state laws will supersede city or county laws or ordinances.

Leases

As stated earlier, a **LEASE** is a rental agreement for a set term. (see form 6, p.195.) It can be as short as a few weeks or for several years, but it requires the tenant to stay for the entire period. A rental agreement does not require the tenant to stay beyond each rental period. Most California landlords opt for the rental agreement.

The following are some disadvantages of a lease.

◆ The landlord cannot take back the property until the lease expires or the tenant breaches the lease. For example, the landlord could not evict the tenant in order to move into the property.

◆ If a tenant moves out before the lease expires, the landlord is required to *mitigate* (minimize) damages by making a reasonable effort to rent the property. Failure to do so will relieve the tenant of the obligation to pay rent. A judge may even say the landlord did not try hard enough if he or she is unable to rent the property.

◆ Collection of back rent is difficult at best, especially since most tenants move because they cannot afford the rent.

◆ California Civil Code, Section 1951.4, allows a landlord to collect rent for the remainder of a lease if the tenant moves out without attempting to re-rent the property. Sample leases, such as those of the California Apartment Association, do not contain the required language. However, if your tenant rents from you because his or her job requires frequent relocation and the rental market is not good, you might want to try adding this wording to the lease. The required wording to put into the lease is in the statute and must read in substantially the following form.

> *The lessor has the remedy described in California Civil Code Section 1951.4 (lessor may continue lease in effect after lessee's breach and abandonment and recover rent as it becomes due, if lessee has right to sublet or assign, subject only to reasonable limitations).*

Essentially, this forces a landlord to follow two additional requirements:
   1. the landlord must allow the tenant continued access to the property and
   2. the tenant must be allowed to assign or sublet the property.

On the other hand, a lease may be desirable in certain situations.

◆ If you spend money on improvements specifically for this tenant (common in commercial leasing, but unusual in leasing residential property), a lease would ensure the tenant remains long enough to justify those costs.

◆ If your property is difficult to rent, even the psychological obligation may result in the tenant staying longer than with a rental agreement. Also, you may be able to get back rent if the tenant moves out before the lease expires. If the property is tough to rent, you do not lose much.

Lease Term

If you use a lease, how long of a term should you require? The most common lease lengths are six months and one year. If you lease for a longer term, or if the tenant has the right to renew the lease, you may want to include a rental increase. There are two common ways to do this.

   1. Simply state the increase in the lease. For example, state that the rent beginning on the first day of the thirteenth month of the lease shall automatically increase from $1,000 per month to $1,100 per month. You may want to express this by giving the exact date of the increase.

2. Tie the rent to a government inflation index. Pick one of the indexes that measures inflation and state that the rent shall increase by the same percentage that the index increased for the prior twelve months.

There are many ways to increase rent by passing on to the tenant the landlord's increased costs of the property. This could include increases in taxes, insurance, maintenance, and so on. These formulas may also be combined. However, these are most commonly used in commercial leasing and are beyond the scope of this book.

Required Clauses

There is no special form to create a lease or rental agreement. However, a lease must contain the following minimum information to be valid:

- ◆ name of lessor (landlord) or lessor's agent;
- ◆ name of lessee (tenant);
- ◆ description of the premises;
- ◆ rental rate;
- ◆ starting date;
- ◆ termination date (lease only); and,
- ◆ granting clause ("Lessor hereby leases to Lessee...").

There have been cases where a lease has been held to be valid where one or more of these terms has been omitted if there was an objective means to determine the missing term, but such exceptions are beyond the scope of this book.

Disclosure Requirements

Landlords in California must make certain *disclosures* to prospective tenants. All disclosures should be made in writing. A **CALIFORNIA LANDLORD DISCLOSURES** form is included in Appendix D of this book. (see form 13, p.217.) Disclosures may also be made in the lease or rental agreement itself. These disclosures include the following.

- ◆ If your property is within one mile of a former military base where ammunition or explosives were kept, you must disclose this to a prospective tenant. You can find out if the government ever owned property within a one-mile radius of your property from the county recorder's office or from a title company.
- ◆ If a tenant is going to pay for utilities outside of the tenant's unit, you must disclose this. Most modern units are separately metered. However, if the tenant's meter includes utilities for which the tenant is not normally responsible, disclose it in writing and make some arrangement in writing for proration or reimbursement.
- ◆ The presence of environmental hazards, such as asbestos and lead-based paint, must be disclosed. If your building was constructed prior to 1981, assume there is asbestos present.

If your building was constructed before 1979, there is a good chance it has both asbestos and lead-based paint.

◆ Any demolition to the property for which a permit application has been made must be disclosed.

◆ Prospective tenants must be notified if the property is to be brought to market rate rent by terminating a subsidy contract. Before this law went into effect in 2004, only existing tenants had to be notified.

◆ If the building is over one story high, emergency safety procedures must be posted and tenants must be given a booklet or pamphlet describing the procedures. These must not only conform to the California Health and Safety Code, but must also be approved by the fire marshal. It may also be required that these disclosures be in a language other than English if the lease or rental agreement was negotiated in another language.

◆ California Civil Code, Section 1632, requires that if a lease or rental agreement is negotiated in Spanish, the tenant must receive a Spanish translation of the lease or agreement before signing. The English language lease or agreement is then binding. The translation may be submitted to the Department of Consumer Affairs for an opinion as to whether it is an accurate translation. The California Apartment Association has lease forms with approved Spanish translations. The law has recently been expanded to cover not only Spanish, but Chinese, Tagalog, Vietnamese, and Korean.

OSHA

The U.S. Occupational Safety and Health Administration (OSHA) has both written information and software that will help you identify the presence of asbestos and give you legal ways to eliminate the potential danger. Remember that you may be liable to workers as well as tenants.

EPA

In 1996, the EPA and the U.S. Department of Housing and Urban Development issued regulations requiring notices to be given to tenants of rental housing built before 1978 that there may be *lead-based paint* present and that it could pose a health hazard to children. This applies to all housing except housing for the elderly or zero-bedroom units (efficiencies, studio apartments, and so on). It also requires that a pamphlet about lead-based paint, titled *Protect Your Family from Lead in Your Home*, be given to prospective tenants. The recommended disclosure form is included in Appendix D. (see form 12, p.215.)

The rule is contained in the *Federal Register*, Vol. 61, No. 45, March 6, 1996, pages 9064-9088. More information and copies of the pamphlet can be obtained from the *National Lead Information Center* at 800-424-5323. The information can also be obtained on the Internet at **www.epa.gov/lead**.

Both the U.S. Environmental Protection Agency (EPA) and the California Department of Health Services can help you determine if your property has lead-based paint and what to do about it. Both agencies have booklets that you must give to tenants.

Service of Process and Payment of Rent

New disclosure laws require disclosure of the name, address, and telephone number of the owner or manager for the purpose of *service of process* (where a tenant should serve the papers in order to sue you) and payment of rent. (California Civil Code, Sections 1961–1962.7.)

If you only have an oral agreement, you still must furnish this information to the tenant in writing within fifteen days of your oral agreement. If you have a written agreement (lease or rental agreement), you must furnish a copy to the tenant within fifteen days of the tenant signing it. You must also furnish a copy of the lease or rental agreement to the tenant once a year upon request.

> **Landlord Tip**
>
> The applicable code sections for payment of rent are contained in Appendix A. Read them carefully before deciding how to accept rent. There are also optional posting requirements that are not recommended. You do not want the information available to everyone.

You are allowed to use a post office box for an address to receive rent, but it is conclusively presumed that you received the rent if the tenant proves it was properly mailed (you take the risk of lost mail). You may also require the tenant to pay rent by deposit to your bank account or electronically. You must, of course, give the tenant the necessary information to do this. For deposits to your account, the bank must be within five miles of the property.

Suggested Clauses

The following clauses are not required by any law but are suggested to help you avoid potential problems during the tenancy.

   ◆ *Security or damage deposit clause.*
   ◆ *Use clause*, which is a provision limiting use of the property.

> **NOTE:** *Under the California Health and Safety Code, Section 1597.40, a tenant may use the property as a day care business even if prohibited by the lease or local zoning ordinances. The tenant must first obtain a state license to operate a day care facility on the property, and, after obtaining the license, give the landlord at least a thirty-day notice before starting the business. The maximum security deposit laws still apply, but the landlord may raise the deposit above that of other tenants.*

   ◆ *Maintenance clause*, which spells out who is responsible for what maintenance.
   ◆ *Limitation on landlord's liability for acts beyond his or her control.* It is not legal for a landlord to attempt to limit liability for his or her own acts, but a landlord may limit liability for acts of others beyond his or her control.

◆ *Limitation on assignment of the lease or subletting by tenant.*

◆ *Clause granting attorney's fees for enforcement of the lease.*

◆ *Clause putting duty on the tenant for his or her own insurance.*

◆ *Late fee and fee for bounced checks.*

◆ *Limitation on number of people living in the unit.* This can be a reasonable number based on the size of the unit, but if it causes discrimination against families with children, it could be illegal and subject the landlord to fines.

NOTE: *The safe-harbor rule is a limit of two people per bedroom plus one additional. A landlord could go below that if the landlord had a record of renting to families with children and did not use the limit to avoid children.*

◆ *In a condominium, a clause stating that the tenant must comply with all rules and regulations of the condominium.*

◆ *Requirement that if locks are changed, the landlord is given a key.* Forbidding tenants to change locks may subject the landlord to liability for a break-in.

◆ *Limitation on pets.* Landlords may and usually do prohibit pets except with the landlord's written permission. If you allow pets, be aware of some possible problems. (A landlord may be liable for an injury caused by a tenant's dog if the landlord knew or should have known of the animal's dangerous tendencies and did nothing about it. (*Uccello v. Laudenslayer*, 44 Cal. App. 3rd 504 (1975).))

Landlord Tip

It is not advised that you specify the security deposit is to be used for damage caused by the pet, as this may prevent you from using the extra deposit to cover damages caused by the tenant.

If the pet is a wild animal, you only have to know that the tenant is keeping it to be *strictly liable*—it is presumed dangerous. If the tenant posts signs warning of a dangerous dog, your insurance may refuse to cover the damage, arguing that the danger was known.

You may not forbid dogs necessary for a blind, deaf, or otherwise disabled tenant, nor increase the security deposit in such a situation. Usually, though, you may increase the security deposit for pets.

You may not raise the security deposit beyond the legal limit, regardless of the tenant's pets. This will be further discussed in Chapter 3 in the section on security deposits.

A **PET AGREEMENT** form is contained in Appendix D. (see form 4, p.191.)

◆ *Limitation on where cars may be parked*, such as not on the lawn.

◆ *Limitation on storage of boats, RVs, etc., on the property.*

◆ *In commercial leases, there should be clauses regarding the fixtures, insurance, signs, renewal, eminent domain, and other factors related to the business use of the premises.*

◆ *A clause to protect the landlord if it is necessary to dispose of property left behind by a tenant.* (See the section on "Property Abandoned by Tenant" in Chapter 8, page 64.)

◆ *Attorney's fees.* The lease will control attorney's fees. If the landlord requires the tenant to pay reasonable attorney's fees if the landlord sues and wins, the landlord is automatically required to pay the tenant's reasonable attorney's fees if the tenant wins.

Landlords put payment of attorney's fees into the lease because most suits are brought by the landlord and won by default. The problem is that most of the judgments won are not collectable.

NOTE: *A court may award attorney's fees even if not required by the lease. This usually happens when the court feels that one of the parties should be punished for especially bad behavior.*

Oral Leases

A rental agreement or lease of property for one year or less does not have to be in writing to be valid. The problem, of course, is proving the terms of the oral agreement. Even the most honest people often remember things differently, especially as time passes.

It is best not to use oral leases or rental agreements, even with friends or relatives. Better still— do not use oral leases or rental agreements, *especially* with friends or relatives.

Problem Clauses

Even though both the landlord and tenant sign that they agree to all the terms of a lease, some clauses may not be valid. The law does not allow tenants to give up certain rights. Landlords and tenants cannot agree to an illegal activity. Sometimes a clause is so unfair that a court will refuse to enforce it even if it is technically legal. The best advice is to use common sense and offer a lease that is fair to the tenant while still protecting your interests.

Unconscionable Clauses

If a judge feels that a clause in a rental agreement is grossly unfair, it may be ruled *unconscionable*. Certain provisions in leases are simply prohibited. The prohibited provisions fall into two broad categories.

1. A tenant cannot waive the right to a *habitable dwelling*. These rights are set forth in the California Civil Code, Sections 1941 and 1942. However, the landlord and tenant may agree to the tenant maintaining, repairing, or improving the property. Also, the California Civil Code, Section 1942.1, allows the parties to agree in writing to submit any controversy over the condition of the property to arbitration.
2. The tenant cannot waive the legal remedies provided for in the California Civil Code, Sections 1942.4 and 1953, such as the right to withhold rent or to sue the landlord.

Another problem is a clause in a lease that gives the landlord an illegal advantage over the tenant. A court could decide that the offending clause is unenforceable or it could declare the entire lease invalid.

Clauses by which the tenant agrees to give up a legal right are the most common unconscionable clauses. Examples are clauses in which the tenant:

◆ agrees to pay more rent than the local rent control ordinance allows;

◆ agrees to a *nonrefundable* security deposit;

◆ agrees not to sue the landlord for improper maintenance that causes injury;

◆ gives up the right to withhold rent as allowed by law;

◆ allows the landlord to enter the property without giving adequate notice; and,

◆ gives the landlord the right to evict by *self-help* or without following the legal notice requirements.

Any such clauses—as well as others that a court determines are illegal, against public policy, or unconscionable—will not be enforced.

Buried Clauses

If a lease contains a clause that adversely affects a tenant or might be considered controversial, it should not be *buried* in the lease. It should be pointed out to and initialed by the tenant. If not, a court would be more likely to refuse to enforce the provision. Boldface, eight-point type is the standard for words or clauses that should be noticed. The addition of initials by the tenant would make it difficult to argue that you buried the clause.

Security Deposits

Under California law, any money given to the landlord by the tenant that is above the normal rent is considered a *refundable security deposit*. It does not matter whether you call it nonrefundable, a fee, last month's rent, or a larger first month's rent—it is refundable by law.

The maximum amount allowed is two months' rent for an unfurnished unit and three months' rent for a furnished unit. A tenant with a pet may be charged a deposit greater than that of tenants without pets and it is not considered discriminatory, but it may not exceed the allowable amount.

Water Beds

Under the California Civil Code, Section 1940.5, if your certificate of occupancy was issued after January 1, 1973, you may not prohibit a tenant from having a waterbed. However, the bed must conform to industry standards and the tenant must protect the landlord with insurance. Also, you can require up to the amount of one-half month's rent as an additional security deposit.

Guarantee

One way to protect yourself, especially when renting to young tenants, is to require a guarantee of the lease or rental agreement. With a parent or other relative on the hook, a tenant is much less likely to damage the premises or to abscond without paying the rent. A GUARANTEE OF LEASE/RENTAL AGREEMENT is included in this book in Appendix D. (see form 11, p.213.)

Options

Both residential and nonresidential leases may contain clauses that grant the tenant an *option* to extend the lease for another term or several terms. These options often provide for an increase in rent during the renewal periods.

NOTE: *A clause that automatically renews a lease is required to be in at least eight-point, boldface type. (California Civil Code, Section 1945.5.)*

Option to Purchase

An option to purchase gives the tenant the right, but not the obligation, to purchase the property at some future date, at a preset price. The tenant may elect to *exercise the option* (i.e., buy the property) at any time during the lease, or be limited to some more specific time. If a lease contains an option to purchase, it will usually be enforceable exactly according to its terms.

An option to purchase is usually not a good deal for the landlord. The disadvantage of an option to purchase is that if the option price is less than the market value, the tenant exercises the option (buys). If the option price is greater than the market value, the tenant does not buy.

The advantages of an option to purchase are that a tenant may be willing to sign a longer lease, pay higher rent, and take better care of the property.

Right of First Refusal

The *right of first refusal* may be used as an alternative to the option to purchase. Tenants will often express an interest in purchasing the property if the landlord ever decides to sell. With a right of first refusal, you give the tenant the right to match any offer you receive and are willing to accept from another buyer.

If you wish to give your tenants any rights to purchase as part of the lease, it is suggested that you either have an attorney prepare the agreement or consult a book on the subject.

Forms

There is no special form that must be used to create a lease or rental agreement. However, there are minimum requirements, as explained earlier. For example, an exchange of letters that contained these requirements would be sufficient to create a contract.

This book contains suggested lease forms. Forms may also be obtained from the *California Apartment Association* in Sacramento by calling 800-967-4222 or visiting **www.caanet.org**. Forms regarding court procedures can usually be obtained from the court clerk. Several other books on the subject contain forms and lease clauses. If your situation requires special clauses, you should either consult such a book or a real estate attorney.

Be careful to choose a good lease form. Some forms on the market do not comply with California law and can be dangerous to use. Forms 6–9 in this book are leases and rental agreements developed and used by the author. They are free of legalese and intended to be easily understandable by both parties. You may also need to use forms 12 and 13.

As examples of the importance of proper forms, the 2006 lease form has a mandatory change concerning Megan's Law and the sixty-day notice requirement is no longer in effect. You can no longer ask for bank account numbers on the rental application. In 2007, there will probably be other changes. Joining an organization such as the California Apartment Association can keep you current for both forms and laws.

Payment

Before allowing a tenant to move in, be sure that the tenant has good funds for his or her first month's rent, and especially for the security deposit. This means you should clear the check, or get cash or a cashier's check. This is even more important if the security deposit is a large amount, such as two months' rent. If the security deposit check bounces after the tenant has moved in, you have nothing to secure unpaid rent if you decide to evict. A credit check should avoid the problem, but it does not hurt to be careful.

You may not require cash as the only method of payment for rent or the security deposit, unless a tenant's check has bounced.

Photos or Video

Even if a tenant signs something stating that the unit was in good repair at the beginning of the rental, the old adage of a picture being worth a thousand words is true. A witness to the date you took the pictures or made the video is also helpful. Before and after photos are excellent proof of damage.

Signatures

If you do not have the proper signatures on the lease, you could have problems enforcing it or evicting the tenants.

Landlord

If the property is owned by more than one person, then it is best to have all owners sign the lease.

Tenants

In most cases, it is best to have all adult occupants sign the lease so that more people will be liable for the rent.

Initials

Some landlords have places on the lease for the tenants to write their initials. This is usually done next to clauses that are unusual or very strongly pro-landlord, such as where the tenant is paying utilities for more than just the tenant's unit.

Initials of both landlord and tenant should also be placed wherever any part of the printed form is changed.

Notary

A lease does not need to be *notarized* to be valid. In fact, a landlord should not allow his or her signature on a lease to be notarized because the lease could then be recorded in the public records, which would be an *encumbrance* on the landlord's title and could cause a problem if the landlord then tries to sell the property.

Cosigners and Guarantors

If you have someone sign the lease or rental agreement to ensure payment by the tenant, that individual must also sign any subsequent changes to the agreement, especially rent increases.

Backing Out of a Lease

A lease is a contract that is valid when signed. As long as there is no fraud or illegality involved, neither party may back out. Sometimes, prospective tenants sign leases and then never move in, for various reasons. Usually, the most serious consequence is that the landlord keeps all or part of a deposit, if one has been given. On a long-term lease for a hard-to-rent property, you may want to consult a lawyer to explore the chances of successfully suing for damages. If the property is fairly easy to rent at the same amount of money, filing suit is not worth the effort and expense.

Rescission

Contrary to the beliefs of some tenants, there is no law allowing a *rescission* period for a lease (backing out of the lease). Once a lease has been signed by both parties, it is legally binding.

Illegality

If a lease is entered into for an illegal purpose, then it is void and unenforceable by either party. For example, you could not legally lease your property for the storage of stolen goods or for a house of prostitution.

Chapter 3:
Handling Security Deposits

The law regarding security deposits is controlled by the California Civil Code, Section 1950.5. It applies to rentals that are longer than thirty days, but not to short-term rentals such as hotels, motels, and vacation homes.

Amount

Under California law, any money given to the landlord by the tenant above the normal rent is considered a refundable *security deposit*. It does not matter if you call it a nonrefundable deposit, a cleaning fee, a moving-in fee, last month's rent, or a larger first month's rent payment. Any amount paid at the beginning of the tenancy that is above one month's rent is considered a security deposit and must comply with the law.

The *maximum amount* allowed is two months' rent for an unfurnished unit and three months' rent for a furnished unit. A tenant with a pet may be charged a larger deposit than a tenant without a pet, without liability for discrimination. In either case, the amount may not exceed the two- or three-month limit. A tenant with a waterbed may be charged a maximum of one-half month's rent over these amounts.

Interest and Bank Account

California law does not require that security deposits be kept in a trust account or separate from other money of the landlord. Also, there is no state law that the landlord pay interest on the deposits. However, some cities have local ordinances with such requirements. At the time of publication, the following cities had ordinances covering deposits. If you rent property in any of these cities, you should obtain a copy of the ordinance. As with any list in this book, there may be changes. Check your local city or county, even if it is not on the list.

◆ Berkeley
◆ Cotati
◆ East Palo Alto
◆ Hayward
◆ Los Angeles
◆ San Francisco
◆ Santa Cruz
◆ Santa Monica
◆ Watsonville
◆ West Hollywood

Keeping the Deposit

California Civil Code, Section 1950.5, allows a landlord to deduct only the following items from the security deposit:

◆ unpaid rent;
◆ repair for damages caused by the tenant or the tenant's guest or licensee, exclusive of normal wear and tear;
◆ cleaning after the tenant leaves (cleaning for the purpose of keeping a portion of the deposit is defined as returning the unit to its condition when the tenant moved in); and,
◆ return of personal property or appurtenances if the security deposit agreement calls for it.

The landlord may deduct *damages* from a security deposit, but may not deduct normal wear and tear. What is normal is a question of fact that only a judge or jury can decide using a *standard of reasonableness.* A hole in a wall is clearly not normal. An apartment needing paint after a tenant lived there ten years is normal. Between those, you have to use your best judgment. If you have any doubts, you should get a second opinion from a disinterested person or an attorney. A landlord making a claim on a deposit should *always* take pictures of the damage.

Itemized Statement

The law requires that the landlord give the tenant both an itemized statement and receipts for work done and materials used (if deducting their cost from the deposit) for damages and cleaning. This must be done by first-class mail or personal delivery within twenty-one calendar days after the tenant vacates the unit. It can be done before the tenant vacates, but not before notice to vacate is given by either landlord or tenant. If you have a fixed-term lease, proper notice is no earlier than sixty calendar days before the lease expires.

There are two exceptions—if the total to be deducted for repair or cleaning is $125 or less, or if the tenant signs a waiver. The waiver must be signed by the tenant after the notice to terminate the tenancy by either party or within sixty days of expiration of a fixed-term lease (same as the rules above). The itemized statement is still required and the tenant may request receipts within fourteen days after receipt of the itemized statement, even if the tenant signed a waiver.

If the work cannot be completed within twenty-one days, an estimate can be given. Within fourteen days after the work is completed or receipts are received from the contractor, the receipts must be furnished to the tenant. If you cannot get receipts from the contractor, you must give the tenant the name, address, and phone number of the contractor.

The law specifically states that the landlord (or landlord's employee) may do the work. A reasonable amount may be charged or reasonable estimate given if the work cannot be completed within the allotted time.

California Civil Code 1950.5 (f)(2)(A) If the landlord or landlord's employee did the work, the itemized statement shall reasonably describe the work performed. The itemized statement must include the time spent and the reasonable hourly rate charged.

You should be as detailed as possible in case you are later taken to court by the tenant. You should only take *legitimate* deductions from the deposit, as listed previously in "Keeping the Deposit" on page 34. If you claim things that are not legitimate, the court can assess a penalty of $600, in addition to forcing you to return the deposit. An **ITEMIZED SECURITY DEPOSIT DISPOSITION** form is included in this book as form 22 on page 235. When noting the damages to the premises, you should take photographs or have someone who is disinterested observe the damage.

Address

If the tenant provided you with a new address, you should send the itemized statement there. If not, you should send it to the address of the property. If the tenant has not filed a *change of address notice* with the post office, your notice will be returned to you and will serve as your proof that you complied with the law.

If you wish to learn the tenant's new address, you should write "Address Correction Requested" on the envelope, and you will receive the new address from the post office for a very small fee.

If you try to send the tenant the balance of a deposit but cannot find the tenant, then the money is considered abandoned and is supposed to be turned over to the State of California.

Liquidated Damages

Some leases have clauses allowing a landlord to keep the entire deposit or a certain portion of it if the tenant leaves before the lease is up. Where the clause has been considered a *liquidated damages clause*, it has usually been upheld. However, where it has been considered a penalty, it has been thrown out. It is not possible to say for certain whether a clause will be considered one or the other, because judges have a wide leeway in their rulings. Usually the decision depends upon who the judge considers the good guy and the bad guy in the case.

Example:

In one case, an automatic $200 re-rental fee was considered acceptable. (Lesatz v. Standard Green Meadows, 416 N.W.2d 334 (Mich. App. 1987).)

In another case, an automatic $60 cleaning fee was considered a penalty, and therefore illegal. (Albregt v. Chen, 477 N.E.2d 1150 (Ohio App. 1985).)

In a California case, an additional $65 fee in a lease resulted in a civil penalty against the landlord of $271,000 plus $40,000 in attorney fees. (People v. Parkmerced Co., 244 Cal. Rptr. 22 (Cal. App. Div. 1988).)

Damage Exceeds Deposit

If, as happens in many cases, the damages exceed the deposit, then you should show this in the itemized statement. You can sue the tenant in small claims court for the balance, but this is rarely worth the effort and expense.

Eviction

The statement and receipt rule applies even if you evict the tenant.

Full Statement

You might want to write on the back of the check, "Accepted in full payment of claims against security deposit." However, this might make a tenant want to immediately sue. A check without this language might be cashed by the tenant who plans to sue later but never gets around to it.

Walk Through

Effective 2003, the law requires you to inform the tenant of the right to request an inspection of the property for purposes of possible deductions from the security deposit. This must be done in writing within a reasonable time after either you or the tenant has given notice to terminate the tenancy. The walk-through must take place within two weeks of the tenant's date to vacate.

If the tenant does not make the request, an inspection before the tenant vacates is not required. The tenant can also make the request and then change his or her mind. A written waiver signed by both you and the tenant is necessary. If the tenant makes the request, you then agree upon a time to inspect. The tenant may opt to be present or not to be present.

The tenant can change his or her mind and waive the request in writing. This waiver must be signed by you and the tenant. You must then give the tenant a forty-eight hour notice before you arrive for the inspection. After you inspect the unit, you must give the tenant, at that time, a list of those items you intend to deduct from the deposit.

The purpose of this law is to avoid dispute later over deductions from the security deposit. For example, you inspect the unit and it needs cleaning. The tenant says it is dirty because he or she is moving and it will be clean and repaired before he or she leaves. At least you and the tenant have an opportunity to discuss what you feel is a problem.

You do not have to give the tenant a dollar amount at this time for the work you feel needs to be done. You also are not held to only those things on the list you give the tenant in two instances—if you cannot discover the damage because of the tenant's possessions (a hole in the wall behind a picture or the couch) or if the damage takes place after the inspection. Read the rules in California Civil Code, Section 1950.5, in Appendix A.

Selling or Buying a Property

If you sell a property while holding a security deposit, you should transfer the security deposit to the new owner. You are allowed to deduct for rent owed and for damages caused by the tenant.

If you buy property where tenants have put up security deposits, you should be sure to get a correct accounting from the seller and have the deposits transferred to you at closing or have them deducted from your amount owed. You will be liable for them when the tenants move out. To protect themselves, buyers sometimes request statements from each tenant confirming the amount of the deposits.

Chapter 4:
Responsibility for Maintenance

The duty of a landlord to maintain the property has increased over the years. Today, the first thing a tenant does when something goes wrong is to call the landlord to fix it. This is true even if the tenant caused the problem. This chapter examines the actual legal duties of the landlord and the tenant to maintain the property.

Landlord's Duties

Your duties as a landlord are created in two ways. You must do what you agree to do (this is your *contractual duty*) and you must also do what the law requires you to do.

The contract between the parties, whether a written lease or a verbal agreement, can impose an obligation on the landlord to provide certain types of maintenance. For example, if the lease allows use of a swimming pool or states that the landlord will paint the unit, then the landlord would be obligated under the contract to maintain the pool and to paint as agreed. However, since landlords typically provide the lease agreements, excessive promises are not usual and this issue rarely comes up.

Landlord Tip

If you have a tenant that you trust who is handy, you may allow the tenant to make minor repairs and be reimbursed for the cost of materials. This not only saves you money, but gives the tenant more privacy and the good feeling of being trusted. Always set a maximum dollar amount and do this only with a tenant you know is trustworthy.

Statutes

State law requires the landlord to keep the premises *habitable*. California Civil Code, Section 1941.1, defines *habitable premises* as having:

> *(a) effective waterproofing and weather protection of roof and exterior walls, including unbroken windows and doors;*

(b) plumbing or gas facilities that conformed to applicable law in effect at the time of installation, maintained in good working order;

(c) a water supply approved under applicable law that is under the control of the tenant, capable of producing hot and cold running water, or a system that is under the control of the landlord, that produces hot and cold running water, furnished to appropriate fixtures, and connected to a sewage disposal system approved under applicable law;

(d) heating facilities that conformed with applicable law at the time of installation, maintained in good working order;

(e) electrical lighting, with wiring and electrical equipment that conformed with applicable law at the time of installation, maintained in good working order;

(f) building, grounds, and appurtenances at the time of the commencement of the lease or rental agreement, and all areas under control of the landlord, kept in every part clean, sanitary, and free from all accumulations of debris, filth, rubbish, garbage, rodents, and vermin;

(g) an adequate number of appropriate receptacles for garbage and rubbish, in clean condition and good repair at the time of the commencement of the lease or rental agreement, with the landlord providing appropriate serviceable receptacles thereafter and being responsible for the clean condition and good repair of the receptacles under his or her control; and,

(h) floors, stairways, and railings maintained in good repair.

In addition, for the place to be considered habitable, there must also be dead bolt locks on unit entrances, as required by Civil Code Section 141.3 (see Appendix A) and a properly strapped water heater. (Effective January 1, 2004, local governments are allowed to fine the landlord for a violation. You have thirty days to comply after you are cited.)

The common sense definition of *lacking habitability* is having serious defects that make it very difficult or impossible for the tenant to reside on the property. Cosmetic defects are not included. As previously explained, the landlord may create a duty for cosmetic defects by agreement.

Code Violations

Besides the habitability requirement of the statutes, there are various health codes both at the state and local level. Some of these are contained in the California Health and Safety Code, Section 17920.3, and some are in Title 25 of the California Code of Regulations. Most local governments also have building codes, such as the Uniform Housing Code.

You should be aware that governmental bodies can levy fines of hundreds of dollars a day for minor violations. Ignoring notices of violation can be expensive.

Whenever you receive a governmental notice, you should read it very carefully and follow it to the letter. One landlord, who sold his property and thought the problem was solved, was fined $11,000 ($500 a day for the last twenty-two days he owned the property) for a violation. After you correct a violation, be sure that the governmental body that sent the notice gives you written confirmation that you are in compliance.

Waiver of Landlord's Duties

As a basic rule, landlords cannot get out of their duty to do maintenance by putting it on the tenant. (California Civil Code, Section 1942.1.) However, the statute contains an exception where the parties agree that the tenant will do the maintenance in exchange for lower rent.

As a practical matter, only a small number of units would be suitable for tenant maintenance, such as the single family house.

NOTE: *There must be a true agreement for reduced rent. If the court decides that the tenant has simply waived the right to the landlord's duty to repair and maintain the property, the agreement will not be enforced.*

Tenant's Duties

The duties of a tenant are set forth by California Civil Code, Section 1941.2, as follows.

> (a) *No duty on the part of the owner to repair a dilapidation shall arise under Section 1941 or 1942 if the resident is in substantial violation of any of the following affirmative obligations, provided the resident's violation contributes substantially to the existence of the dilapidation or interferes substantially with the owner's obligation under Section 1941 or 1942 to effect the necessary repairs:*
>
> > (1) *to keep that part of the premises which he occupies and uses clean and sanitary as the condition of the premises permits;*
> >
> > (2) *to dispose from his dwelling unit of all rubbish, garbage and other waste, in a clean and sanitary manner;*
> >
> > (3) *to properly use and operate all electrical, gas, and plumbing fixtures and keep them as clean and sanitary as their condition permits;*
> >
> > (4) *not to permit any person on the premises with his permission to willfully or wantonly destroy, deface, damage, impair, or remove any part of the structure or dwelling unit or the facilities, equipment, or appurtenances thereto, nor himself do any such thing; and/or,*
> >
> > (5) *to occupy the premises as his abode, utilizing portions thereof for living, sleeping, cooking, or dining purposes only which were respectively designed or intended to be used for such occupancies;*

(b) Paragraphs (1) and (2) of subdivision (a) shall not apply if the owner has expressly agreed in writing to perform the act or acts mentioned therein.

The landlord may agree to perform the requirements of paragraphs (1) and (2). The agreement must be in writing.

Tenant's Remedies

If the landlord has failed to comply with his or her duty to do proper maintenance, the law offers the tenant several possible remedies, depending on the severity of the situation.

Withholding Rent

If a landlord violates the maintenance requirements of the statutes or the health and safety codes, and such violation renders the premises *uninhabitable*, then the tenant can withhold all or part of the rent until proper repairs are made.

Whether the tenant is legally entitled to withhold rent can only be determined in court, meaning the landlord would need to bring an action to either collect the rent or evict the tenant. Since this is time-consuming, expensive, and risky, the landlord would be well advised to work with the tenant to correct the alleged problems and have the rent paid voluntarily.

However, the claim that rent is being withheld for a maintenance violation is most often made after the tenant has been taken to court for failure to pay rent. Unfortunately, the law does not require the tenant to give the notice in writing or to produce proof of delivery, so a tenant can claim to have given notice of withholding rent for a maintenance violation after an eviction has been started.

Repair and Deduct

If the problem with the premises renders the premises *untenantable* and the landlord fails to remedy it within a reasonable time, then the tenant is allowed to make the repair and deduct the cost from the next month's rent under California Civil Code, Section 1942. This remedy cannot be used more than twice in a twelve-month period.

Whether the premises are untenantable is a legal question that would depend on the facts of the situation. A clogged toilet or a broken window in the winter would most likely make the premises untenantable, while a slight drip in a faucet or a burned-out bulb where other light is available probably would not.

What is a reasonable time in which to remedy the situation is also a legal question that depends on the facts. The law says that thirty days is clearly reasonable. But a much shorter time would also be reasonable for many problems.

The tenant must give the landlord reasonable notice of the problem before using this remedy. The notice can be verbal and does not have to be in writing. The problem cannot be caused by the tenant or a violation of the tenant's duties.

If the premises are actually untenantable and the landlord refuses, after a reasonable amount of time, to remedy the situation, the tenant also has the option of moving out. A tenant using this remedy where there is substantial time remaining on the lease is taking a risk that he or she will be sued for breach of the lease.

Moving Out

If the premises are actually untenantable, then the landlord would be wasting time tracking the tenant down and filing a suit. If the situation is minor and used as an excuse to break the lease, the landlord might want to take the matter to court. If so, the landlord should be prepared with photographs and witnesses to prove that the condition of the premises was not as bad as claimed.

Chapter 5:
Landlord's Liabilities

The law of liability for injuries and crime on rental property has changed considerably over the last couple decades. The law for hundreds of years—that landlords were not liable—was overturned and landlords are now often liable, even for conditions that are not their fault.

General Rules of Landlord Liability

The landlord has a duty to make conditions safe or adequately warn of dangerous conditions. However, warning is only a temporary safeguard until the premises can be made safe. This duty applies not only to what is usually thought of as dangerous conditions, such as a broken step or cracked walkway, but also to the actions of others. This means criminal acts by tenants and non-tenants may create liability for the landlord.

There are three ways for a landlord to create liability—through *intentional acts*, *negligence*, and *strict liability*.

Intentional Acts

An *intentional act* is one that the landlord affirmatively does. For example, a landlord assaults a tenant. Assault, by definition, is intentional. It is both a crime and a *tort*. This means the landlord could be both prosecuted for the crime (fined or jailed) and sued by the tenant in civil court for damages (money).

Harassing a tenant or defrauding a tenant out of property can result in a $2,000 fine. This does not preclude the tenant from suing the landlord or pursuing criminal charges.

Negligence

The basis of the vast majority of liability is *negligence*. In order to have liability for negligence, four elements must be present.

Duty. The defendant (landlord) must owe a duty to the plaintiff (the one who is suing). That duty will extend to almost anyone who is injured on the property—not just a tenant.

Owing a duty to the plaintiff means that the relationship between the parties requires that the defendant must use reasonable care to avoid damage to the plaintiff. For example, if a visitor to the building saw a discarded banana peel on the ground, the visitor would have no duty to remove it and would not be liable for any subsequent injury caused by someone slipping on it. The landlord, seeing the same peel, would have a duty to remove it, and would incur liability for a subsequent injury.

A duty may sometimes be created by the landlord where none previously existed. For example, there may be no duty to have an alarm system in the building. However, if the landlord installs one, he or she may be liable if there is failure to keep it in good working order and someone is injured because it failed.

Breach of duty. A breach of duty is the failure to use *reasonable care*. This is usually what is contested. If the landlord did everything he or she reasonably could to prevent the damage or injury to the plaintiff, he or she is not liable. The problem is that *reasonableness* is subjective. A judge or jury may have a much different idea of what is reasonable than the landlord.

The term *standard of care* refers to what constitutes reasonableness. For example, someone attempting to give first aid to an automobile accident victim would be held to a higher standard if he or she were a doctor than someone without medical training. The standard of care may be greater if the landlord makes promises beyond the normal standards. These promises commonly concern safety from crime, and are contained in advertisements and in direct communication with the tenant.

Causation. The breach of duty by the landlord must have caused the plaintiff's injury or damages. If you had an inadequate lock on a door (failure to use reasonable care), but the burglar came in through the window, there was no causation.

Damages. The plaintiff must be injured or suffer some loss as a result of the negligent conduct of the landlord.

Another common basis for a landlord's liability is what is called *negligence per se*. This is a presumed or automatic failure to use reasonable care, and it arises when a landlord violates a law. A common example would be failing to fence off a swimming pool. (You still need a duty, causation, and damages to be liable for negligence.)

Strict Liability

Strict liability is like negligence, except there is no need to prove breach of duty. The basis of strict liability is an unusually *dangerous activity*. If a landlord were having a fireworks display and something went wrong that caused injury, the fact that the landlord used reasonable care would not be a defense. The same would be true if a landlord allowed a tenant to keep what would normally be considered a wild animal and someone were injured by it.

Accidents

The word *accident* can have two meanings. It can mean something that happens without fault by anyone. It can also mean something that could have (or should have) been prevented. The second meaning is the one that creates liability.

Areas Under the Landlord's Control

A landlord is liable for failure to use reasonable care in keeping areas under the landlord's control safe for the tenants and others who may use them. This means that the landlord is liable if:

- ◆ the landlord created the dangerous condition;
- ◆ the dangerous condition would have been discovered by a reasonable inspection; or,
- ◆ the landlord knew of the dangerous condition. (The California Supreme Court reversed its previous ruling that a landlord could be strictly liable for a dangerous condition that did not meet the above test of liability. (*Peterson v. Superior Court of Riverside County* (10 Cal. 4th 1185).))

Areas Not Under the Landlord's Control

The general rule is that a landlord is not liable for injuries on parts of the premises not under his or her control, except:

- ◆ where there is a danger known to the landlord;
- ◆ where there is a violation of law in the condition of the premises;
- ◆ where there is a preexisting defect in construction; or,
- ◆ where the landlord undertakes to repair the premises or is required by the lease to make the repairs.

Pets

The same rules that apply to accidents caused by dangerous conditions apply to injuries caused by pets. If the landlord knows that a pet owned by a tenant is dangerous, then the landlord can be liable if the pet injures someone. Some courts have even held landlords liable when a tenant's dog bit a friend who was visiting the tenant.

How can a landlord know if a tenant's pet is dangerous? With most common types of cats and dogs, the landlord will not know unless someone reports to the landlord that the pet is vicious.

However, if the pet is obviously dangerous, such as possibly a pit bull or definitely a poisonous snake, then the landlord is assumed to know the condition is dangerous and would be liable for any injuries.

Crimes Against Tenants

Another area where liability of landlords has been greatly expanded is in the area of crimes against tenants. The former theory of law was that a person could not be held liable for deliberate acts of third parties. However, that theory has recently been abandoned in favor of a theory that a landlord must protect tenants from crimes.

The theory is that where the landlord can foresee the possibility of criminal attack, the landlord must take precautions to prevent it. However, the law is still evolving in this area, and some courts have said that this means any time an attack is possible the landlord must protect the tenant. This would include nearly every tenancy, especially in urban areas.

There are several ways a landlord may be liable for crimes committed on the premises, including the following.

◆ *Renting to a tenant who is dangerous, when the landlord knows or should have known of the danger.* (Of course, it is difficult to know whether an applicant is dangerous. Using a person's looks to make such a determination could make the landlord liable for discrimination. If a tenant turns out to be dangerous after beginning a rental and the landlord fails to terminate the tenancy, the landlord could be liable for crimes committed by the tenant.)

◆ *Dangerous conditions.* (If windows do not lock properly, halls are not well-lit, or bushes create good hiding places for muggers, this can create liability for the landlord.)

◆ *Inadequate security.* (In high crime urban areas, some courts have ruled that landlords can be liable for crimes if they fail to provide protection for their tenants and their guests in the form of security guards.)

◆ *Broken promises.* (If a lease or advertisement for the property promises certain types of security, such as locked garages or security guards, then the landlord can be liable for failing to provide these or for letting them fall out of repair. Even general terms in advertising, such as "safe" or "secure," can cause a landlord to be liable if there is a crime committed.)

Crimes by Tenants Against Non-Tenants

Another evolving area of law where landlords were previously not liable, but are now subject to liability, involves crimes by tenants against non-tenants. Landlords who know of a tenant's criminal activity and do nothing to remove the tenant from the premises may be liable to the injured third party. This area of liability for landlords is still developing, and it is unclear to what extent a landlord can be held responsible to third parties for a tenant's crimes.

Protection from Liability

With juries awarding multimillion dollar verdicts, the owner of rental property is at great risk in the event of an injury to a tenant. The following sections cover some of the ways you can protect yourself.

Insurance

Insurance is the most important thing a landlord can have for protection from liability. Even the most careful landlord can have problems. Fortunately, an *umbrella liability policy*, offering coverage of a million dollars or more, can be available at a reasonable fee. However, insurance alone is not enough. There are many verdicts awarded each year that exceed insurance limits.

Tenant Relations

By maintaining *good relations* with tenants, a landlord can avoid bad feelings that inspire lawsuits. Even serious matters are often overlooked or settled easily when people have a good relationship. If at all possible, you should seek to stay on good terms with your tenants.

Asset Protection

Every person with substantial assets, especially risky assets like rental property, should use *asset protection techniques*. Such techniques make personal assets untouchable from all types of claims. For example, you can keep equity in a homestead, pension plan, family limited partnership, or certain types of trusts.

Contractual Protections

It is not legal for a landlord to provide in the lease that he or she is not liable for his or her own acts of negligence or for other liabilities that the law specifically places on the landlord. However, the landlord can sometimes avoid liability by putting duties that can result in liability on the tenant. For example, if a lease put the responsibility for certain maintenance or for repair of a lock on a tenant, then the landlord *might* be free from liability if a defect in either of these causes an injury.

This might not be upheld by a court in every case, but it offers one more line of defense that might dissuade a trial lawyer from taking the case. It would be most useful in a single family home or duplex, but might not work well in a building with more apartment units.

Security Guards

In some inner-city apartment complexes where crime is common, landlords may be required to provide armed guards or face liability. Again, insurance is a must and this additional cost will have to be covered by rent increases.

Background Checks

There are two kinds of background check reports. One is a financial report—the credit report. The law is clear that you can, with the applicant's permission, get a credit report. It is also clear that poor credit is a legitimate reason to deny a rental unit, as long as you use the same standard for all applicants.

The other type of report is the *investigative* report. Generally, these have been criminal background checks (discussed later), but a new issue is currently emerging that involves whether checking court records for *unlawful detainer* actions (evictions) against the applicant is investigative. If it is decided that it is, a procedure of notification to the applicant must be followed, which is different from notification for a credit report. A clear answer to this question has not currently been decided.

The type of report that is definitely investigative is the criminal background check. There is no requirement that you do a criminal background check. The following are some advantages and disadvantages to having a criminal background check performed.

The obvious advantage is to deny a rental unit to someone who is a danger to other tenants or to the property. Convictions for crimes such as sexual assault, burglary, or arson are examples of the types of crimes that could endanger other tenants or the property.

However, you should ask yourself further questions if a prospective tenant turns out to be a convicted criminal. How long ago did the crime take place? Was it the type of crime that would affect the normal obligations of a tenant? Were there several arrests but no convictions? What about crimes that were plea bargained down to misdemeanors? The tendency is to refuse a rental unit as soon as you see a criminal record, but the law says that you cannot do that.

Suppose you decide to rent to an applicant who later attacks another tenant. Are you then liable because you knew of the tenant's past crimes, making the attack *foreseeable*?

The procedure is relatively simple. Tell the applicant that you are going to do a criminal background check. The applicant may simply withdraw the application. If not, within three days of ordering the report, give the applicant a written statement saying that the report has been ordered. Include a box that the applicant can check that says that the applicant wants a copy of the report. If the box is checked, give the applicant a written copy of the report within three days of when you receive it.

Because the law is unclear, you should consult a lawyer to create a plan to be sure that you are not discriminating against applicants, and yet, are not opening yourself up to liability for later foreseeable crimes or torts by those you accept. This is one area of the law that carries major adverse consequences if you do it wrong.

Another problem involves registered sex offenders. Under *Megan's Law*, you can now look up registered sex offenders on the Internet, including their addresses. If you rent to one, it is likely that your other tenants will find out, and many will protest or vacate. If you refuse to rent based on Megan's Law information, you violate California law. If you get the information from another source, you do not violate the law.

To illustrate further how confusing the present situation is, if you are receiving any federal housing subsidies, the law is different. The federal law conflicts with California law. Federal law requires you to refuse renting to those convicted of certain crimes, whereas California law may not allow you to refuse renting for the same crimes. Consult a lawyer before doing criminal background checks and for further help deciphering the laws associated with them.

Proposition 65

Proposition 65 requires a business with ten or more employees to post a warning of unsafe drinking water or chemicals that may cause harm or birth defects. It had little impact on rental property until recently, when lawsuits were filed against property owners. The suits alleged that owners violated the law by not warning of tobacco smoke and some common household chemicals.

The law does not require that you specify any or all possible hazards. There are about 750 chemicals on the current list, which changes on a regular basis. However, since some chemicals on the list may be present in any rental unit, you should post the warning.

A notice in large, boldface type (the law says *clear and reasonable* type) similar to form 49 on page 297 should be posted.

In addition, it is advisable to let your tenants know that your property is not some sort of toxic waste dump. This can be done with a letter stating that the law (Proposition 65) requires posting if there are known dangerous chemicals. These chemicals include secondhand tobacco smoke, car exhaust fumes, and common pesticides used in landscaping. Indicate that you are posting the warning to comply with the law and know of no specific chemicals to be present that are not usually associated with an apartment complex.

You may also attach the Office of Environmental Health Hazard Assessment (OEHHA) fact sheet for tenants. It also states that property owners are posting for protection against lawsuits even if there are no dangerous chemicals present. Download it from the OEHHA website at **www.oehha.ca.gov/prop65/pdf/Prop65tenants.pdf**, or use the one provided in Appendix D. (see form 49, p.297.)

Mold

The problem of mold is a fairly recent development. Mold has been around for a long time, but agencies responsible for protecting our environment have only recently begun to address the problem in rental housing. The federal Environmental Protection Agency (EPA) and the California Department of Health Services have established guidelines to protect tenants against harm from mold.

The guidelines include identification, prevention, remedies, and disclosure. Visit the EPA website at **www.epa.gov/iaq/largebldgs/graphics/iaq.pdf** for detailed information with diagrams to identify the most likely places to find mold and how to correct the problem. The site shows simple and practical ways to prevent mold, as well as what to do when the problem is extensive. The California Department of Health Services has guidelines on its website at **www.dhs.ca.gov**, as well as links to other helpful publications.

The law is still evolving on this issue, and landlord responsibility and liability will become clearer within the next few years. It is clear, however, that if the landlord knows or should have known that mold exists on the rental property, he or she could be sued for a lot of money. If there is a complaint about mold, it should be responded to immediately. If the landlord does not know what to do, he or she can bring in a company that does inspections. The company will be able to recommend corrective measures.

Chapter 6:
Changing the Terms of the Tenancy

The landlord/tenant relationship is no different from any other relationship—it will very likely change over time. The original situation may change, requiring a change in the agreement between the parties. This can be as simple as raising the rent to keep up with the market, or it can be more complicated, such as a tenant leaving before the lease expires and wanting someone else to take over his or her obligations. The ability to change the original terms of the tenancy will be governed by the agreement between the parties (lease or rental agreement) and the requirements of the law.

Assignment or Sublease by Tenant

Sometimes a tenant will seek to turn over all or part of the premises to a third party. This can be done in one of two ways—an assignment or a sublease.

Assignments

In an *assignment*, a tenant assigns all of his or her interest in a lease to another party, who then takes over the tenant's position. The new tenant takes the place of the original tenant and deals directly with the landlord. The new tenant pays rent directly to the landlord.

Sublease

In a *sublease*, the original tenant leases all or part of the property to a third party. This new party (called a *subtenant* or *sublessee*) is responsible to the original tenant (called the *sublessor*). The original tenant is still responsible to the landlord. The sublessee pays his or her rent to the sublessor, who then pays his or her rent to the landlord.

Validity

Subleases and assignments are allowed unless prohibited by the terms of the lease. However, even if prohibited by the lease, a problem arises as California law places a *duty to mitigate* on the landlord. This means that a landlord has a duty to make reasonable efforts to rent the property in the event the tenant leaves before the end of the lease term. If your tenant offers you a new tenant who is reasonably acceptable, you cannot say no and still hold the original tenant liable for rent for the balance of the lease term.

Approval

The safest way to handle a sublease or assignment is to require the landlord's written consent. This way you can screen the proposed new tenant and make a more informed decision as to whether to allow the sublease or assignment. This will also help in the event of eviction. You must specifically evict an assignee or subtenant.

Waiver

Express consent (with words) to the sublease or assignment may be waived by *implied consent* (by conduct). Accepting rent from the new tenant, or knowingly allowing a guest to stay beyond the time specified in the lease or rental agreement, may waive your right to later object.

Landlord Tip

If you raise the rent by a notice, remember that you must give sixty days' notice if the increase is more than 10% in one year.

Modifying the Lease

You may raise the rent or security deposit if more people are going to occupy the unit. You may draw up a new lease that all adult occupants will sign or you may use a thirty-day notice for a rental agreement. Be careful to check rent control laws if applicable to your property, and do not exceed the maximum allowed security deposit.

Sale of Property by Landlord

A landlord has the right to sell property covered by a lease, but the new owner takes the property subject to the terms of any existing lease. The new owner cannot cancel the old lease or raise the rent while the lease is still in effect (unless the lease has provisions allowing the landlord to do so).

When selling property, the contract should make it clear to the buyer that the sale is subject to existing leases. Otherwise, the buyer may sue for failure to deliver the premises free and clear of other claims.

At closing, the leases should be assigned to the buyer. Also, any security deposits need to be transferred to the buyer or returned to the tenants. When the buyer inspects the property, any damage found should be deducted from the deposit, if it is to be returned to the tenant.

If you transfer the security deposit to the buyer, send the tenant a letter containing the buyer's name and address, notification of the transfer of the security deposit, and an itemized statement of any deductions for unpaid rent or damage to the property. The buyer may then demand that the tenant bring the security deposit back up to the agreed-upon amount.

Foreclosures

When property is purchased at a foreclosure sale, the leases of the tenants are terminated if they were signed after the effective date of the mortgage (usually the date it was recorded).

Raising the Rent

If a tenancy is for a set term (such as a one-year lease) at a specified rent, then you cannot raise the rent until the term ends, unless this right is spelled out in the lease. If the tenancy is month to month, then you would be able to raise the rent by giving notice at least thirty days in advance. This is based upon the requirement of thirty days' notice to terminate the tenancy.

To raise the rent in a month-to-month tenancy, you can use form 16 on page 223. In such a case, the tenant would probably not have to give thirty days' notice if he or she decided not to stay until the end of the month. This is because by raising the rent, you would be terminating the previous tenancy and making the tenant an offer to enter into a new tenancy at a different rental rate.

California Civil Code, Section 1946, allows the parties to shorten the notice period when the rental agreement is created to as little as seven days. However, there is confusion about raising rent by a seven-day notice; therefore, a thirty-day agreement in the rental agreement is advised. You may also raise the security deposit to reflect the increase in rent. The same notice requirements apply.

How to Raise the Rent

Most commonly, rent is increased on the date it is due (usually the first of the month). This is not a legal requirement, and rent may be raised on any date if the proper notice is given. If you raise the rent in the middle of a rental period, you must prorate the rent. This means you must figure out how much rent is due before and after the increase to the next usual rent payment date.

Most rent increases are accomplished by mailing a notice to the tenant. California Civil Code, Section 827, allows mailing as an acceptable form of notice without first attempting to serve the tenant personally. Personal service is still allowed, and California Code of Civil Procedure, Section 1162, contained in Appendix A, describes what you must do should you wish to use it.

You may use the regular mail, but you must be able to prove that you sent it to the right address with proper postage. This can be done by affidavit. It is easier to do it by sending certified mail. (You can also send overnight mail and even a fax if your tenant has agreed to it in writing, but the recommended way is to send it by certified mail.)

Notice Requirements for Mailing

If you use the mail, you must allow extra time for your notice. If mailed in California, allow five extra days. If mailed outside of California but within the United States, allow ten extra days. If mailed outside the United States, allow twenty extra days.

Example: *If you send a notice on June 1ˢᵗ from within California, make it effective no earlier than July 6ᵗʰ.*

If you raise the rent more than 10% in a one-year period, you must give a sixty-day notice. The 10% increase does not have to be all at once. For example, if you raise the rent by 5% in January and 6% in July, the July increase will require a sixty-day notice. You are still required to add the extra time for mailing.

The relevant code sections (California Civil Code, Section 827 and California Code of Civil Procedure, Section 1013) are contained in Appendix A.

> **Warning:** Rent control or any other government program, such as subsidized housing, may affect your ability to raise rents and security deposits, as well as the procedure for doing so.

Modifying the Lease

If you agree to modify the terms of your lease with a tenant, you should put it in writing. If you do not and you allow a tenant to do things forbidden in the lease, you may be found to have waived your rights. A simple modification form, AMENDMENT TO LEASE/RENTAL AGREEMENT, is included in this book. (see form 10, p.211.)

Chapter 7:
Problems During the Tenancy

Even if you find good tenants and draw up a good and fair lease or rental agreement, there will always be problems. This chapter examines some of these problems from the legal perspective. It points out what the law allows and forbids you to do when problems arise.

Landlord's Access to the Premises

California Civil Code, Section 1954, is specific as to a landlord's right to enter a tenant's unit. According to the statute, the landlord has the right to enter a tenant's unit:

- ◆ in an emergency (the statute does not define *emergency*);
- ◆ to make necessary or agreed-upon repairs, decorations, alterations, improvements, or services;
- ◆ to show the unit to prospective buyers, mortgagees, tenants, or workmen;
- ◆ when the unit has been abandoned or surrendered;
- ◆ pursuant to a court order; or,
- ◆ by invitation or consent of the tenant.

Notice

Except in cases of emergency, abandonment, or surrender, the landlord can enter only during normal business hours. The statute does not define normal business hours. Some lease forms call for entry between 8 a.m. and 6 p.m., Monday through Saturday.

Except in cases of emergency, abandonment, or surrender, or when it is impracticable, reasonable notice must be given. The statute defines reasonable notice time as twenty-four hours.

The law allows a landlord to enter a unit without giving the tenant twenty-four hours' written notice when the tenant makes a request for repairs or other service.

The notice to the tenant must be in writing. It can be handed to the tenant, or if no one is at the unit, it can be handed to someone of suitable age in the unit or slipped under the door where the tenant usually enters.

NOTE: *California Civil Code, Section 1953, prohibits a tenant's waiver of rights under Section 1954.*

Violations by the Tenant

A tenant may violate a lease in several ways. The most common is the failure to pay rent when it is due. Other violations of the lease terms can be as minor as keeping a cat or small bird not allowed under the terms of the lease, or extremely serious problems like dealing drugs or assaulting another tenant. Some violations can be corrected (e.g., pay the back rent or give up the pet) to avoid eviction, and the landlord must give the tenant the opportunity to do so. Other violations, like assaulting another tenant, can result in eviction without giving the tenant a chance to make amends.

Rent Due Date

Under California law, unless otherwise stated in a lease or rental agreement, rent is due on the last day of each rental period, unless otherwise agreed. (California Civil Code, Section 1947.) For this reason, you should clearly spell out in the lease that the rent is due at the beginning of each rental period.

Vacating Early

If a tenant *vacates* (moves out) the property before the end of the lease, he or she is still liable for the rent until the end of the lease. However, the landlord cannot just sit back and wait for the end of the lease. The landlord has a duty to try to find a new tenant and credit the rent received from the new tenant to the amount owed by the old tenant. The landlord may also hold the old tenant liable for any reasonable costs of finding a new tenant, such as running an ad or doing a credit check on the new tenant.

Bad Checks

Your policy concerning payment by check and bounced checks should be set out in your rental agreement. In addition, you should post your charges, if any, where the rents are paid.

If you get a bad check, you may consider the rent to be unpaid and may serve the tenant with a THREE-DAY NOTICE TO PAY RENT OR QUIT. (see form 23, p.237.)

Under California Civil Code, Section 1719, you may also demand payment from the tenant by sending certified mail that states the amount of the check and the amount of any charges. If you make this demand and the check is not made good within thirty days, you are entitled to three times the amount of the check, up to $1,500. The maximum you may charge for a bounced check is $25 for the first check and $35 for each check after that.

A **NOTICE OF DISHONORED CHECK AND DEMAND FOR PAYMENT** is included in this book in Appendix D. (see form 21, p.233.) Use this form only for bad checks due to insufficient funds or a closed account. If the tenant stopped payment, you must use a different procedure as explained in California Civil Code, Section 1719, in Appendix A. A tenant is not liable if a stop payment is ordered for a good faith statement.

Keep in mind that if a rent check bounces, you are much better off giving the tenant a **THREE-DAY NOTICE TO PAY RENT OR QUIT** (see form 23, p.237) than a thirty-day notice to make a check good. However, you can do both and possibly collect triple damages after the tenant leaves.

If a tenant gives you a bad check and then moves before making the check good, you may want to hold the check and periodically call the bank to see if any money is in the account. You can usually get a bank to cash a check less than six months old. If you redeposit a bounced check and it bounces again, the bank will mutilate it (punch holes in it) and you will not be able to later cash it.

Damage to the Premises

Minor damage by the tenant, even if intentional, must be repaired by the landlord, although the tenant may be billed for the cost involved. If the tenant does not pay, the landlord may sue for the amount due.

Major damage done by the tenant may relieve the landlord of the duty to keep the unit habitable. This is discussed further in Chapter 4. The landlord may bill the tenant for the damage and sue if it is not paid.

The landlord may also serve the tenant with a **THREE-DAY NOTICE TO COMPLY OR QUIT** or obtain an injunction against the tenant doing further damage. (see form 24, p.239.) These are difficult options without an attorney.

Lease Violations

If the tenant violates the lease—for example by making too much noise, having a pet, or allowing too many people to live in the premises—the landlord has three options. If the breach is curable, a **THREE-DAY NOTICE TO COMPLY OR QUIT** can be sent. If the breach is incurable, either a three- or thirty-day notice to quit can be given. The procedure, and definitions of curable and incurable, are explained in detail in Chapter 9.

Violations by the Landlord

A landlord may violate the lease contract in ways that give a tenant a range of remedies, from allowing the tenant to withhold rent to allowing the tenant to break the lease and move out. In some cases, the tenant may even successfully sue the landlord for damages caused by the violation.

Retaliatory Conduct

The landlord may not *retaliate* against a tenant who has exercised any rights under California Civil Code, Section 1942.5. These rights include:

- ◆ lodging a written or verbal complaint with the landlord;
- ◆ making a complaint to any government agency;
- ◆ filing a lawsuit or arbitration proceeding; and,
- ◆ receiving a judgment or arbitration award.

Retaliation includes raising rent, decreasing services, and eviction. The burden is on the tenant to prove that the landlord is retaliating and not acting for some legitimate reason. The landlord's action must be within 180 days of the tenant's action, against which the tenant claims that the landlord is retaliating.

If a landlord's action to raise rent, decrease services, or evict is disputed, the landlord must prove the legitimate purpose. As a practical matter, a landlord must have a provable reason that is not retaliatory in order to raise rent, reduce services, or evict. Penalties for violation may include punitive damages and attorney's fees.

Interrupting Utilities

Under California Civil Code, Section 789.3, a landlord who terminates or interrupts utilities such as water, heat, light, electricity, gas, elevator, garbage collection, or refrigeration can be held liable for up to $100 per day ($250 minimum) in damages, plus attorney's fees and actual damages suffered by the tenant.

Failure to Make Repairs

If the building becomes uninhabitable, the tenant has two duties.

1. *Notify* the landlord, either orally or in writing.
2. Give the landlord a *reasonable time* to make the repairs. A reasonable time will vary with the type of repair necessary. More than thirty days is generally considered unreasonable for most repairs. The time may be much shorter for repairs such as no heat in the winter or broken water pipes.

If the landlord fails to repair in a reasonable time, the tenant then has three options.

1. *Move*, even if this would violate the terms of a lease or rental agreement.
2. *Repair and deduct*, which means that the tenant may make the necessary repairs and deduct an amount not to exceed one month's rent. This may be done not more than twice in a twelve-month period. (California Civil Code, Section 1942.)
3. *Withhold rent*, which is a more complex remedy. The tenant refuses to pay rent until the defect is corrected and may demand reduced rent for the time that the property was not in proper condition.

The tenant must have the rent available and cannot use this as a way to avoid paying rent. If a court demands, or the landlord and tenant agree to, a reduced rent, the tenant must pay the reduced rent within three days if notice is given.

Receivership and Relocation

In extreme cases, the California Health and Safety Code, Section 17980.7(c), allows for a receiver to be appointed to take over operation of the building, make necessary repairs, and pay for the tenant's moving and relocation until the repairs are made.

Tax Consequences of Failure to Repair

Under California Health and Safety Code, Section 17980.7(b) 1 and 2, if the condition of the property violates state or local codes, and the landlord does not make the necessary repairs within six months, the landlord may lose the tax advantages of the property, such as deductions for interest and depreciation allowed under California Revenue and Taxation Code, Sections 17274 and 24436.6.

Local governments can require a landlord to make repairs within thirty days. If the landlord fails to comply, he or she can be required to submit personal information, such as his or her Social Security number or business identification number. This makes it easier to enforce the loss of tax advantages.

NOTE: *These are state, not federal, rules.*

Destruction of the Premises

If the premises are damaged by fire, earthquake, or other casualty, the rights of both landlord and tenant are usually spelled out in the lease. If the lease does not cover this situation, or if the rental is under an oral agreement, then California law provides that upon total destruction of the premises, the lease terminates. (California Civil Code, Section 1933.) If the premises are only partially destroyed, then the tenant has the option of terminating the tenancy upon giving notice. (California Civil Code, Section 1932.)

Chapter 8:
Problems at the End of the Tenancy

Some problems arise or are discovered only when the tenancy ends. These may include a tenant staying beyond the agreed-upon term, damaging the property, or leaving personal property behind.

Tenant Holding Over

Sometimes a tenant will refuse to vacate the premises at the end of the lease or rental period. At the end of a lease term, no notice is required by either landlord or tenant. However, it has become so common for the tenant to stay after the end of the lease that it is wise to take a practical approach.

◆ If you do not want the tenant to leave, accept rent. This will create a month-to-month tenancy. If you wish to raise the rent, serve a thirty-day notice before the lease term expires.

◆ If you want the tenant to leave, serve a **THIRTY-DAY NOTICE OF TERMINATION OF TENANCY.** It will take effect at the end of the lease term. (see form 26, p.243.)

Damage to the Premises

If you find damage at the end of a tenancy, you may deduct the amount of the damage from the security deposit. However, the notice requirements as spelled out in Chapter 3 must be followed.

If the damages exceed the amount of the security deposit, the landlord may sue the tenant. If suing in small claims court, the following rules apply.

◆ An individual cannot ask for more than $7,500 in a claim.

Landlord Tip

Remember that the security deposit should not be used as the last month's rent. This could leave an insufficient amount to cover damage to the property.

♦ Corporations and other entities cannot ask for more than $5,000.

♦ You can file as many claims as you want for up to $2,500 each, but you can only file two claims in a calendar year that ask for more than $2,500.

♦ You can only sue a guarantor for up to $4,000 ($2,500 if the guarantor does not charge for the guarantee). A *guarantor* is a person who promises to be responsible for what another person owes.

Property Abandoned by Tenant

Tenants often leave personal property behind when they move. It is usually of little value, and in most cases, the landlord throws it away. This is not, however, what the law requires. The landlord must mail to the former tenant or other person who may own the property a **NOTICE OF RIGHT TO RECLAIM ABANDONED PROPERTY**. (see form 44, p.287 and form 45, p.289.) The tenant then has eighteen days from the date of the mailing to reply. The notice may be sent to the property if the landlord does not know where the former tenant may be.

If there is no reply to the notice, the landlord has certain options based on the value of the property.

♦ If the property is worth less than $300, the landlord may do as he or she pleases with it.

♦ If the property is worth $300 or more, the landlord must sell it at a public auction and the proceeds—less the costs for storage, advertising, and selling the property—must be turned over to the local county. The owner of the property then has one year to claim the money.

There are specific requirements regarding the sale of a former tenant's property, including providing notice of the sale to the former tenant, advertising, and hiring a bonded public auctioneer. Check California Government Code, Section 6066, and California Civil Code, Section 1988, for the details. Also consult with the auctioneer, who should be familiar with the procedure.

As a practical matter, these auctions rarely occur. The tenant usually either does not leave personal property valued at $300 or more behind, or he or she comes back to claim it.

Back Rent

If the tenant owes rent, you may recover it from the proceeds of the auction only if you have a judgment against the tenant and properly execute the judgment. If you have a judgment, contact the court clerk or marshal's office for the procedure to levy against the proceeds of the auction.

If the tenant contacts the landlord for the return of the property, refusal to return it until unpaid rent is paid is not allowed. Although the landlord may insist on storage charges, it may not be worth the possibility of a lawsuit, even if the landlord wins.

Vehicles

If the tenant leaves a motor vehicle on the property, the landlord can often get the police to tow it away and take responsibility for its disposal. However, some cities have different procedures, and they may say it is the landlord's responsibility. If so, you can usually find out the procedure from a towing company. Most likely they will tow it, sell it, and deduct their fees from the proceeds. If there are excess proceeds, you may be able to levy on them for any back rent judgment.

Chapter 9:
Terminating a Tenancy

A tenancy may be terminated in several ways. Unless the tenancy is terminated properly, you cannot regain possession of the premises. If you file for eviction without properly terminating the tenancy, the tenant may win the case and you may be ordered to pay damages to the tenant, as well as the tenant's attorney's fees.

Tenancies with No Specific Term

When there is no specific term, either party may terminate by giving written notice based on the rental period. A month-to-month requires at least a thirty-day notice. A week-to-week tenancy requires at least a seven-day notice. (California Civil Code, Section 1946.)

The law does not require the termination to coincide with the payment of rent. If a tenant who pays rent on the first of each month gives a thirty-day notice to vacate on the tenth, the tenant may legally vacate thirty days later without liability for rent after that date. The rent is due and payable to and including the date of termination.

In most cases, you do not have to give a good reason to terminate a tenancy. In fact, you do not have to give any reason. However, you cannot terminate a tenancy for an illegal reason, such as retaliation or discrimination. In public housing and some rent-controlled areas, you must have a good reason. There are special rules that you must carefully follow.

To terminate a month-to-month tenancy, use a **THIRTY-DAY NOTICE**. (see form 26, p.243.) To terminate a week-to-week tenancy, use a seven-day notice. For a weekly rental, or a rental where the tenant has agreed in writing to seven days' notice, you can change the "30" to "7" on the notice.

Landlord Tip

If you are under rent control or have Section 8 housing, always check the requirements. Your notice requirement can be as much as ninety days.

You should personally attempt to hand the notice to the tenant at the property. If the tenant is not there, you should next try to serve him or her at work, if you know where the tenant works. If neither of these are successful, you can serve another adult at the property and mail a second copy to the tenant. If there is no other adult at the property, you can post a copy on the front door of the property and mail a second copy to the tenant. You can also send the notice by certified or registered mail, but you must add five days to the time given to the tenant.

Expiration of Rental or Lease Term

When the term of a lease ends, the tenant is expected to vacate the property without notice. This is different from some states, where a lease is presumed to be renewed unless the tenant gives the landlord notice that he or she is leaving. If you believe that a tenant may not be expecting to leave at the end of the lease, or if you would simply like to be sure it is understood, you can use the LETTER TO VACATING TENANT. (see form 17, p.225.)

If you accept rent after the lease terminates, it is presumed to convert to a *periodic* (month-to-month) tenancy. You will then need to give a thirty-day notice.

If your property is subject to local rent control, you will probably need good cause to terminate. Check your local ordinance regarding your right to terminate or to increase the rent.

Special requirements apply to public housing. For more information, see the section on "Special Rules for Public Housing" on page 72.

Early Termination by Tenant

There are several reasons for a tenant to terminate the tenancy early. Some of them are legally justified and some not.

Destruction of Premises

If the premises are destroyed, such as by fire or earthquake, the tenant may immediately vacate the premises and terminate the rental. (California Civil Code, Section 1933.)

Premises Uninhabitable

If the premises are damaged so that they have become *uninhabitable,* as defined in California Civil Code, Section 1941.1, and the landlord has not improved (or cannot improve) the conditions within a reasonable time, the tenant may vacate the premises and terminate the rental.

Remedies for Breach by Tenant

If the tenant leaves the premises before the end of the lease agreement without the legal right to do so, the tenant has breached the agreement. The landlord then has two options.

1. The landlord may relet the property and sue the tenant for the unpaid rent during the time the property was vacant. The landlord's duty to mitigate is met if reasonable efforts are used to find another tenant.

2. The landlord may ignore the duty to mitigate and hold the tenant liable for the unpaid rent until the lease expires. California Civil Code, Section 1951.4 allows this only if the lease contained a notice to the tenant of the landlord's intent to do this, and the lease:
   ◆ allowed subletting or assignment;
   ◆ allowed subletting or assignment with reasonable standards or conditions; or,
   ◆ allowed subletting or assignment with the landlord's consent, which will not be unreasonably withheld.

Abandonment

If the tenant leaves early by abandoning the property, you must choose which of the following procedures to follow.

First, be certain that the tenant has in fact left with no intent to return. If you simply assume that the tenant has abandoned the property and rent it to another tenant, you will be liable if the original tenant returns. Check the obvious signs, such as removal of furniture, clothing, and other personal items. Telephone the tenant's workplace, references, and bank. Once you believe that the tenant has gone for good, you have the following options.

◆ You may re-rent the property and take the chance that the tenant does not return. This saves the time and money of following the formal legal procedures, but may create liability if the tenant returns.

◆ You may follow either of two legal remedies.

1. You may serve a **THREE-DAY NOTICE TO PAY RENT OR QUIT**, followed by an unlawful detainer action. (see form 23, p.237.) This is the more expensive of the two remedies.

2. You may serve a **NOTICE OF BELIEF OF ABANDONMENT** pursuant to California Civil Code, Section 1951.3. (see form 27, p.245.) The section requires that the rent be due and unpaid for at least fourteen days, and that the landlord has sufficient reason to believe that the tenant has abandoned the property.

Landlord Tip

Check the rental application. If you make a few phone calls and are unable to find anyone who knows the whereabouts of the tenant, you will have reason to believe that the tenant has abandoned the premises.

The law allows for service either personally or by first-class mail. Since abandonment almost always involves not knowing the location of the tenant, service by mail will probably be used. The landlord should mail to the property address unless there is another address where the landlord believes the tenant can be reached. Again, this will seldom be the case. If the tenant does not reply in writing within eighteen days after the date of the mailing, stating that there is no intent to abandon and giving an address for legal service, the landlord may reenter and take possession of the premises.

The landlord may enter the property at any time before taking possession for reasons of health and safety.

It is tempting to just take back the unit when you think a tenant has abandoned it. In most cases, you will be correct and there will not be a problem. However, if you are wrong and you have not followed the proper procedure, you could be in for an expensive lawsuit. Unless you are certain that the tenant is not coming back, the loss of rent by following the proper procedure may be a small price to pay.

Early Termination by Landlord

A landlord may terminate a tenancy before the end of the term for three reasons—failure to pay rent, failure to cure a curable breach of a covenant or condition of the lease, and commitment of an incurable breach of a covenant or condition. You are required to attach a copy of the lease to your notice or complaint when a violation of a provision in the lease is the reason for the notice.

Failure to Pay Rent

Failure to pay rent is the most common reason for eviction. The landlord must serve a **THREE-DAY NOTICE TO PAY RENT OR QUIT**. (see form 23, p.237.) The notice may be served any time after the rent is due. The unlawful detainer action may be brought on the fourth day after the notice is served.

There is no grace period for rent payment unless the lease states one. However, allowing a tenant to continually pay rent late may modify your agreement or waive your right to rent on the agreed-upon date. Many landlords routinely serve a **THREE-DAY NOTICE TO PAY RENT OR QUIT** any time the rent is late. This preserves their right to insist on rent as agreed to in the lease or rental agreement.

A **Three-Day Notice to Pay Rent or Quit** is included in Appendix D as form 23. This must be completed and served exactly as required by law or you could lose your eviction suit. The most important requirements follow.

Calculating the Three Days

This may sound simple, but many landlords have lost their case by making an error here. First, you must not serve the notice until the day after the rent is due. Even if the tenants tell you they cannot pay the rent on the day it is due, you must wait until the next day to serve the notice. Next, if the due date was a Saturday, Sunday, or legal holiday, you cannot serve the notice until the day after the next business day. Third, you cannot count the day of service of the notice in the three days. Fourth, if the third day of the three-day notice is a Saturday, Sunday, or legal holiday, you cannot file your eviction until the day after the next business day.

Example: *Suppose rent is due on the 25th of the month, and December 25th falls on a Friday. Since that day is a holiday, rent would not be due until Monday the 28th. You would serve the notice on the 29th, and since the 1st of January is a holiday followed by a weekend, the third day would be the 4th of January. Therefore, you could not file your suit until the 5th.*

Calculating the Amount Due

On a **Three-Day Notice to Pay Rent or Quit**, you can only demand rent that is actually past due, not late fees or any other amounts due under the rental agreement.

Serving the Notice

You should personally attempt to hand the notice to the tenant at the property. If the tenant is not there, you should next try to serve him or her at work, if you know where that is. If neither of these is successful, you can serve another adult at the property and mail a second copy to the tenant. If there is no other adult at the property, you can post a copy on the front door of the property and mail a second copy to the tenant. The three-day period starts the day after both of these things have been accomplished.

In some areas, it is possible to hire an off-duty peace officer to deliver the notice in full uniform, and thus possibly have a more serious effect on the tenant.

Curable Breach

A *curable*, but uncured, breach of a covenant or condition is a situation in which you want a tenant to stop doing something that violates the lease. Examples would include getting a pet or having a guest stay longer than permitted. A **Three-Day Notice to Comply or Quit** can be used for these situations. (see form 24, p.239.)

If the problem is not corrected, the unlawful detainer action may be filed on the fourth day after the notice is served. In using this notice, you should calculate the three days and serve the notice as explained in the section on "Failure to Pay Rent."

Incurable Breach

An *incurable breach* of a covenant or condition is a situation in which the tenant has done something so bad that you simply want him or her out. Perhaps the tenant has left and moved someone in without your consent, has caused severe damage to the property, or has assaulted another tenant. For this, you would use a **THREE-DAY NOTICE TO QUIT.** (see form 25, p.241.) This remedy may be difficult to use and an attorney is recommended. The biggest problem is knowing whether a court will consider the action of the tenant to be incurable, or if you will be told you should have sent the **THREE-DAY NOTICE TO COMPLY OR QUIT.** (see form 24, p.239.) When in doubt, it is best to use the **THREE-DAY NOTICE TO COMPLY OR QUIT** first, or if the tenancy is month-to-month, to use a **THIRTY-DAY NOTICE OF TERMINATION OF TENANCY.** (see form 26, p.243.) In using this notice, you should calculate the three days and serve the notice as explained on page 71.

Drug-Dealing Tenants

Knowingly allowing a drug-dealing tenant to remain in possession of the unit may subject a landlord to liability for damage or injury to other tenants, tenants' guests, workers, neighbors, and anyone else who could foreseeably be damaged or injured. In extreme cases, forfeiture of the property could result.

The other side of the problem is that to accuse someone of dealing drugs could subject the landlord to liability. Use of a thirty-day notice is recommended, because no reason for the termination must be stated.

If you have a fixed-term lease with your tenants, or your property is subject to rent control or other limitations, and you suspect a tenant of dealing drugs, you should consult an attorney.

Special Rules for Public Housing

For nonpayment of rent, the landlord must give the tenant fourteen days' notice rather than a three-day notice and it must be mailed or hand delivered, not posted. (Code of Federal Regulations, Title 24, Section 866.4(1)(2) (24 C.F.R. Sec. 866.4(1)(2)).) The notice must inform the tenant of his or her right to a *grievance procedure.* At least one court has held that both a fourteen-day notice and a three-day notice must be given. (*Stanton v. Housing Authority of Pittsburgh,* 469 F. Supp. 1013 (W.D. Pa.1977).) Other courts have disagreed. (*Ferguson v. Housing Authority of Middleboro,* 499 F. Supp. 334 (E.D. Ky 1980).)

For breach of the terms of the lease other than payment of rent, a thirty-day notice must be given (except in emergencies), and it must inform the tenant of the reasons for termination, the right to reply, and the right to a grievance procedure. (24 C.F.R. Sec. 366(4)(1).) If the tenant requests a grievance hearing, a second notice must be given, even if the tenant loses in the hearing. (*Ferguson v. Housing Authority of Middleboro*, 499 F. Supp. 432 (E.D. Ky 1980).)

Section 236 Apartments

Section 236 is a HUD program that helps low-income families obtain rental housing. Tenants pay rent based on a percentage of their income (30% with a formula for exclusions and deductions) with HUD setting a maximum that can be paid, called the *market rent*. The landlord can benefit with guarantees of payment as well as mortgage guarantees and lower mortgage interest rates. For further information, contact your local HUD office or go to **www.hud.gov**.

For nonpayment of rent, tenants must be given the three-day notice and be advised that if there is a judicial proceeding, they can present a valid defense. Service must be by first-class mail or hand-delivered or placed under the door. (24 C.F.R. Sec. 450. 4(a).)

For breach of the terms of the lease other than payment of rent, the tenant must first have been given notice that in the future, such conduct would be grounds for terminating the lease. The notice of termination must state when the tenancy will be terminated and specifically why it is being terminated, and it must advise the tenant of the right to present a defense in the eviction suit. (24 C.F.R. Sec. 450.)

Section 8 Apartments

Under 24 C.F.R. Sec. 882.215(c)(4), the landlord must notify the housing authority in writing at the commencement of the eviction proceedings. Also, the paragraph on page 71 concerning breach of a lease other than payment of rent applies to Section 8 housing as well.

Death of a Tenant

If a lease contains a clause binding the *heirs, successors, and assigns* of the lessee, then the lease continues after the death of the tenant unless cancelled by the lessor and the heirs. Otherwise, it is a personal contract that expires at death.

As a practical matter, you will probably want to re-rent the property as soon as possible. However, you should make arrangements for the storage of the decedent's property or you may be liable for it. If you know the decedent's closest relative, you can probably be safe in turning over the property to him or her. (Be sure to get a signed receipt.) However, if you think there is any chance there will be disputed claims to the property, give it only to a person who has been appointed executor of the estate.

Option to Cancel

Some landlords like to use a lease form giving them an option to cancel the lease. However, when a lease allows one party to cancel it at will, the lease is generally not considered binding and the courts will allow either party to cancel it at will. A lease will probably be held to be valid if the option to cancel is contingent upon some event. For example, a lease that gave the landlord the option to cancel if the property were taken for road right-of-way purposes would probably be valid.

Chapter 10:
Evicting a Tenant

This chapter explains the basic steps for filing an eviction case against a tenant. In most cases, service of the first notice or the filing of the complaint is enough to convince the tenant to move. Tenants rarely file an answer, so these forms usually do the trick. However, an eviction case can get very complicated and may require pleadings that are beyond the scope of this book. There are books on the market on the subject of evictions that explain in minute detail the more complicated procedures. If your eviction gets complicated, you may want to consult one of these books or an attorney.

Self-Help by Landlord

The only way a landlord may recover possession of a dwelling unit is if the tenant voluntarily surrenders it to the landlord or abandons it, or if the landlord gets a court order giving him or her possession.

Under California Civil Code, Section 789.3, landlords are specifically forbidden to use *self-help* methods to evict tenants, such as interrupting utilities, changing locks, removing doors or windows, or removing the tenant's personal belongings from the unit. Violation of this law subjects the landlord to liability for a penalty of up to $100 per day, plus attorney's fees and any other actual damages suffered by the tenant.

Settling with the Tenant

Although in a vast majority of evictions the tenants do not answer the complaint and the landlord wins quickly, some tenants can create nightmares for landlords. Clever tenants and legal aid lawyers can delay the case for months. Vindictive tenants can destroy the property with little worry of ever paying for it. This is why lawyers sometimes advise their landlord clients to offer the tenant a cash settlement to leave. For example, a tenant may be offered $200 to be out of the premises and leave it clean within a week. Of course, it hurts to give money to a tenant who already owes you money, but it could be cheaper than the court costs of an unlawful detainer action, vacancy time, and damage to the premises. You will have to make your own decision based upon your tenant.

Grounds for Eviction

A tenant can be evicted for one or more of these reasons:

- ◆ violating one or more of the terms of the lease;
- ◆ failing to leave at the end of the term; or,
- ◆ violating California law regarding the duties of tenants.

Violations of the Lease

The most common violation of the lease by a tenant is the failure to pay the rent. However, a tenant can also be evicted for violating other terms of the rental agreement, such as disturbing other tenants.

Failure to Leave

A tenant may also be evicted for failing to leave after being served with a thirty-day notice when there is a month-to-month tenancy. The tenant need not have done anything wrong, and the landlord need not state a reason for asking the tenant to leave.

Duties of Tenants

As explained in Chapter 4, there are certain requirements of the tenant regarding maintenance. If the tenant violates these requirements, he or she can be evicted.

Limitations on Evictions

The reason for asking a tenant to leave cannot be for the purpose of retaliation or discrimination. Also, regulations on property subject to government control (e.g., public housing, subsidized housing, and rent control property) may not only require that the landlord state a reason, but also may have limitations on the reasons that justify an eviction.

Terminating the Tenancy

It is an ancient rule of law that an eviction suit cannot be filed until the tenancy is legally terminated. There are cases from as far back as the 1500s in which evictions were dismissed because the landlord failed to properly terminate the tenancy. If you make the same mistake, do not expect it to be overlooked by the judge. What the judges often do in cases where the tenancy has not been properly terminated is order the landlord to pay the tenant's attorney's fees and start the procedure again.

Termination for Cause

The tenancy may terminate by natural expiration or by action by the landlord. If you need to evict a tenant whose tenancy has not expired, you should carefully read Chapter 9 and follow the procedures to properly terminate the tenancy.

Termination by Expiration

If parties to a lease do not agree to renew or extend the agreement, then it automatically ends at its expiration date. (This is different from some areas in which the lease is automatically renewed unless notice is given that it is not being renewed.)

Using an Attorney

If your lease or rental agreement provides for the landlord to recover attorney's fees, the law allows the same for the tenant. There are also other situations in which you could be required by California law to pay your tenant's attorney's fees. Because of this, it is important to do an eviction exactly as required. In some cases, the tenant may just be waiting for the eviction notice before leaving the premises. In such a case, the landlord may regain the premises no matter what kind of papers are filed.

In other cases, tenants with no money and no defenses have retained free lawyers, who find technical defects in the case. This can cause a delay in the eviction and cause the landlord to be ordered to pay the tenant's attorney's fees. A simple error in your court papers can cost you the case.

A landlord needing to do an eviction should consider the costs and benefits of using an attorney, compared to doing it without an attorney. One possibility is to file the case without an attorney and hope the tenant moves out. If the tenant stays and fights the case, an attorney can be hired to finish the case. Some landlords who prefer to do their evictions themselves start by paying a lawyer for a half-hour or hour of time to review the facts of the case and point out problems. You may also be able to find an attorney to give you advice as questions come up.

When it is Advisable to Hire an Attorney

While a landlord has the right to evict a tenant without using an attorney, there are several instances when it is advisable to at least consult with a real estate attorney before proceeding.

These include when:
- ◆ your tenant has a lawyer;
- ◆ your tenant contests the eviction;
- ◆ you are evicting based on the tenant's drug dealing or other misconduct, and are serving a notice that requires stating a reason for the eviction;
- ◆ you are serving a seven-day notice when a thirty-day notice would normally be used;
- ◆ your property is subject to rent control, or is public or subsidized housing;
- ◆ your tenant is also an employee of yours, such as a manager (this may be avoided if you used an attorney when you hired the tenant as your manager);
- ◆ your tenant files bankruptcy; or,
- ◆ your tenant is in the military.

Tenant Represented by an Attorney

Whenever a tenant has an attorney, the landlord should also have one. Otherwise, you risk the following types of problems.
- ◆ A winning tenant was awarded $8,675 in attorney's fees that was figured at $150 an hour and then doubled.
- ◆ In a suit by a cooperative association against a tenant for $191.33 in maintenance fees and to enforce the association rules, the tenant won the suit and was awarded $87,375 in attorney's fees.
- ◆ An argument that a legal aid organization was not entitled to attorney's fees did not win. The landlord had to pay $2,000 for twenty hours of the legal aid attorney's time in having the case dismissed.

Selecting an Attorney

It is, of course, important to find an attorney who both knows landlord/tenant law and charges reasonable fees. There are many subtleties of the law that can be missed by someone without experience. Some attorneys who specialize in landlord/tenant work charge very modest fees unless the case gets complicated. Others charge an hourly rate that can add up to thousands of dollars. Check with other landlords or a local apartment association for names of good attorneys. You also might try calling the manager of a large apartment complex in the area.

The California Bar Association certifies *specialists* in the various areas of law. An attorney becomes a specialist by proving experience and taking an examination. Consult your county association for a list of specialists.

Fees

If you get a security deposit at the beginning of the tenancy and start the eviction immediately upon a default, then the deposit should be nearly enough to cover the attorney's fee.

NOTE: *A landlord can represent him- or herself in court and does not have to use an attorney. A landlord's agent, such as the apartment manager, can also represent the landlord. However, it is considered the unauthorized practice of law for any other person who is not an attorney to represent a party in court.*

Forms

Each county in the state makes its own rules regarding forms. Some have their own required forms, some have optional forms, and some do not have forms. The forms included in this book should work in most areas. Before using them, you should ask your court clerk if the court has any required or recommended forms.

NOTE: *Special forms have been authorized for Downey, El Cajon, and North Santa Barbara. Contact your court clerk to obtain them.*

Court Procedures

An eviction is started by filing a *complaint* against the tenant. An eviction suit is called an *unlawful detainer* action. The complaint must be filed in *municipal court* (formerly called justice court) and a filing fee must be paid. Small claims court no longer hears eviction cases. Superior courts will only hear cases involving claims of damages in excess of $25,000. If your damages are over $25,000, you should consult an attorney.

NOTE: *Before you may file a complaint, you must have given the tenant either a three-day notice or a thirty-day notice. See Chapter 9 for information about which type of notice is required in your situation and how to calculate the three or thirty days correctly.*

Complaint

A COMPLAINT—UNLAWFUL DETAINER is included in this book as form 30 in Appendix D. You should go over it carefully and be sure to fill it out completely and accurately.

Civil Case Cover Sheet

The next form you need to fill out is the CIVIL CASE COVER SHEET. (see form 29, p.249.) It is very straightforward and easy to fill out. It is primarily used for statistical purposes to let the courts keep track of what types of cases are being filed.

Summons

The third form you need to file is the SUMMONS. (see form 31, p.255.) This is an important form and must be completed correctly. It is the notice to the tenants that they are being sued. It should include the names of all adults living in the premises. If there are people living there whose names you do not know, you should list their names as John Doe, Jane Doe, etc.

You are responsible for properly filling out all forms. If you are using an eviction service to serve the summons, the service should know how to do it and be able to advise you. If you are doing it yourself and are not sure that you are doing it right, ask the court clerk to take a quick look at it. There will be directions either on the document itself or on a separate instruction sheet. Again, the clerk or eviction service can guide you if necessary.

Prejudgment Claim of Right to Possession

If there are any adults living at the premises whose names you do not know, or if you think someone other than your tenant may claim to be living there, you should prepare a PREJUDGMENT CLAIM OF RIGHT TO POSSESSION. (see form 32, p.259.) This is served with the SUMMONS (form 31) and COMPLAINT—UNLAWFUL DETAINER (form 30), and provides legal notice to everyone at the premises.

The claimant then has ten days to file a PREJUDGMENT CLAIM OF RIGHT TO POSSESSION. (see form 32, p.259.) If this is not done, the claim cannot be made when the marshal or sheriff comes to actually evict the tenant. If you do not do this and someone you have not served claims to have a right to live there, it will delay your eviction.

Copies

You will need to have an original of all of the above forms and a copy of the COMPLAINT—UNLAWFUL DETAINER for each defendant. (see form 30, p.251.) You will need two copies of each PREJUDGMENT CLAIM OF RIGHT TO POSSESSION for each person you expect to serve. (see form 32, p.259.) You do not need extra copies of the CIVIL CASE COVER SHEET. You should make a copy of everything for your own file.

Filing

Once you have prepared the papers, you need to file them in the judicial district where the property is located. This is usually done personally, but you may have your process server do it or the clerk may let you file by mail. Call your clerk to find out if this is possible.

Service of Process

A copy of both the COMPLAINT—UNLAWFUL DETAINER and the SUMMONS is *served* upon the tenants by the sheriff, a marshal, a private process server, or any adult person other than the plaintiff. However, if you will be using the PREJUDGMENT CLAIM OF RIGHT TO POSSESSION, only a sheriff, a marshal, or private process server may serve them.

A process server may cost a few dollars more than the sheriff, but can often get service quicker and may be more likely to serve the papers personally, allowing you to get a money judgment. A process server will also make it more likely that the service and completion of the **Summons** are done properly than if you have a friend or relative do it.

The best way to serve the papers is to personally hand them to the tenant or to leave them in his or her presence if he or she refuses to take them. With this type of service, the case will proceed more quickly and allow you to get a money judgment.

If the process server is unable to serve the tenant personally, the papers can be handed to another adult member of the household or they can be served by posting one copy on the property and mailing an additional copy to each tenant. However, these methods have strict rules that must be followed. If you decide to post and mail a copy, then you must petition for a judge's permission. If you need to use either of these methods, you should hire a process server or consult an attorney.

Public Housing

In Section 8 housing, the local housing authority must be notified in writing before the tenant can be served with the eviction. (24 C.F.R. Sec. 882.215(c)(4).) The papers served on the tenants are the copy of the **Complaint—Unlawful Detainer** with a copy of the **Summons** stapled on top. (see form 30, p.251 and form 31, p.255.) If there are parties whose names you do not know, they must be given the **Complaint—Unlawful Detainer**, the **Summons**, and the **Prejudgment Claim of Right to Possession**.

Return of Service

After service is made, the person performing the service must return the original summonses (the ones with the court seals on them) to the court with the backs filled out completely.

Wait Five Days

After the **Complaint—Unlawful Detainer** and **Summons** have been served on the defendants, they have five days (excluding the day they are served and any legal holidays) to file an answer. At this point, most tenants move out. If they have not filed an answer, you can request that a default be entered on the sixth day (unless it falls on a Saturday or Sunday—then it would be entered on Monday). If the tenants have filed any type of answer with the court, you cannot get a default.

Default

If the tenant has not answered the summons, you have three options on how to proceed.

Option One

The easiest and fastest procedure is to have the clerk enter the *default* (the tenant did not file an answer) and judgment for possession. The drawback is that you may not be able to get a money judgment, but since it probably would not be collectable, you may not mind. To use this procedure, you would need a **REQUEST FOR ENTRY OF DEFAULT** (form 33), **CLERK'S JUDGMENT FOR POSSESSION—UNLAWFUL DETAINER** (form 34), and a *Writ of Execution* (available from the court).

In filling out form 33, mark the box for a "Clerk's Judgment" and mark boxes "1. c" and "1. e.(1)." In forms 33 and 34, do not fill in any of the areas regarding monetary amounts. On both of these forms, be sure to fill in the sections about whether the **PREJUDGMENT CLAIM OF RIGHT TO POSSESSION** (form 32) was served. (1.e.(1) on form 33 and 9 on form 35.) File these with the court clerk with the appropriate filing fee and the court should issue your *Writ of Execution*.

If you do wish to get a money judgment at the same time you are requesting the default, you can ask that a hearing be set before a judge for a money judgment. Unfortunately, not all counties allow this procedure, even though the plain words of the statute allow it. To do this, complete a second set of forms 33, 34, and 35, but on form 33 you should check boxes "1.c" and "1.d," and fill in the monetary amounts under lines 2 and 5. On form 35, complete the monetary amounts on lines 11 through 18.

Option Two

The second option is to set a hearing and get a judgment for possession and money damages from a judge. This may take much longer than getting a default through the clerk. If you want the tenants out quickly, you may prefer to forgo the money judgment. For this procedure, you need forms 33, 35, and either form 36 or a judgment form provided by your clerk. To fill out form 33, check the box for a court judgment, and then check the boxes for "1.c" and "1.d," and fill in the information under 2. Also, on both forms 33 and 35, be sure to fill in the sections about whether the **PREJUDGMENT CLAIM OF RIGHT TO POSSESSION** was served.

Option Three

The third option is to apply for a judgment for possession and money damages from a judge by using a declaration instead of testimony at a hearing. For this, you would prepare the forms the same as in the second option, except that you would check boxes under 1.e.(2) and 4.a, 4.b, and 4.c. You would need form 37 or to type the information from form 37 on legal paper (with numbers down the left side). Ask your clerk what is required.

Military Personnel

Special rules apply to military personnel. There will not be a default entered on a tenant who is a member of the military unless the tenant has an attorney. Consult an attorney if your tenant is in the military and refuses to leave. If the tenant is in the military, but his or her spouse is not and the spouse is on the lease, you can proceed against the nonmilitary spouse. Always contact the tenant's commanding officer before beginning eviction. This will usually resolve the matter.

Tenant's Motion

If the tenant files any type of legal motion, such as a *Motion to Strike* or a *Motion to Quash*, it is obvious that he or she either knows the law or is being helped by someone who does. Unless you have experience in a similar case, you should seek the advice of an attorney familiar with tenant evictions.

Jury Demand

If the tenant demands a jury trial, especially if he or she also has an attorney, you should consult an attorney, because the case will be much more complicated than without a jury.

Discovery Requests

A request for discovery by a tenant is another sign that you need to consult an attorney. *Discovery* is a process in which parties can ask each other questions (either written ones called *interrogatories* or oral ones called *depositions*) under oath. They can also subpoena each other's records, including bank statements and charge card receipts. Failure to respond can result in being held in contempt of court and giving false information can result in a criminal charge of perjury.

A tenant may file an *answer* to your complaint in the form of a letter to the court, or he or she may use the court answer form, in which boxes are checked to respond to your allegations. If the letter simply gives an excuse as to why the rent is unpaid or denies that your complaint is correct, you can move ahead to the next section in this book on "Setting the Trial."

If the tenant checked the "Affirmative Defenses" boxes on the form answer, or if the tenant includes affirmative defenses in the letter or files a counterclaim, you should seek the advice of an attorney. If you do not, the minimum you should do is file a response to the tenant's defenses (denying they are true if they are not) or an answer to the counterclaim (denying the allegations that are untrue).

Setting the Trial

The next step will be setting a trial date. This is done by filing either a *Memorandum to Set Civil Case for Trial* or a *Request for Trial Setting*, depending on the county you are in. This form can be obtained from the court clerk. The trial date will be set and a trial will follow in approximately two or three weeks. If you win, the same steps to evict should be taken as with the default judgment. If you lose, you will have to begin again. Unless you know precisely how to win the next time, consult an attorney.

If no one shows up at the hearing except you, explain to the judge that you are ready to proceed. The judge may ask you questions or to read your complaint under oath. The judge may have a judgment form or may ask you for one. You can use the JUDGMENT—UNLAWFUL DETAINER in Appendix D, unless your county has its own form. (see form 37, p.271.)

Tenant's Attorney

If the tenant shows up with an attorney and you were not told previously, you should ask the judge for a *continuance* to get your own attorney. If you make a mistake and lose, you may have to pay the tenant's attorney's fees.

Defenses

If the tenant does appear for the hearing, he or she will probably present one or more of the following defenses. The particular defenses may depend on your reason for eviction.

◆ If you are evicting for nonpayment of rent, the tenant may argue that you failed to keep the building habitable, which excuses the nonpayment of rent. If the tenant had notified you of repairs that you failed to make before you served your three-day notice, this could be a winning argument. Even worse would be if you had been cited by a government inspector for health or safety violations.

◆ If you are not evicting for nonpayment of rent, the more common arguments are retaliation, discrimination, or violation of a rent control ordinance. These, as well as habitability, were covered earlier.

◆ The tenant may always argue that you did not follow proper legal procedure in serving your NOTICE or SUMMONS and COMPLAINT—UNLAWFUL DETAINER. Failing to properly fill out the forms may result in you having to start over.

Stipulation

You should arrive for the trial early, and if you see the tenant is present, try to discuss the matter and see if something can be worked out. Since there is no way of knowing how a trial will turn out—and even the best cases have been lost over a small mistake—most lawyers prefer to settle a case whenever possible. This will allow you to recover some back rent and avoid the hassle of cleaning and re-renting the unit. If you wish to settle with the tenant and come to an agreement by which the rent will be paid over time, then you can enter into a stipulation to delay the case. A *stipulation* is a contract entered into a court record.

If you can work out a satisfactory arrangement with the tenant, you may file a STIPULATION FOR ENTRY OF JUDGMENT in the case. (see form 38, p.273.) A judgment will then be issued that reflects this agreement. A typical stipulation might allow the tenant to stay for a slightly longer time than if eviction procedures were followed and call for some periodic payments of past-due rent. If the arrangement you have worked out with the tenant does not fit this form, you can retype it to conform to your agreement.

Once the case is filed, you should never accept any rent from the tenant without signing a stipulation. If you do, your case can be dismissed and you will have to start over again with a new Notice and Complaint—Unlawful Detainer.

Presenting Your Case

To win your case, you will need to prove the claims in your complaint and rebut the defenses, answers, and counterclaims of the tenant. Much of your proof will be your own testimony, but you can also use evidence, such as a copy of the lease and any notices or photos of any damages. It is also helpful to have a witness who can verify what you have said.

The trial usually proceeds in the following eight-step order, but ask your judge before you start because he or she may prefer a less formal procedure.
    1. Opening remarks by the judge
    2. Landlord's opening statement
    3. Tenant's opening statement
    4. Landlord's testimony and evidence
    5. Tenant's testimony and evidence
    6. Landlord's rebuttal and closing argument
    7. Tenant's closing argument
    8. Landlord's rebuttal to tenant's closing argument

Opening Statement

In your opening statement, tell the judge what the case is about and what you plan to prove.

Testimony and Evidence

In your testimony and evidence, go point by point through your complaint and state the facts of the case, presenting evidence wherever it is available. Photos and copies of notices sent to the tenant are very useful.

Rebuttal

In your rebuttal, point out what parts of the tenant's evidence are untrue (if any), and argue that even if some points are true, you should win the case anyway because they do not constitute a legal defense.

In your rebuttal to the tenant's closing argument, point out the flaws in the tenant's argument, show any inconsistencies in his or her testimony, counter any of the tenant's legal arguments with your own, and summarize why you are entitled to win in spite of the tenant's presentation of the case.

Closing Argument

In your closing argument, summarize your case and again point out what parts of the tenant's evidence are untrue (if any). Also, argue that even if some points are true, you should win the case anyway because they do not constitute a legal defense.

Judgment

Once both sides have finished their presentation, the judge may announce a decision or say that the case will be taken under *advisement*. The reason for the latter may be that the judge wants to research the law or perhaps thinks the parties are too emotional and might get upset.

If a decision is made on the spot, you should present your proposed JUDGMENT—UNLAWFUL DETAINER. (see form 37, p.271.) If it is taken under advisement, you will receive the judgment in the mail within a few days. If it does not arrive within a few days, you can call the judge's secretary for the status of your case, but do not make a pest of yourself.

If you win the case, you will need to bring a prepared *Writ of Execution* to the court clerk along with the fee. The Writ of Execution form is only available from the court.

The Writ of Execution is then taken to the office of the sheriff or marshal, along with written authorization, instructions to carry out the writ, and the sheriff's fee. The marshal or sheriff will prepare a five-day notice to vacate, and will serve it or post it at the property. After five days, the marshal or sheriff will physically remove the tenant from the property.

Once the tenant leaves, you may have to deal with personal property left behind. Abandoned personal property is discussed in Chapter 8. California law does not allow you to claim the proceeds from auctioning off the tenant's personal property unless you have a judgment. This would apply to back rent that the tenant owes.

Tenant's Appeal

A tenant has thirty days to file a notice of appeal. The appeal from the municipal court is to the appellate department of the superior court.

The tenant's appeal does not necessarily delay eviction, unless the judge grants a *stay* and the tenant deposits rent with the court. If your tenant feels strongly enough to deposit rent with the court, consult an attorney. Since the *Writ of Possession* gives the tenant twenty-four hours to vacate the property, the tenant will have to act immediately if he or she wants to stop the eviction.

Tenant's Bankruptcy

If a tenant files bankruptcy, all legal actions against him or her must stop immediately. This provision is automatic from the moment the bankruptcy petition is filed. (11 U.S.C. Sec. 362.) If you take any action in court, seize the tenant's property, try to impose a landlord's lien, or use the security deposit for unpaid rent, you can be held in contempt of federal court.

It is not necessary that you receive formal notice of the bankruptcy filing. Verbal notice is sufficient. If you do not believe the tenant, then you should call the bankruptcy court to confirm the filing.

The stay lasts until the debtor (the tenant) is discharged or the case is dismissed, or until the property is abandoned or voluntarily surrendered.

The landlord may ask for the right to continue with the eviction by filing a *Motion for Relief from Stay* and paying the filing fee. A hearing is held within thirty days. It may be held by telephone. The motion is governed by Bankruptcy Rule 9014. The requirements of how the tenant must be served are contained in Bankruptcy Rule 7004. For such a hearing, the services of an attorney are usually necessary.

If the tenant filed bankruptcy after a judgment of eviction has been entered, there should be no problem lifting the automatic stay since the tenant has no interest in the property. (*In re Cowboys, Inc.*, 24 B.R. 15 (S.D. Fla. 1982).)

The bankruptcy stay only applies to amounts owed to the landlord at the time of filing the bankruptcy. Therefore, the landlord can sue the tenant for eviction and rent owed for any time period *after* the filing of the bankruptcy petition, unless the bankruptcy trustee assumes the lease. The landlord can proceed during the bankruptcy without asking for relief from the automatic stay under three conditions. (*In re Knight*, 8 B.R. 925 (D.C. Md. 1981).)

1. The landlord can only sue for rent due after the filing.
2. The landlord cannot sue until the trustee rejects the lease. (If the trustee does not accept the lease within sixty days of the *Order for Relief*, then Section 365(d)(1) provides that it is deemed rejected.)
3. The landlord must sue under the terms of the lease and may not treat the trustee's rejection as a breach.

In a Chapter 13 (reorganization) bankruptcy, the landlord should be paid the rent as it comes due.

If your tenant files bankruptcy and you decide it is worth hiring a lawyer, you should locate an attorney who is experienced in bankruptcy work. Prior to the meeting with the attorney, you should gather as much information as possible (type of bankruptcy filed, assets, liabilities, case number, and so on).

Landlord's Appeal

The United States legal system allows one chance to bring a case to court. If you did not prepare for your trial, or thought you would not need to do something like call a witness, and you lost, you do not have the right to try again. If someone lied at trial and that party was believed by the judge or jury, there is usually not much that can be done. However, in certain limited circumstances you may be able to have your case reviewed.

♦ If the judge made a mistake in interpreting the law that applies to your case, that is grounds for reversal.

♦ If new evidence is discovered after the trial that could not have been discovered before the trial, then a new trial might be granted, but this is not very common.

♦ There are certain other grounds for rehearing, such as misconduct of an attorney or errors during the trial, but these matters are beyond the scope of this book.

If you wish to appeal your case, you should consult with an attorney or review a book in the law library on California appellate practice. However, if you want to remove the tenant quickly, you should just file a new eviction action. It is much quicker than the appeals process.

Satisfaction of Judgment

If, after a judgment has been entered against the tenant, the tenant pays the amount due, it is the landlord's responsibility to file an **ACKNOWLEDGMENT OF SATISFACTION OF JUDGMENT**. (see form 43, p.285.)

NOTE: *Occasionally, someone will write to the publisher and say that they followed this book, but the judge gave the tenants extra time to move or acted in some other manner that is contradictory to what is said in this book. Remember, most times a case will go smoothly, but judges may interpret the law differently, and judges do sometimes make mistakes or make an exception when the case seems to warrant it. If your case gets complicated, you should invest in an experienced landlord/tenant attorney who can finish your case quickly.*

Chapter 11:
Money Damages and Back Rent

Trying to collect a judgment against a former tenant is usually not worth the time and expense. Most landlords are just glad to regain possession of the property. Tenants who do not pay rent usually do not own property that can be seized, and it is very difficult to garnish wages. However, former tenants occasionally come into money. Some landlords have been surprised many years later when called by a title insurance company wanting to pay off a former tenant's judgment to clear a property lien. Therefore, it is usually worthwhile to at least put a claim for back rent into an eviction complaint.

Making a Claim

If a tenant moved out owing rent or leaving damage to the property, you can file a suit in small claims court. Be sure you know where the tenant lives or works, because you must have the papers served on the tenant in order to get a judgment.

To make a claim against a tenant for back rent in an eviction, you should check the boxes in the COMPLAINT—UNLAWFUL DETAINER that request past-due rent and damages. (see form 30, p.251.) If you have not checked these boxes, you can later file a separate suit in small claims court for both back rent and damage to the premises. Also, you should instruct your process server to attempt personal service rather than posting. Keep in mind that if the tenant avoids the process server, it may take a lot longer to get him or her out.

Uncontested Eviction

In order to get a money judgment, you must get a judgment signed by a judge rather than the clerk. If you used the clerk's default and judgment for your eviction, then you must file a separate small claims case for money damages. However, you have the following options to get a money judgment with your eviction suit.

- ◆ If your county allows it, you can request a money judgment from a judge at the same time as you request the clerk's judgment for possession.
- ◆ You can have a hearing before a judge for both a money judgment and possession.
- ◆ You can use a sworn declaration instead of a court hearing.

These procedures are explained in Chapter 10.

Contested Eviction

If the tenant files a response in the case and you are required to set a trial, the issue of rent owed can be brought up at the trial. If the tenant moves out prior to trial, you should still attend the trial both to obtain a judgment that you are entitled to possession and for a money judgment.

If the tenant does not attend the trial but is still in the unit, there will be rent owed for the time from the trial to the actual day the tenant moves out. Therefore, you should ask the judge to retain jurisdiction until those amounts can be ascertained. (Different judges may have different procedures for doing this.) Otherwise, you may have to file a separate suit in small claims court.

Amount

You are entitled to a judgment against the tenant for the rent due, damage to the premises, and the costs of your lawsuit, if any.

Rent

Under California law, in a month-to-month tenancy you are entitled to rent for the entire month of the final month in which the tenant leaves, even if he or she moved out early in the month.

If the tenant signed a lease, you are entitled to rent for the entire term of the lease, less any rent you receive by renting to someone else, plus any costs of finding a new tenant. For this reason, you should wait until the end of the lease term to be able to accurately assess your damages.

Damage to the Premises

You may seek compensation from the tenant for damage to the premises. This does not include *normal wear and tear*. (See "Keeping the Deposit" in Chapter 3.) These amounts cannot be awarded in your eviction suit, but you can deduct them from the security deposit or sue for them in small claims court.

Costs

The legal costs that you may collect are the filing fees, process server fees, and sheriff fees.

Collecting Your Judgment

As mentioned earlier in this chapter, it is usually not worth the trouble to get a judgment against a tenant, and attempting to collect it may be futile, but in some cases you may be able to collect. Assuming that you have already applied the tenant's security deposit toward the judgment, you can take the following actions to collect what you are owed.

Finding Assets

You will need to know a tenant's assets. If you have a tenant application with bank account numbers, employer name and address, and automobile descriptions, you may be able to use those if they are still current. A common technique to find out a person's bank balance is to call the bank and say something like *Would a check for $1,000 against account number 0123456789 be good today?* If not, call later (or another branch) and ask the same of a check for $500 and so on, until you know the approximate balance. If there is enough to make it worth your while, you can begin garnishment as explained in the next section.

If you do not have any information about the tenant's accounts or assets, you are allowed to order the tenant to appear in court and disclose this information under oath.

Examination of the Debtor

To schedule an examination of the debtor, you need to fill out and file an APPLICATION AND ORDER FOR APPEARANCE AND EXAMINATION. (see form 40, p.277.) Once this is signed by the judge, it will need to be personally served on the tenant. This is best done by the sheriff or a process server. The order must be served at least ten days prior to the date of the examination.

At the examination, the debtor will be required to answer under oath the questions that you ask. Failing to answer truthfully could subject the tenant to a fine or even jail time. You should use the JUDGMENT DEBTOR QUESTIONNAIRE and ask each question on both pages. (see form 41, p.279.) Once you know what the debtor owns, you can garnish it, levy upon it, or put a lien on it.

Garnishing Property

Garnishment is a legal procedure for seizing cash owed to a person, such as money in a bank or credit union, or earnings held by an employer. It is accomplished by using a *Writ of Execution* form used to get possession, but you check the "Execution (Money Judgment)" box. Get a Writ of Execution form from the court.

Money in an account is easy to seize, but wages are not. Under federal law, you can only garnish 25% of the amount over $154.50 that a person earns per week. Also, under California law, a person may claim a higher exemption if the money is needed for support.

Before preparing the form, you should call the clerk to find out what the current fee is, then make four copies and file three of them and the original with the clerk.

Levying on Property

A *levy* is a legal procedure where a sheriff takes control of an item of personal property, such as a vehicle, furniture, or business equipment. The problem with this is the exemptions. The first $2,300 equity in a car is exempt, as are most household items, up to $6,075 in jewelry and antiques, and $6,075 in business tools. Also, the sheriff's fee for the levy is hundreds of dollars. Unless the tenant is quite wealthy, a levy will probably not be very useful.

Filing a Lien

Even if the tenants have no property now, some time in the future they may inherit or buy real estate. A court judgment becomes a lien on all real property owned by the judgment debtor in every county where an **ABSTRACT OF JUDGMENT** is recorded. (see form 46, p.291.) The judgment lien is valid for ten years and is renewable for an additional ten years.

Even if you do not have much hope of collecting, it does not hurt to record your judgment in a few counties where the tenant may try to buy property in the future. The tenant who cannot afford to pay rent today may be in the market to buy property (or may inherit property) many years from now. Also, it will be a blot on his or her credit, which he or she may later want to clear up by paying you.

Chapter 12:
Self-Service Storage Space

When real property is rented for the storage of personal property and not as a residence, different rules of law apply. This is understandable, since you are not dealing with people (tenants) but with things. You do not, for example, have to make the premises habitable. You also do not have the leverage of eviction because the renter is not losing a place to live. The rules are generally more favorable to the landlord in self-storage rentals than the rules for renting to people.

Applicability

The rental of space in self-storage facilities is controlled by the California Business and Professional Code, beginning with Section 21700.

A *self-storage facility* is real property used to store personal property. It is not a warehouse, a garage, or another part of a private residence. It cannot be used as a residence. If you rented out a garage separately, and not as part of a residence rental, it could qualify.

Rental Agreement

In addition to the occupant's name and address, the rental agreement must also have a space for the occupant to provide an alternative address (although the occupant is not required to give one). (California Business and Professional Code, Section 21712.) If the landlord wishes to have the ability to sell the stored property in order to satisfy unpaid rent, the agreement must so provide.

Termination for Unpaid Rent

If the rent is unpaid for fourteen days, the landlord may terminate the agreement by sending a notice to the renter's last known address and the alternative address, if any, given in the rental agreement.

Late Fees

Late fees may be charged for unpaid rent. The owner of a self-service storage facility may assess a *reasonable* late payment fee if an occupant does not pay the entire amount of the rental fee specified in the rental agreement. The late fee is subject to the following requirements.

◆ No late payment fee shall be assessed unless the rental fee remains unpaid for at least ten days after the date specified in the rental agreement for payment of the rental fee.

◆ The amount of the late payment fee must be specifed in the renter's rental agreement.

◆ Only one late payment fee may be assessed for each rental fee payment that is not paid on the day specified in the rental agreement.

◆ A *reasonable late payment fee* is one that does not exceed the following:

   ◆ ten dollars ($10), if the rental agreement provides for monthly rent of sixty dollars ($60) or less;

   ◆ fifteen dollars ($15), if the rental agreement provides for monthly rent greater than sixty dollars ($60) but less than one hundred dollars ($100); or,

   ◆ twenty dollars ($20) or 15% of the monthly rental fee, whichever is greater, if the rental agreement provides for monthly rent of one hundred dollars ($100) or more.

Liens

A *lien* against property means that the property may be used to secure the debt. If the rent on a storage unit is not paid, the contents can be used (sold) to pay what is owed. Liens take priority over the debts of general creditors. There may be more than one lien on the same property. Usually, first in time determines the priority. The owner of a self-storage facility has a lien for rent, labor, or other charges on the property stored in the unit. (California Business and Professional Code, Section 21702.) It does not matter whose property it is—the lien attaches to any property in the unit on the date it is brought to the facility.

The lien on a vehicle or vessel is subject to prior liens. In other words, if the car or boat is not free and clear, that lien takes priority over the storage lien.

The California Business and Professional Code sets forth the instructions for how the lien sale is to be carried out. It even includes the forms that should be sent to the occupant. A copy of this form, the Preliminary Lien Notice, is included as form 47 in Appendix D of this book.

Chapter 13:
Mobile Home Parks

Mobile homes in California require different eviction procedures, depending on several factors, such as the classification of the unit as a *mobile home* or a *recreational vehicle* (RV), and the ownership of the unit.

If the landlord owns the unit, the eviction procedures are the same as described earlier for houses or apartments. The procedures are more difficult when the landlord owns the land (e.g., trailer park), but not the RV or mobile home. This is because the unit may be sold to pay for the back rent. You are evicting the *unit*, not just the *tenant*. This is the procedure described below.

The distinction between an RV and a mobile home depends on two factors.
1. If the unit requires a moving permit to go onto public roads, it is a mobile home.
2. If the unit does not require a moving permit, it still may be considered a mobile home if it occupies a mobile home space or occupies an RV space for more than nine months.

NOTE: *To add to the confusion, units such as motor coaches and camping trailers are always considered RVs. When in doubt, check California Civil Code, Sections 798 and 799.*

Procedure

As of January 1, 2006, the rental agreement does not allow for a *right of first refusal* clause. This is a clause allowing the landlord to purchase the mobile home by matching the price the owner is willing to accept from a third party. The law does not prevent a separate agreement for a right of first refusal, but if you put it in your rental agreement, you will not be able to enforce it if the owner decides to sell.

Once you have determined that you are dealing with a mobile home, you follow a procedure somewhat similar to an eviction from a house or apartment.

◆ Serve a **Three-Day/Sixty-Day Notice**. (see form 23, p.237.) Three days is the time for payment of rent and the sixty days is the time to remove the mobile home before you can take further action.

◆ File a **Complaint—Unlawful Detainer** (form 30), **Summons** (form 31), and (optional) **Prejudgment Claim of Right to Possession** (form 32). These are the same as house and apartment evictions, but you must wait sixty days before you can file them.

◆ File a **Request for Entry of Default**. (see form 33, p.261.) In contested cases, follow the same rules as for houses or apartments. After you win, file for a *Writ of Execution*. At this time, you will be given a date when the marshal will lock out the tenant.

Taking Possession

After the lockout, you are not finished. You do not own the unit, so you cannot take possession as you would your house or apartment. You must have the unit removed or sold, or you must take ownership yourself. The procedure depends on whether the tenant or a third party is the owner.

If the tenant is both the registered and the legal owner, return the *Writ of Possession* to the court and obtain from the court a Writ of Execution of the judgment. Deliver the Writ of Execution and instructions to the marshal to sell the unit to pay the judgment. The unit will be sold at auction, through a lien sale like a foreclosure. You would become the owner if there was no one willing to pay enough to satisfy the judgment. The title you receive should then be taken to the Housing and Community Development Agency to clear the title in your name.

If there is a different legal owner, you must give notice to the legal owner, wait the statutory period (minimum of ten days) for the owner to pay you, and publish a notice before holding the sale. You must also give notice to any other lienholders. The procedure is similar to foreclosure.

Abandoned Property

If a unit is abandoned, you have three options.

1. Follow the unlawful detainer procedures as described on page 80.
2. Follow the procedure for abandonment. (California Civil Code, Section 798.61.) The difference between the abandoned mobile home and an abandoned apartment is that the rent on the mobile home must be unpaid for more than sixty days before you may proceed.
3. If there are lienholders, contact them for payment or a lienholder's sale to raise the money for payment.

Rent Control

There are over seventy local governments that have some form of rent control for mobile homes. Check the city and county offices where the property is located. They may have special requirements different from those in this chapter.

Chapter 14:
New and Changing Laws

Local laws and California laws are constantly changing. There is no practical way to update a book often enough to keep up with these changes, but you can get the most up-to-date information available from other sources.

The *California Apartment Association* (CAA) keeps track of all changes that will affect rental housing. Ideally, you should become a member. This will give you access to forms and other valuable help in managing your rental property. The CAA has forms, for example, that have been revised twice in a matter of months. Since no book can be reprinted every few months to keep up with such changes, it is worth your time to be a member of the CAA.

If you do not become a member, at least check the website on a regular basis for information that may affect your property. The website address is **www.caanet.org**.

Glossary

A

actual damages. Money lost by the plaintiff due to the wrongful acts of the defendant. This differs from other types of damages, such as punitive or liquidated.

agent. One who acts on behalf of another (called the principal) with authority to commit the principal to a contract.

assignment. A transfer of rights, such as those of a lease. The person receiving the rights is called the assignee; the one transferring the rights is called the assignor. A transfer of duties is called a delegation.

B

back rent. Commonly describes rent that is more than one rental period in arrears, although it can mean any unpaid rent that is due.

bad faith. Acting with intent to do wrong rather than simply making a mistake.

breach. Violating the terms of a contract without a legal excuse.

buried clauses. Clauses in a contract that are difficult to find unless the contract is read very carefully. The law requires certain clauses to be in a specific size or bold type, or to be located in an easy to see place, such as just above where the parties will sign.

C

causation. A necessary element to collect damages. The plaintiff must show that the defendant's conduct caused the damages to the plaintiff.

complaint. The initial filing of a lawsuit. The plaintiff files the complaint alleging the reason for the suit and the defendant then must file an answer.

contempt of court. Violation of a court order or improper behavior in a courtroom.

cosigner. One who signs to secure the debt of another. The cosigner is just as liable as the debtor, unless otherwise agreed.

court hearing. A general term covering any number of court proceedings. It differs from a trial in that there is no jury and may be based on legal, rather than factual, issues.

credit report. A history of the debts of a person with emphasis on whether the debts were paid as agreed. The report is commonly used by prospective lenders, landlords, and employers.

curable breach. A violation of a contract that can be corrected. A landlord can send a notice to a tenant demanding that the tenant correct the violation of the lease before beginning eviction.

D

damages. The financial harm done to the defendant. Examples could be the tenant's failure to pay the rent or physical damage to the property.

default. Failure to fulfill an obligation, rather than actively doing something wrong. Failure to pay rent is the most common.

defendant index. A list of cases filed by the name of the defendant. This lets the researcher see all the cases filed in the past against a particular person.

deposition. Questioning a witness outside the courtroom. The witness may have an attorney, but rules of questioning are not as strict as in court questioning.

discovery. The giving of information to the opposing side in a lawsuit. Modern legal theory is that surprises are less likely to produce a just result than openness. A criminal defendant does not, of course, have to give incriminating information to a prosecutor, but a prosecutor must give exculpatory information to a defendant.

duty to mitigate. The obligation of the plaintiff to hold damages to a minimum. A landlord's obligation to try to re-rent the property after a tenant moves out before the lease ends is an example.

E

eviction. The process of removing a person from property. Removing a tenant is the most common type.

F

fictitious name. A name other than the name of the person. It does not have to be for a wrongful purpose. For example, Joe Smith owns his building in the name of Smith's Resort.

G

garnishment. The taking of a person's wages to pay a debt. There must first be a judgment against the person and there are rules as to the procedures to follow and the maximum that can be taken from a pay period.

guarantor. One who agrees to be liable for the debt of another. A guarantor of payment is liable the same as the debtor (primary liability). A guarantor of collection is liable only after the creditor has been unable to collect from the debtor (secondary liability).

guaranty. Agreeing to be liable for the debt of another.

H

habitability. A condition fit for human occupancy. A landlord has a duty to have the rental unit fit for the tenant to live in, such as having heat and working plumbing. This is a minimum standard required by law. The standard agreed to by the parties may be much higher.

I

implied authorization. Authority of an agent implied by his or her position, even if there is no actual authority. If a building manager, for example, collects rent against the wishes of the owner, but the owner has not informed the tenant that the manager has no authority to do this, the tenant is not responsible for any loss suffered by the owner if the manager keeps the money.

incurable breach. A violation of a contract that is so severe the landlord simply wants the tenant out of the residence.

injunction. A remedy to prevent a person from doing something, rather than collecting damages for the harm caused. If you want the factory next to your building to stop emitting noxious fumes, you could sue for an injunction to make it stop.

intentional acts. Those acts that are deliberately done. Intentional wrongdoing is generally considered more serious than carelessness (negligence) or acts for which one is strictly liable.

interest (as in an interest in property). A right in property. It may be the right of an owner, the right to occupy as a tenant, or some lesser right as to travel across the property (easement right).

interest-bearing account. An account earning money simply for being in the account. Some money held by a landlord, such as security deposits, may be placed in such accounts.

interrogatories. Questions submitted by parties to a lawsuit to the opposing side. They are in written form, rather than verbal questions, as in a deposition.

J

judgment. The decision of a court. It will determine if the plaintiff is entitled to damages (if the plaintiff won) and for how much.

just cause. A legal and lawful reason to bring a legal action.

L

landlord. An owner of property who rents the property to a tenant.

landlord/tenant law. That portion of real property law dealing with the legal relationship between an owner of property (landlord) and one who rents the property (tenant).

lease. A contract between a landlord and a tenant setting forth the rights and duties agreed to by each. It differs from a rental agreement in that it has a definite termination date.

levy. A collection, seizure, or assessment.

liability. Legal responsibility to do, or refrain from doing, something. This means you can be sued (be liable) for failure to carry out this responsibility.

liens. Money encumbrances against property. Examples would be mortgages or deeds of trust (voluntary liens), or judgments and tax liens (involuntary liens).

liquidated damages. A preset estimate of damages should the contract be breached, when actual damages would be difficult to determine. Common in real estate sales contracts. For example, the buyer loses the deposit if he or she *breaches* the contract. The amount must be reasonable or it will be considered a penalty and void.

M

management company. A business that takes care of property for the owner. It may be responsible for collecting rents, maintenance, leasing to and evicting tenants, or all of these.

N

negligence. Failure to use reasonable care by one who has a duty to do so. The failure must cause damages to the plaintiff. If a landlord, for example, fails to use reasonable care to keep a building safe, and this failure causes injury to a tenant, the landlord would be liable for negligence.

negligence per se. Negligence from violating a statute (law). For example, if the law says that you must have a fence around your pool and you do not, injury caused by not having the fence would be negligence per se.

notary. One who is licensed by the state to attest to the authenticity of a signature. In order to have almost all documents recorded, the signature on the document must be notarized.

notice. Informing of something that has happened or is going to happen. Recording a deed, for example, would give notice that a transfer of ownership has taken place. A notice to quit would tell the tenant to move within a given time in the future.

notice to quit. Informing a tenant to leave the property or face eviction. The notice could simply demand that the tenant leave, or be conditional, such as pay the rent owed or leave.

O

on-site manager. A person who lives on the property and is responsible for the day-to-day activities, such as collection of rent, maintenance, and showing the property to prospective tenants.

option. The choice of entering into a contract. For example, a lease could give the tenant the option (right but not obligation) to extend beyond the expiration date or the option to purchase the property.

ordinances. County and city laws. They are called statutes at the state or federal level.

P

punitive damages. Money the defendant must pay as a punishment or to set an example (also called exemplary damages) for especially bad behavior. Requires more than simple breach or negligence.

R

reasonable care. The care a reasonably prudent person would take under the circumstances. Failure to use reasonable care is required to prove *negligence*.

rent. The periodic payment of money in exchange for the right to possession of the property.

rent control. Governmental regulations setting maximum rents and rules for eviction beyond normal contract law.

rent control board. A group that monitors and enforces rent control.

rescission. Returning the parties to a contract to their positions before the contract. This may not always be possible as the subject matter of the contract cannot always be returned.

retaliatory evictions. Demanding a tenant leave in response to a legitimate action taken by the tenant, such as reporting the landlord for health code violations. If the eviction is considered retaliatory, it is illegal.

right of first refusal. Giving a tenant the right to match any offer to buy the property. The tenant must *first refuse* to buy before the owner can sell to a third party.

S

safe-harbor rule. Any rule considered within the law or disclaimers to avoid liability.

screening. Checking the background of a prospective tenant. This may include a credit report, verification of employment, reference of a prior landlord, and so on.

security deposit. Money deposited with the landlord, in addition to rent, to be used if the tenant fails to pay the agreed upon rent or causes damage to the property.

service of process. The delivery of the paperwork necessary to begin a lawsuit. A landlord must inform tenants where service of process can be received.

standard of care. How much a person must do to avoid damage to another to whom a duty is owed. The law sets minimum standards for a landlord's operation of a rental property for the health and safety of the tenant. The standard may be raised by agreement of the parties or promises by the landlord.

statutes. Laws passed by the federal congress or state legislators. County and city laws are called *ordinances.*

stay. A court order to stop a legal process in progress. For example, a bankruptcy court could stay (stop) an eviction or foreclosure proceeding. The owner or lender would then have to ask the court to lift the stay (grant a relief of stay).

stipulation. Agreement between the parties to a legal dispute on a specific point. This eliminates the need to prove the point.

strict liability. Holding one responsible for damages even though reasonable care was used to prevent the damage or injury. The plaintiff must still show that the defendant owed a duty to the plaintiff and that the plaintiff's actions caused the damages.

sublease. A lease between a tenant and a third party (subtenant). Subleasing is allowed unless the lease specifically prohibits it. Usually, the lease states that approval of the landlord is required.

T

tenant. One who rents real property. The tenant receives the right to occupy the property in exchange for the payment of money (*rent*).

U

unconscionable clause. A clause in a contract that is so unfair (although not against the law) that a court cannot in good conscience enforce it. The clause must be unfair at the formation of the contract, and the court can choose to enforce the rest of the contract.

unlawful detainer. The name for the legal action to evict someone from property.

W

waiver. The giving up of a right. For example, accepting late rent without charging the agreed upon late charge may be a waiver of future right to the late charge.

Z

zoning. The specified allowable use of property as set forth by county or city ordinance, or by master plan.

Appendix A:
California Statutes

This appendix contains selected California statutes that pertain to the landlord/tenant relationship. The following sections are covered.

- ◆ California Civil Code, Section 827—Raising Rent
- ◆ California Civil Code, Section 1719—Bad Checks
- ◆ California Civil Code, Sections 1940 through 1954.1—Landlord/Tenant Renting Real Estate
- ◆ California Civil Code, Sections 1954.50 through 1954.535—Rent Control
- ◆ California Civil Code, Sections 1961 through 1962—Multiunit Buildings
- ◆ California Civil Code, Sections 1980 through 1991—Abandoned Property
- ◆ California Code of Civil Procedure, Section 1013 through 1013a—Procedures for Changing a Lease
- ◆ California Code of Civil Procedure, Section 1162—Raising Rent

You can read the laws in their entirety by visiting **www.leginfo.ca.gov** and clicking on "California Law," then selecting a code or entering a key word in the search bar.

CALIFORNIA CIVIL CODE SECTION 827

(a) Except as provided in subdivision (b), in all leases of lands or tenements, or of any interest therein, from week to week, month to month, or other period less than a month, the landlord may, upon giving notice in writing to the tenant, in the manner prescribed by Section 1162 of the Code of Civil Procedure, change the terms of the lease to take effect, as to tenancies for less than one month, upon the expiration of a period at least as long as the term of the hiring itself, and, as to tenancies from month to month, to take effect at the expiration of not less than 30 days, but if that change takes effect within a rental term, the rent accruing from the first day of the term to the date of that change shall be computed at the rental rate which obtained immediately prior to that change; provided, however, that it shall be competent for the parties to provide by an agreement in writing that a notice changing the terms thereof may be given at any time not less than seven days before the expiration of a term, to be effective upon the expiration of the term. The notice, when served upon the tenant, shall in and of itself operate and be effectual to create and establish, as a part of the lease, the terms, rents, and conditions specified in the notice, if the tenant shall continue to hold the premises after the notice takes effect.

(b)(1) In all leases of a residential dwelling, or of any interest therein, from week to week, month to month, or other period less than a month, the landlord may increase the rent provided in the lease or rental agreement, upon giving written notice to the tenant, as follows, by either of the following procedures:

(A) By delivering a copy to the tenant personally.

(B) By serving a copy by mail under the procedures prescribed in Section 1013 of the Code of Civil Procedure.

(2) If the proposed rent increase for that tenant is 10 percent or less of the rental amount charged to that tenant at any time during the 12 months prior to the effective date of the increase, either in and of itself or when combined with any other rent increases for the 12 months prior to the effective date of the increase, the notice shall be delivered at least 30 days prior to the effective date of the increase, and subject to Section 1013 of the Code of Civil Procedure if served by mail.

(3) For an increase in rent greater than the amount described in paragraph (2), the minimum notice period required pursuant to that paragraph shall be increased by an additional 30 days, and subject to Section 1013 of the Code of Civil Procedure if served by mail. This paragraph shall not apply to an increase in rent caused by a change in a tenant's income or family composition as determined by a recertification required by statute or regulation.

(c) If a state or federal statute, state or federal regulation, recorded regulatory agreement, or contract provides for a longer period of notice regarding a rent increase than that provided in subdivision (a) or (b), the personal service or mailing of the notice shall be in accordance with the longer period.

SECTION 1719

1719. (a)(1) Notwithstanding any penal sanctions that may apply, any person who passes a check on insufficient funds shall be liable to the payee for the amount of the check and a service charge payable to the payee for an amount not to exceed twenty-five dollars ($25) for the first check passed on insufficient funds and an amount not to exceed thirty-five dollars ($35) for each subsequent check to that payee passed on insufficient funds.

(2) Notwithstanding any penal sanctions that may apply, any person who passes a check on insufficient funds shall be liable to the payee for damages equal to treble the amount of the check if a written demand for payment is mailed by certified mail to the person who had passed a check on insufficient funds and the written demand informs this person of (A) the provisions of this section, (B) the amount of the check, and (C) the amount of the service charge payable to the payee. The person who had passed a check on insufficient funds shall have 30 days from the date the written demand was mailed to pay the amount of the check, the amount of the service charge payable to the payee, and the costs to mail the written demand for payment. If this person fails to pay in full the amount of the check, the service charge payable to the payee, and the costs to mail the written demand within this period, this person shall then be liable instead for the amount of the check, minus any partial payments made toward the amount of the check or the service charge within 30 days of the written demand, and damages equal to treble that amount, which shall not be less than one hundred dollars ($100) nor more than one thousand five hundred dollars ($1,500). When a person becomes liable for treble damages for a check that is the subject of a written demand, that person shall no longer be liable for any service charge for that check and any costs to mail the written demand.

(3) Notwithstanding paragraphs (1) and (2), a person shall not be liable for the service charge, costs to mail the written demand, or treble damages if he or she stops payment in order to resolve a good faith dispute with the payee. The payee is entitled to the service charge, costs to mail the written demand, or treble damages only upon proving by clear and convincing evidence that there was no good faith dispute, as defined in subdivision (b).

(4) Notwithstanding paragraph (1), a person shall not be liable under that paragraph for the service charge if, at any time, he or she presents the payee with written confirmation by his or her financial institution that the check was returned to the payee by the financial institution due to an error on the part of the financial institution.

(5) Notwithstanding paragraph (1), a person shall not be liable under that paragraph for the service charge if the person presents the payee with written confirmation that his or her account had insufficient funds as a result of a delay in the regularly scheduled transfer of, or the posting of, a direct deposit of a social security or government benefit assistance payment.

(6) As used in this subdivision, to "pass a check on insufficient funds" means to make, utter, draw, or deliver any check, draft, or order for the payment of money upon any bank, depository, person, firm, or corporation that refuses to honor the check, draft, or order for any of the following reasons:

(A) Lack of funds or credit in the account to pay the check.

(B) The person who wrote the check does not have an account with the drawee.

(C) The person who wrote the check instructed the drawee to stop payment on the check.

(b) For purposes of this section, in the case of a stop payment, the existence of a "good faith dispute" shall be determined by the trier of fact. A "good faith dispute" is one in which the court finds that the drawer had a reasonable belief of his or her legal entitlement to withhold payment. Grounds for the entitlement include, but are not limited to, the following: services were not rendered, goods were not delivered, goods or services purchased are faulty, not as promised, or otherwise unsatisfactory, or there was an overcharge.

(c) In the case of a stop payment, the notice to the drawer required by this section shall be in substantially the following form:

NOTICE

To: _____
       (name of drawer)

_____ is the payee of
       (name of payee)
a check you wrote for $ _____
                 (amount)

The check was not paid because you stopped payment, and the payee demands payment. You may have a good faith dispute as to whether you owe the full amount. If you do not have a good faith dispute with the payee and fail to pay the payee the full amount of the check in cash, a service charge of an amount not to exceed twenty-five dollars ($25) for the first check passed on insufficient funds and an amount not to exceed thirty-five dollars ($35) for each subsequent check passed on insufficient funds, and the costs to mail this notice within 30 days after this notice was mailed, you could be sued and held responsible to pay at least both of the following:

(1) The amount of the check.

(2) Damages of at least one hundred dollars ($100) or, if higher, three times the amount of the check up to one thousand five hundred dollars ($1,500).

If the court determines that you do have a good faith dispute with the payee, you will not have to pay the service charge, treble damages, or mailing cost.

If you stopped payment because you have a good faith dispute with the payee, you should try to work out your dispute with the payee.

You can contact the payee at:

_____

(name of payee)

_____

(street address)

_____

(telephone number)

You may wish to contact a lawyer to discuss your legal rights and responsibilities.

_____

(name of sender of notice)

(d) In the case of a stop payment, a court may not award damages or costs under this section unless the court receives into evidence a copy of the written demand which, in that case, shall have been sent to the drawer and a signed certified mail receipt showing delivery, or attempted delivery if refused, of the written demand to the drawer's last known address.

(e) A cause of action under this section may be brought in small claims court by the original payee, if it does not exceed the jurisdiction of that court, or in any other appropriate court. The payee shall, in order to recover damages because the drawer instructed the drawee to stop payment, show to the satisfaction of the trier of fact that there was a reasonable effort on the part of the payee to reconcile and resolve the dispute prior to pursuing the dispute through the courts.

(f) A cause of action under this section may be brought by a holder of the check or an assignee of the payee. A proceeding under this section is a limited civil case. However, if the assignee is acting on behalf of the payee, for a flat fee or a percentage fee, the assignee may not charge the payee a greater flat fee or percentage fee for that portion of the amount collected that represents treble damages than is charged the payee for collecting the face amount of the check, draft, or order. This subdivision shall not apply to an action brought in small claims court.

(g) Notwithstanding subdivision (a), if the payee is the court, the written demand for payment described in subdivision (a) may be mailed to the drawer by the court clerk. Notwithstanding subdivision (d), in the case of a stop payment where the demand is mailed by the court clerk, a court may not award damages or costs pursuant to subdivision (d), unless the court receives into evidence a copy of the written demand, and a certificate of mailing by the court clerk in the form provided for in subdivision (4) of Section 1013a of the Code of Civil Procedure for service in civil actions. For purposes of this subdivision, in courts where a single court clerk serves more than one court, the clerk shall be deemed the court clerk of each court.

(h) The requirements of this section in regard to remedies are mandatory upon a court.

(i) The assignee of the payee or a holder of the check may demand, recover, or enforce the service charge, damages, and costs specified in this section to the same extent as the original payee.

(j) (1) A drawer is liable for damages and costs only if all of the requirements of this section have been satisfied.

(2) The drawer shall in no event be liable more than once under this section on each check for a service charge, damages, or costs.

(k) Nothing in this section is intended to condition, curtail, or otherwise prejudice the rights, claims, remedies, and defenses under Division 3 (commencing with Section 3101) of the Commercial Code of a drawer, payee, assignee, or holder, including a holder in due course as defined in Section 3302 of the Commercial Code, in connection with the enforcement of this section.

SECTION 1940-1954.535

1940. (a) Except as provided in subdivision (b), this chapter shall apply to all persons who hire dwelling units located within this state including tenants, lessees, boarders, lodgers, and others, however denominated.

(b) The term "persons who hire" shall not include a person who maintains either of the following:

(1) Transient occupancy in a hotel, motel, residence club, or other facility when the transient occupancy is or would be subject to tax under Section 7280 of the Revenue and Taxation Code. The term "persons who hire" shall not include a person to whom this paragraph pertains if the person has not made valid payment for all room and other related charges owing as of the last day on which his or her occupancy is or would be subject to tax under Section 7280 of the Revenue and Taxation Code.

(2) Occupancy at a hotel or motel where the innkeeper retains a right of access to and control of the dwelling unit and the hotel or motel provides or offers all of the following services to all of the residents:

(A) Facilities for the safeguarding of personal property pursuant to Section 1860.

(B) Central telephone service subject to tariffs covering the same filed with the California Public Utilities Commission.

(C) Maid, mail, and room services.

(D) Occupancy for periods of less than seven days.

(E) Food service provided by a food establishment, as defined in Section 113780 of the Health and Safety Code, located on or adjacent to the premises of the hotel or motel and owned or operated by the innkeeper or owned or operated by a person or entity pursuant to a lease or

similar relationship with the innkeeper or person or entity affiliated with the innkeeper.

(c) "Dwelling unit" means a structure or the part of a structure that is used as a home, residence, or sleeping place by one person who maintains a household or by two or more persons who maintain a common household.

(d) Nothing in this section shall be construed to limit the application of any provision of this chapter to tenancy in a dwelling unit unless the provision is so limited by its specific terms.

1940.1. (a) No person may require an occupant of a residential hotel, as defined in Section 50519 of the Health and Safety Code, to move, or to check out and reregister, before the expiration of 30 days occupancy if a purpose is to avoid application of this chapter pursuant to paragraph (1) of subdivision (b) of Section 1940.

(b) In addition to any remedies provided by local ordinance, any violation of subdivision (a) is punishable by a civil penalty of five hundred dollars ($500). In any action brought pursuant to this section, the prevailing party shall be entitled to reasonable attorney's fees.

1940.2. (a) It is unlawful for a landlord to do any of the following for the purpose of influencing a tenant to vacate a dwelling:

(1) Engage in conduct that violates subdivision (a) of Section 484 of the Penal Code.

(2) Engage in conduct that violates Section 518 of the Penal Code.

(3) Use, or threaten to use, force, willful threats, or menacing conduct constituting a course of conduct that interferes with the tenant's quiet enjoyment of the premises in violation of Section 1927 that would create an apprehension of harm in a reasonable person. Nothing in this paragraph requires a tenant to be actually or constructively evicted in order to obtain relief.

(4) Commit a significant and intentional violation of Section 1954.

(b) A tenant who prevails in a civil action, including an action in small claims court, to enforce his or her rights under this section is entitled to a civil penalty in an amount not to exceed two thousand dollars ($2,000) for each violation.

(c) An oral or written warning notice, given in good faith, regarding conduct by a tenant, occupant, or guest that violates, may violate, or violated the applicable rental agreement, rules, regulations, lease, or laws, is not a violation of this section. An oral or written explanation of the rental agreement, rules, regulations, lease, or laws given in the normal course of business is not a violation of this section.

(d) Nothing in this section shall enlarge or diminish a landlord's right to terminate a tenancy pursuant to existing state or local law; nor shall this section enlarge or diminish any ability of local government to regulate or enforce a prohibition against a landlord's harassment of a tenant.

1940.5. An owner or an owner's agent shall not refuse to rent a dwelling unit in a structure which received its valid certificate of occupancy after January 1, 1973, to an otherwise qualified prospective tenant or refuse to continue to rent to an existing tenant solely on the basis of that tenant's possession of a waterbed or other bedding with liquid filling material where all of the following requirements and conditions are met:

(a) A tenant or prospective tenant furnishes to the owner, prior to installation, a valid waterbed insurance policy or certificate of insurance for property damage. The policy shall be issued by a company licensed to do business in California and possessing a Best's Insurance Report rating of "B" or higher. The insurance policy shall be maintained in full force and effect until the bedding is permanently removed from the rental premises. The policy shall be written for no less than one hundred thousand dollars ($100,000) of coverage. The policy shall cover, up to the limits of the policy, replacement value of all property damage, including loss of use, incurred by the rental property owner or other caused by or arising out of the ownership, maintenance, use, or removal of the waterbed on the rental premises only, except for any damage caused intentionally or at the direction of the insured, or for any damage caused by or resulting from fire. The owner may require the tenant to produce evidence of insurance at any time. The carrier shall give the owner notice of cancellation or nonrenewal 10 days prior to this action. Every application for a policy shall contain the information as provided in subdivisions (a), (b), and (c) of Section 1962 and Section 1962.5.

(b) The bedding shall conform to the pounds-per-square foot weight limitation and placement as dictated by the floor load capacity of the residential structure. The weight shall be distributed on a pedestal or frame which is substantially the dimensions of the mattress itself.

(c) The tenant or prospective tenant shall install, maintain and remove the bedding, including, but not limited to, the mattress and frame, according to standard methods of installation, maintenance, and removal as prescribed by the manufacturer, retailer, or state law, whichever provides the higher degree of safety. The tenant shall notify the owner or owner's agent in writing of the intent to install, remove, or move the waterbed. The notice shall be delivered 24 hours prior to the installation, removal, or movement. The owner or the owner's agent may be present at the time of installation, removal, or movement at the owner's or the owner's agent's option. If the bedding is installed or moved by any person other than the tenant or prospective tenant, the tenant or prospective tenant shall deliver to the owner or to the owner's agent a written installation receipt stating the installer's name, address, and business affiliation where appropriate.

(d) Any new bedding installation shall conform to the owner's or the owner's agent's reasonable structural specifications for placement within the rental property and shall be consistent with floor capacity of the rental dwelling unit.

(e) The tenant or prospective tenant shall comply with the minimum component specification list prescribed by the manufacturer, retailer, or state law, whichever provides the higher degree of safety.

(f) Subject to the notice requirements of Section 1954, the owner, or the owner's agent, shall have the right to inspect the bedding installation upon completion, and periodically thereafter, to insure its conformity with this section. If installation or maintenance is not in conformity with this section, the owner may serve the tenant with a written notice of breach of the rental agreement. The owner may give the tenant three days either to bring the installation into conformity with those standards or to remove the bedding, unless there is an immediate danger to the structure, in which case there shall be immediate corrective action. If the bedding is installed by any person other than the tenant or prospective tenant, the tenant or prospective tenant shall deliver to the owner or to the owner's agent a written installation receipt stating the installer's name and business affiliation where appropriate.

(g) Notwithstanding Section 1950.5, an owner or owner's agent is entitled to increase the security deposit on the dwelling unit in an amount equal to one-half of one months' rent. The owner or owner's agent may charge a tenant, lessee, or sublessee a reasonable fee to cover administration costs. In no event does this section authorize the payment of a rebate of premium in violation of Article 5 (commencing with Section 750) of Chapter 1 of Part 2 of Division 1 of the Insurance Code. (h) Failure of the owner, or owner's agent, to exercise any of his or her rights pursuant to this section does not constitute grounds for denial of an insurance claim.

(i) As used in this section, "tenant" includes any lessee, and "rental" means any rental or lease.

1940.6. (a) The owner of a residential dwelling unit or the owner's agent who applies to any public agency for a permit to demolish that residential dwelling unit shall give written notice of that fact to:

(1) A prospective tenant prior to the occurrence of any of the following actions by the owner or the owner's agent: (A) Entering into a rental agreement with a prospective tenant. (B) Requiring or accepting payment from the prospective tenant for an application screening fee, as provided in Section 1950.6. (C) Requiring or accepting any other fees from a prospective tenant. (D) Requiring or accepting any writings that would initiate a tenancy.

(2) A current tenant, including a tenant who has entered into a rental agreement but has not yet taken possession of the dwelling unit, prior to applying to the public agency for the permit to demolish that residential dwelling unit.

(b) The notice shall include the earliest possible approximate date on which the owner expects the demolition to occur and the approximate date on which the owner will terminate the tenancy. However, in no case may the demolition for which the owner or the owner's agent has applied occur prior to the earliest possible approximate date noticed.

(c) If a landlord fails to comply with subdivision (a) or (b), a tenant may bring an action in a court of competent jurisdiction. The remedies the court may order shall include, but are not limited to, the following:

(1) In the case of a prospective tenant who moved into a residential dwelling unit and was not informed as required by subdivision (a) or (b), the actual damages suffered, moving expenses, and a civil penalty not to exceed two thousand five hundred dollars ($2,500) to be paid by the landlord to the tenant.

(2) In the case of a current tenant who was not informed as required by subdivision (a) or (b), the actual damages suffered, and a civil penalty not to exceed two thousand five hundred dollars ($2,500) to be paid by the landlord to the tenant.

(3) In any action brought pursuant to this section, the prevailing party shall be entitled to reasonable attorney's fees.

(d) The remedies available under this section are cumulative to other remedies available under law.

(e) This section shall not be construed to preempt other laws regarding landlord obligations or disclosures, including, but not limited to, those arising pursuant to Chapter 12.75 (commencing with Section 7060) of Division 7 of Title 1 of the Government Code.

(f) For purposes of this section:

(1) "Residential dwelling unit" has the same meaning as that contained in Section 1940.

(2) "Public agency" has the same meaning as that contained in Section 21063 of the Public Resources Code.

1940.7. (a) The Legislature finds and declares that the December 10, 1983, tragedy in Tierra Santa, in which lives were lost as a result of a live munition exploding in a residential area that was formerly a military ordnance location, has demonstrated (1) the unique and heretofore unknown risk that there are other live munitions in former ordnance locations in California, (2) that these former ordnance locations need to be identified by the federal, state, or local authorities, and (3) that the people living in the neighborhood of these former ordnance locations should be notified of their existence. Therefore, it is the intent of the Legislature that the disclosure required by this section is solely warranted and limited by (1) the fact that these former ordnance locations cannot be readily observed or dis-

covered by landlords and tenants, and (2) the ability of a landlord who has actual knowledge of a former ordnance location within the neighborhood of his or her rental property to disclose this information for the safety of the tenant.

(b) The landlord of a residential dwelling unit who has actual knowledge of any former federal or state ordnance locations in the neighborhood area shall give written notice to a prospective tenant of that knowledge prior to the execution of a rental agreement. In cases of tenancies in existence on January 1, 1990, this written notice shall be given to tenants as soon as practicable thereafter.

(c) For purposes of this section:

(1) "Former federal or state ordnance location" means an area identified by an agency or instrumentality of the federal or state government as an area once used for military training purposes and which may contain potentially explosive munitions.

(2) "Neighborhood area" means within one mile of the residential dwelling.

1940.8. A landlord of a residential dwelling unit shall provide each new tenant that occupies the unit with a copy of the notice provided by a registered structural pest control company pursuant to Section 8538 of the Business and Professions Code, if a contract for periodic pest control service has been executed.

1940.9. (a) If the landlord does not provide separate gas and electric meters for each tenant's dwelling unit so that each tenant's meter measures only the electric or gas service to that tenant's dwelling unit and the landlord or his or her agent has knowledge that gas or electric service provided through a tenant's meter serves an area outside the tenant's dwelling unit, the landlord, prior to the inception of the tenancy or upon discovery, shall explicitly disclose that condition to the tenant and shall do either of the following:

(1) Execute a mutual written agreement with the tenant for payment by the tenant of the cost of the gas or electric service provided through the tenant's meter to serve areas outside the tenant's dwelling unit.

(2) Make other arrangements, as are mutually agreed in writing, for payment for the gas or electric service provided through the tenant's meter to serve areas outside the tenant's dwelling unit. These arrangements may include, but are not limited to, the landlord becoming the customer of record for the tenant's meter, or the landlord separately metering and becoming the customer of record for the area outside the tenant's dwelling unit.

(b) If a landlord fails to comply with subdivision (a), the aggrieved tenant may bring an action in a court of competent jurisdiction. The remedies the court may order shall include, but are not limited to, the following:

(1) Requiring the landlord to be made the customer of record with the utility for the tenant's meter.

(2) Ordering the landlord to reimburse the tenant for payments made by the tenant to the utility for service to areas outside of the tenant's dwelling unit. Payments to be reimbursed pursuant to this paragraph shall commence from the date the obligation to disclose arose under subdivision (a).

(c) Nothing in this section limits any remedies available to a landlord or tenant under other provisions of this chapter, the rental agreement, or applicable statutory or common law.

1941. Section Nineteen Hundred and Forty-one. The lessor of a building intended for the occupation of human beings must, in the absence of an agreement to the contrary, put it into a condition fit for such occupation, and repair all subsequent dilapidations thereof, which render it untenantable, except such as are mentioned in section nineteen hundred and twenty-nine.

1941.1. A dwelling shall be deemed untenantable for purposes of Section 1941 if it substantially lacks any of the following affirmative standard characteristics or is a residential unit described in Section 17920.3 or 17920.10 of the Health and Safety Code:

(a) Effective waterproofing and weather protection of roof and exterior walls, including unbroken windows and doors.

(b) Plumbing or gas facilities that conformed to applicable law in effect at the time of installation, maintained in good working order.

(c) A water supply approved under applicable law that is under the control of the tenant, capable of producing hot and cold running water, or a system that is under the control of the landlord, that produces hot and cold running water, furnished to appropriate fixtures, and connected to a sewage disposal system approved under applicable law.

(d) Heating facilities that conformed with applicable law at the time of installation, maintained in good working order.

(e) Electrical lighting, with wiring and electrical equipment that conformed with applicable law at the time of installation, maintained in good working order.

(f) Building, grounds, and appurtenances at the time of the commencement of the lease or rental agreement, and all areas under control of the landlord, kept in every part clean, sanitary, and free from all accumulations of debris, filth, rubbish, garbage, rodents, and vermin.

(g) An adequate number of appropriate receptacles for garbage and rubbish, in clean condition and good repair at the time of the commencement of the lease or rental agreement, with the landlord providing appropriate serviceable receptacles thereafter and being responsible for the clean condition and good repair of the receptacles under his or her control.

(h) Floors, stairways, and railings maintained in good repair.

1941.2. (a) No duty on the part of the landlord to repair a dilapidation shall arise under Section 1941 or 1942 if the tenant is in substantial violation of any of the following affirmative obligations, provided the tenant's violation contributes substantially to the existence of the dilapidation or interferes substantially with the landlord's obligation under Section 1941 to effect the necessary repairs:

(1) To keep that part of the premises which he occupies and uses clean and sanitary as the condition of the premises permits.

(2) To dispose from his dwelling unit of all rubbish, garbage and other waste, in a clean and sanitary manner.

(3) To properly use and operate all electrical, gas and plumbing fixtures and keep them as clean and sanitary as their condition permits.

(4) Not to permit any person on the premises, with his permission, to willfully or wantonly destroy, deface, damage, impair or remove any part of the structure or dwelling unit or the facilities, equipment, or appurtenances thereto, nor himself do any such thing.

(5) To occupy the premises as his abode, utilizing portions thereof for living, sleeping, cooking or dining purposes only which were respectively designed or intended to be used for such occupancies.

(b) Paragraphs (1) and (2) of subdivision (a) shall not apply if the landlord has expressly agreed in writing to perform the act or acts mentioned therein.

1941.3. (a) On and after July 1, 1998, the landlord, or his or her agent, of a building intended for human habitation shall do all of the following:

(1) Install and maintain an operable dead bolt lock on each main swinging entry door of a dwelling unit. The dead bolt lock shall be installed in conformance with the manufacturer's specifications and shall comply with applicable state and local codes including, but not limited to, those provisions relating to fire and life safety and accessibility for the disabled. When in the locked position, the bolt shall extend a minimum of 13/16 of an inch in length beyond the strike edge of the door and protrude into the doorjamb.

This section shall not apply to horizontal sliding doors. Existing dead bolts of at least one-half inch in length shall satisfy the requirements of this section. Existing locks with a thumb-turn deadlock that have a strike plate attached to the doorjamb and a latch bolt that is held in a vertical position by a guard bolt, a plunger, or an auxiliary mechanism shall also satisfy the requirements of this section. These locks, however, shall be replaced with a dead bolt at least 13/16 of an inch in length the first time after July 1, 1998, that the lock requires repair or replacement. Existing doors which cannot be equipped with dead bolt locks shall satisfy the requirements of this section if the door is equipped with a metal strap affixed horizontally across the midsection of the door with a dead bolt which extends 13/16 of an inch in length beyond the strike edge of the door and protrudes into the doorjamb. Locks and security devices other than those described herein which are inspected and approved by an appropriate state or local government agency as providing adequate security shall satisfy the requirements of this section.

(2) Install and maintain operable window security or locking devices for windows that are designed to be opened. Louvered windows, casement windows, and all windows more than 12 feet vertically or six feet horizontally from the ground, a roof, or any other platform are excluded from this subdivision.

(3) Install locking mechanisms that comply with applicable fire and safety codes on the exterior doors that provide ingress or egress to common areas with access to dwelling units in multifamily developments. This paragraph does not require the installation of a door or gate where none exists on January 1, 1998.

(b) The tenant shall be responsible for notifying the owner or his or her authorized agent when the tenant becomes aware of an inoperable dead bolt lock or window security or locking device in the dwelling unit. The landlord, or his or her authorized agent, shall not be liable for a violation of subdivision (a) unless he or she fails to correct the violation within a reasonable time after he or she either has actual notice of a deficiency or receives notice of a deficiency.

(c) On and after July 1, 1998, the rights and remedies of tenant for a violation of this section by the landlord shall include those available pursuant to Sections 1942, 1942.4, and 1942.5, an action for breach of contract, and an action for injunctive relief pursuant to Section 526 of the Code of Civil Procedure. Additionally, in an unlawful detainer action, after a default in the payment of rent, a tenant may raise the violation of this section as an affirmative defense and shall have a right to the remedies provided by Section 1174.2 of the Code of Civil Procedure.

(d) A violation of this section shall not broaden, limit, or otherwise affect the duty of care owed by a landlord pursuant to existing law, including any duty that may exist pursuant to Section 1714. The delayed applicability of the requirements of subdivision (a) shall not affect a landlord's duty to maintain the premises in safe condition.

(e) Nothing in this section shall be construed to affect any authority of any public entity that may otherwise exist to impose any additional security requirements upon a landlord.

(f) This section shall not apply to any building which has been designated as historically significant by an appropriate local, state, or federal governmental jurisdiction.

(g) Subdivisions (a) and (b) shall not apply to any building intended for human habitation which is managed, directly or indirectly, and controlled by the Department of Transportation. This exemption shall not be construed to affect the duty of the Department of Transportation to maintain the premises of these buildings in a safe condition or abrogate any express or implied statement or promise of the Department of Transportation to provide secure premises. Additionally, this exemption shall not

apply to residential dwellings acquired prior to July 1, 1997, by the Department of Transportation to complete construction of state highway routes 710 and 238 and related interchanges.

1941.4. The lessor of a building intended for the residential occupation of human beings shall be responsible for installing at least one usable telephone jack and for placing and maintaining the inside telephone wiring in good working order, shall ensure that the inside telephone wiring meets the applicable standards of the most recent National Electrical Code as adopted by the Electronic Industry Association, and shall make any required repairs. The lessor shall not restrict or interfere with access by the telephone utility to its telephone network facilities up to the demarcation point separating the inside wiring.

"Inside telephone wiring" for purposes of this section, means that portion of the telephone wire that connects the telephone equipment at the customer's premises to the telephone network at a demarcation point determined by the telephone corporation in accordance with orders of the Public Utilities Commission.

1942. (a) If within a reasonable time after written or oral notice to the landlord or his agent, as defined in subdivision (a) of Section 1962, of dilapidations rendering the premises untenantable which the landlord ought to repair, the landlord neglects to do so, the tenant may repair the same himself where the cost of such repairs does not require an expenditure more than one month's rent of the premises and deduct the expenses of such repairs from the rent when due, or the tenant may vacate the premises, in which case the tenant shall be discharged from further payment of rent, or performance of other conditions as of the date of vacating the premises. This remedy shall not be available to the tenant more than twice in any 12-month period.

(b) For the purposes of this section, if a tenant acts to repair and deduct after the 30th day following notice, he is presumed to have acted after a reasonable time. The presumption established by this subdivision is a rebuttable presumption affecting the burden of producing evidence and shall not be construed to prevent a tenant from repairing and deducting after a shorter notice if all the circumstances require shorter notice.

(c) The tenant's remedy under subdivision (a) shall not be available if the condition was caused by the violation of Section 1929 or 1941.2.

(d) The remedy provided by this section is in addition to any other remedy provided by this chapter, the rental agreement, or other applicable statutory or common law.

1942.1. Any agreement by a lessee of a dwelling waiving or modifying his rights under Section 1941 or 1942 shall be void as contrary to public policy with respect to any condition which renders the premises untenantable, except that the lessor and the lessee may agree that the lessee shall undertake to improve, repair or maintain all or stipulated portions of the dwelling as part of the consideration for rental.

The lessor and lessee may, if an agreement is in writing, set forth the provisions of Sections 1941 to 1942.1, inclusive, and provide that any controversy relating to a condition of the premises claimed to make them untenantable may by application of either party be submitted to arbitration, pursuant to the provisions of Title 9 (commencing with Section 1280), Part 3 of the Code of Civil Procedure, and that the costs of such arbitration shall be apportioned by the arbitrator between the parties.

1942.3. (a) In any unlawful detainer action by the landlord to recover possession from a tenant, a rebuttable presumption affecting the burden of producing evidence that the landlord has breached the habitability requirements in Section 1941 is created if all of the following conditions exist:

(1) The dwelling substantially lacks any of the affirmative standard characteristics listed in Section 1941.1, is deemed and declared substandard pursuant to Section 17920.3 of the Health and Safety Code, or contains lead hazards as defined in Section 17920.10 of the Health and Safety Code.

(2) A public officer or employee who is responsible for the enforcement of any housing law has notified the landlord, or an agent of the landlord, in a written notice issued after inspection of the premises which informs the landlord of his or her obligation to abate the nuisance or repair the substandard or unsafe conditions.

(3) The conditions have existed and have not been abated 60 days beyond the date of issuance of the notice specified in paragraph (2) and the delay is without good cause.

(4) The conditions were not caused by an act or omission of the tenant or lessee in violation of Section 1929 or 1941.2.

(b) The presumption specified in subdivision (a) does not arise unless all of the conditions set forth therein are proven, but failure to so establish the presumption shall not otherwise affect the right of the tenant to raise and pursue any defense based on the landlord's breach of the implied warranty of habitability.

(c) The presumption provided in this section shall apply only to rental agreements or leases entered into or renewed on or after January 1, 1986.

1942.4. (a) A landlord of a dwelling may not demand rent, collect rent, issue a notice of a rent increase, or issue a three-day notice to pay rent or quit pursuant to subdivision (2) of Section 1161 of the Code of Civil Procedure, if all of the following conditions exist prior to the landlord's demand or notice:

(1) The dwelling substantially lacks any of the affirmative standard characteristics listed in Section 1941.1 or violates Section 17920.10 of the Health and Safety Code, or

is deemed and declared substandard as set forth in Section 17920.3 of the Health and Safety Code because conditions listed in that section exist to an extent that endangers the life, limb, health, property, safety, or welfare of the public or the occupants of the dwelling.

(2) A public officer or employee who is responsible for the enforcement of any housing law, after inspecting the premises, has notified the landlord or the landlord's agent in writing of his or her obligations to abate the nuisance or repair the substandard conditions.

(3) The conditions have existed and have not been abated 35 days beyond the date of service of the notice specified in paragraph (2) and the delay is without good cause. For purposes of this subdivision, service shall be complete at the time of deposit in the United States mail.

(4) The conditions were not caused by an act or omission of the tenant or lessee in violation of Section 1929 or 1941.2.

(b) (1) A landlord who violates this section is liable to the tenant or lessee for the actual damages sustained by the tenant or lessee and special damages of not less than one hundred dollars ($100) and not more than five thousand dollars ($5,000).

(2) The prevailing party shall be entitled to recovery of reasonable attorney's fees and costs of the suit in an amount fixed by the court.

(c) Any court that awards damages under this section may also order the landlord to abate any nuisance at the rental dwelling and to repair any substandard conditions of the rental dwelling, as defined in Section 1941.1, which significantly or materially affect the health or safety of the occupants of the rental dwelling and are uncorrected. If the court orders repairs or corrections, or both, the court's jurisdiction continues over the matter for the purpose of ensuring compliance.

(d) The tenant or lessee shall be under no obligation to undertake any other remedy prior to exercising his or her rights under this section.

(e) Any action under this section may be maintained in small claims court if the claim does not exceed the jurisdictional limit of that court.

(f) The remedy provided by this section may be utilized in addition to any other remedy provided by this chapter, the rental agreement, lease, or other applicable statutory or common law. Nothing in this section shall require any landlord to comply with this section if he or she pursues his or her rights pursuant to Chapter 12.75 (commencing with Section 7060) of Division 7 of Title 1 of the Government Code.

1942.5. (a) If the lessor retaliates against the lessee because of the exercise by the lessee of his rights under this chapter or because of his complaint to an appropriate agency as to tenantability of a dwelling, and if the lessee of a dwelling is not in default as to the payment of his rent, the lessor may not recover possession of a dwelling in any action or proceeding, cause the lessee to quit involuntarily, increase the rent, or decrease any services within 180 days of any of the following:

(1) After the date upon which the lessee, in good faith, has given notice pursuant to Section 1942, or has made an oral complaint to the lessor regarding tenantability.

(2) After the date upon which the lessee, in good faith, has filed a written complaint, or an oral complaint which is registered or otherwise recorded in writing, with an appropriate agency, of which the lessor has notice, for the purpose of obtaining correction of a condition relating to tenantability.

(3) After the date of an inspection or issuance of a citation, resulting from a complaint described in paragraph (2) of which the lessor did not have notice.

(4) After the filing of appropriate documents commencing a judicial or arbitration proceeding involving the issue of tenantability.

(5) After entry of judgment or the signing of an arbitration award, if any, when in the judicial proceeding or arbitration the issue of tenantability is determined adversely to the lessor. In each instance, the 180-day period shall run from the latest applicable date referred to in paragraphs (1) to (5), inclusive.

(b) A lessee may not invoke subdivision (a) more than once in any 12-month period.

(c) It is unlawful for a lessor to increase rent, decrease services, cause a lessee to quit involuntarily, bring an action to recover possession, or threaten to do any of those acts, for the purpose of retaliating against the lessee because he or she has lawfully organized or participated in a lessees' association or an organization advocating lessees' rights or has lawfully and peaceably exercised any rights under the law. In an action brought by or against the lessee pursuant to this subdivision, the lessee shall bear the burden of producing evidence that the lessor's conduct was, in fact, retaliatory.

(d) Nothing in this section shall be construed as limiting in any way the exercise by the lessor of his or her rights under any lease or agreement or any law pertaining to the hiring of property or his or her right to do any of the acts described in subdivision (a) or (c) for any lawful cause. Any waiver by a lessee of his or her rights under this section is void as contrary to public policy.

(e) Notwithstanding subdivisions (a) to (d), inclusive, a lessor may recover possession of a dwelling and do any of the other acts described in subdivision (a) within the period or periods prescribed therein, or within subdivision (c), if the notice of termination, rent increase, or other act, and any pleading or statement of issues in an arbitration, if any, states the ground upon which the lessor, in good faith, seeks to recover possession, increase rent, or do any of the other acts described in subdivision (a) or (c). If

the statement is controverted, the lessor shall establish its truth at the trial or other hearing.

(f) Any lessor or agent of a lessor who violates this section shall be liable to the lessee in a civil action for all of the following:

(1) The actual damages sustained by the lessee.

(2) Punitive damages in an amount of not less than one hundred dollars ($100) nor more than two thousand dollars ($2,000) for each retaliatory act where the lessor or agent has been guilty of fraud, oppression, or malice with respect to that act.

(g) In any action brought for damages for retaliatory eviction, the court shall award reasonable attorney's fees to the prevailing party if either party requests attorney's fees upon the initiation of the action.

(h) The remedies provided by this section shall be in addition to any other remedies provided by statutory or decisional law.

1942.6. Any person entering onto residential real property, upon the invitation of an occupant, during reasonable hours or because of emergency circumstances, for the purpose of providing information regarding tenants' rights or to participate in a lessees' association or association of tenants or an association that advocates tenants' rights shall not be liable in any criminal or civil action for trespass.

The Legislature finds and declares that this section is declaratory of existing law. Nothing in this section shall be construed to enlarge or diminish the rights of any person under existing law.

1943. A hiring of real property, other than lodgings and dwelling-houses, in places where there is no custom or usage on the subject, is presumed to be a month to month tenancy unless otherwise designated in writing; except that, in the case of real property used for agricultural or grazing purposes a hiring is presumed to be for one year from its commencement unless otherwise expressed in the hiring.

1944. A hiring of lodgings or a dwelling house for an unspecified term is presumed to have been made for such length of time as the parties adopt for the estimation of the rent. Thus a hiring at a monthly rate of rent is presumed to be for one month. In the absence of any agreement respecting the length of time or the rent, the hiring is presumed to be monthly.

1945. If a lessee of real property remains in possession thereof after the expiration of the hiring, and the lessor accepts rent from him, the parties are presumed to have renewed the hiring on the same terms and for the same time, not exceeding one month when the rent is payable monthly, nor in any case one year.

1945.5. Notwithstanding any other provision of law, any term of a lease executed after the effective date of this section for the hiring of residential real property which provides for the automatic renewal or extension of the lease for all or part of the full term of the lease if the lessee remains in possession after the expiration of the lease or fails to give notice of his intent not to renew or extend before the expiration of the lease shall be voidable by the party who did not prepare the lease unless such renewal or extension provision appears in at least eight-point boldface type, if the contract is printed, in the body of the lease agreement and a recital of the fact that such provision is contained in the body of the agreement appears in at least eight-point boldface type, if the contract is printed, immediately prior to the place where the lessee executes the agreement. In such case, the presumption in Section 1945 of this code shall apply.

Any waiver of the provisions of this section is void as against public policy.

1946. A hiring of real property, for a term not specified by the parties, is deemed to be renewed as stated in Section 1945, at the end of the term implied by law unless one of the parties gives written notice to the other of his intention to terminate the same, at least as long before the expiration thereof as the term of the hiring itself, not exceeding 30 days; provided, however, that as to tenancies from month to month either of the parties may terminate the same by giving at least 30 days' written notice thereof at any time and the rent shall be due and payable to and including the date of termination. It shall be competent for the parties to provide by an agreement at the time such tenancy is created that a notice of the intention to terminate the same may be given at any time not less than seven days before the expiration of the term thereof. The notice herein required shall be given in the manner prescribed in Section 1162 of the Code of Civil Procedure or by sending a copy by certified or registered mail addressed to the other party. In addition, the lessee may give such notice by sending a copy by certified or registered mail addressed to the agent of the lessor to whom the lessee has paid the rent for the month prior to the date of such notice or by delivering a copy to the agent personally.

1946.5. (a) The hiring of a room by a lodger on a periodic basis within a dwelling unit occupied by the owner may be terminated by either party giving written notice to the other of his or her intention to terminate the hiring, at least as long before the expiration of the term of the hiring as specified in Section 1946. The notice shall be given in a manner prescribed in Section 1162 of the Code of Civil Procedure or by certified or registered mail, restricted delivery, to the other party, with a return receipt requested.

(b) Upon expiration of the notice period provided in the notice of termination given pursuant to subdivision (a), any right of the lodger to remain in the dwelling unit or any part thereof is terminated by operation of law. The lodger's removal from the premises may thereafter be effected pursuant to the provisions of Section 602.3 of the Penal Code or other applicable provisions of law.

(c) As used in this section, "lodger" means a person contracting with the owner of a dwelling unit for a room or room and board within the dwelling unit personally occupied by the owner, where the owner retains a right of access to all areas of the dwelling unit occupied by the lodger and has overall control of the dwelling unit.

(d) This section applies only to owner-occupied dwellings where a single lodger resides. Nothing in this section shall be construed to determine or affect in any way the rights of persons residing as lodgers in an owner-occupied dwelling where more than one lodger resides.

1947. When there is no usage or contract to the contrary, rents are payable at the termination of the holding, when it does not exceed one year. If the holding is by the day, week, month, quarter, or year, rent is payable at the termination of the respective periods, as it successively becomes due.

1947.3. (a) (1) Except as provided in paragraph (2), a landlord or a landlord's agent may not demand or require cash as the exclusive form of payment of rent or deposit of security.

(2) A landlord or a landlord's agent may demand or require cash as the exclusive form of payment of rent or deposit of security if the tenant has previously attempted to pay the landlord or landlord's agent with a check drawn on insufficient funds or the tenant has instructed the drawee to stop payment on a check, draft, or order for the payment of money. The landlord may demand or require cash as the exclusive form of payment only for a period not exceeding three months following an attempt to pay with a check on insufficient funds or following a tenant's instruction to stop payment. If the landlord chooses to demand or require cash payment under these circumstances, the landlord shall give the tenant a written notice stating that the payment instrument was dishonored and informing the tenant that the tenant shall pay in cash for a period determined by the landlord, not to exceed three months, and attach a copy of the dishonored instrument to the notice. The notice shall comply with Section 827 if demanding or requiring payment in cash constitutes a change in the terms of the lease.

(3) Paragraph (2) does not enlarge or diminish a landlord's or landlord's agent's legal right to terminate a tenancy.

(b) For the purposes of this section, the issuance of a money order or a cashier's check is direct evidence only that the instrument was issued.

(c) A waiver of the provisions of this section is contrary to public policy, and is void and unenforceable.

1947.7. (a) The Legislature finds and declares that the operation of local rent stabilization programs can be complex and that disputes often arise with regard to standards of compliance with the regulatory processes of those programs. Therefore, it is the intent of the Legislature to limit the imposition of penalties and sanctions against an owner of residential rental units where that person has attempted in good faith to fully comply with the regulatory processes.

(b) An owner of a residential rental unit who is in substantial compliance with an ordinance or charter that controls or establishes a system of controls on the price at which residential rental units may be offered for rent or lease and which requires the registration of rents, or any regulation adopted pursuant thereto, shall not be assessed a penalty or any other sanction for noncompliance with the ordinance, charter, or regulation.

Restitution to the tenant or recovery of the registration or filing fees due to the local agency shall be the exclusive remedies which may be imposed against an owner of a residential rental unit who is in substantial compliance with the ordinance, charter, or regulation.

"Substantial compliance," as used in this subdivision, means that the owner of a residential rental unit has made a good faith attempt to comply with the ordinance, charter, or regulation sufficient to reasonably carry out the intent and purpose of the ordinance, charter, or regulation, but is not in full compliance, and has, after receiving notice of a deficiency from the local agency, cured the defect in a timely manner, as reasonably determined by the local agency.

"Local agency," as used in this subdivision, means the public entity responsible for the implementation of the ordinance, charter, or regulation.

(c) For any residential unit which has been registered and for which a base rent has been listed or for any residential unit which an owner can show, by a preponderance of the evidence, a good faith attempt to comply with the registration requirements or who was exempt from registration requirements in a previous version of the ordinance or charter and for which the owner of that residential unit has subsequently found not to have been in compliance with the ordinance, charter, or regulation, all annual rent adjustments which may have been denied during the period of the owner's noncompliance shall be restored prospectively once the owner is in compliance with the ordinance, charter, or regulation.

(d) In those jurisdictions where, prior to January 1, 1990, the local ordinance did not allow the restoration of annual rent adjustment, once the owner is in compliance with this section the local agency may phase in any increase in rent caused by the restoration of the annual rent adjustments that is in excess of 20 percent over the rent previously paid by the tenant, in equal installments over three years, if the tenant demonstrates undue financial hardship due to the restoration of the full annual rent adjustments. This subdivision shall remain operative only until January 1, 1993, unless a later enacted statute which is chaptered by January 1, 1993, deletes or extends that date.

(e) For purposes of this subdivision, an owner shall be deemed in compliance with the ordinance, charter, or regulation if he or she is in substantial compliance with the applicable local rental registration requirements and applicable local and state housing code provisions, has paid all fees and penalties owed to the local agency which have not otherwise been barred by the applicable statute of limitations, and has satisfied all claims for refunds of rental overcharges brought by tenants or by the local rent control board on behalf of tenants of the affected unit.

(f) Nothing in this section shall be construed to grant to any public entity any power which it does not possess independent of this section to control or establish a system of control on the price at which accommodations may be offered for rent or lease, or to diminish any power to do so which that public entity may possess, except as specifically provided in this section.

(g) In those jurisdictions where an ordinance or charter controls, or establishes a system of controls on, the price at which residential rental units may be offered for rent or lease and requires the periodic registration of rents, and where, for purposes of compliance with subdivision (e) of Section 1954.53, the local agency requires an owner to provide the name of a present or former tenant, the tenant's name and any additional information provided concerning the tenant, is confidential and shall be treated as confidential information within the meaning of the Information Practices Act of 1977 (Chapter 1 (commencing with Section 1798) of Title 1.8 of this part). A local agency shall, to the extent required by this subdivision, be considered an "agency" as defined in subdivision (b) of Section 1798.3. For purposes of compliance with subdivision (e) of Section 1954.53, a local agency subject to this subdivision may request, but shall not compel, an owner to provide any information regarding a tenant other than the tenant's name.

1947.8. (a) If an ordinance or charter controls or establishes a system of controls on the price at which residential rental units may be offered for rent or lease and requires the registration of rents, the ordinance or charter, or any regulation adopted pursuant thereto, shall provide for the establishment and certification of permissible rent levels for the registered rental units, and any changes thereafter to those rent levels, by the local agency as provided in this section.

(b) If the ordinance, charter, or regulation is in effect on January 1, 1987, the ordinance, charter, or regulation shall provide for the establishment and certification of permissible rent levels on or before January 1, 1988, including completion of all appeals and administrative proceedings connected therewith. After July 1, 1990, no local agency may maintain any action to recover excess rent against any property owner who has registered the unit with the local agency within the time limits set forth in this section if the initial certification of permissible rent levels affecting that particular property has not been completed, unless the delay is willfully and intentionally caused by the property owner or is a result of court proceedings or further administrative proceedings ordered by a court. If the ordinance, charter, or regulation is adopted on or after January 1, 1987, the ordinance, charter, or regulation shall provide for the establishment and certification of permissible rent levels within one year after it is adopted, including completion of all appeals and administrative proceedings connected therewith. Upon the request of the landlord or the tenant, the local agency shall provide the landlord and the tenant with a certificate or other documentation reflecting the permissible rent levels of the rental unit. A landlord may request a certificate of permissible rent levels for rental units which have a base rent established, but which are vacant and not exempt from registration under this section. The landlord or the tenant may appeal the determination of the permissible rent levels reflected in the certificate. The permissible rent levels reflected in the certificate or other documentation shall, in the absence of intentional misrepresentation or fraud, be binding and conclusive upon the local agency unless the determination of the permissible rent levels is being appealed.

(c) After the establishment and certification of permissible rent levels under subdivision (b), the local agency shall, upon the request of the landlord or the tenant, provide the landlord and the tenant with a certificate of the permissible rent levels of the rental unit. The certificate shall be issued within five business days from the date of request by the landlord or the tenant. The permissible rent levels reflected in the certificate shall, in the absence of intentional misrepresentation or fraud, be binding and conclusive upon the local agency unless the determination of the permissible rent levels is being appealed. The landlord or the tenant may appeal the determination of the permissible rent levels reflected in the certificate. Any appeal of a determination of permissible rent levels as reflected in the certificate, other than an appeal made pursuant to subdivision (b), shall be filed with the local agency within 15 days from issuance of the certificate. The local agency shall notify, in writing, the landlord and the tenant of its decision within 60 days following the filing of the appeal.

(d) The local agency may charge the person to whom a certificate is issued a fee in the amount necessary to cover the reasonable costs incurred by the local agency in issuing the certificate.

(e) The absence of a certification of permissible rent levels shall not impair, restrict, abridge, or otherwise interfere with either of the following:

(1) A judicial or administrative hearing.

(2) Any matter in connection with a conveyance of an interest in property.

(f) The record of permissible rent levels is a public record for purposes of the California Public Records Act, Chapter 3.5 (commencing with Section 6250) of Division 7 of Title 1 of the Government Code.

(g) Any notice specifying the rents applicable to residential rental units which is given by an owner to a public entity or tenant in order to comply with Chapter 12.75 (commencing with Section 7060) of Division 7 of Title 1 of the Government Code shall not be considered a registration of rents for purposes of this section.

(h) "Local agency," as used in this section, means the public entity responsible for the implementation of the ordinance, charter, or regulation.

(i) Nothing in this section shall be construed to grant to any public entity any power which it does not possess independent of this section to control or establish a system of control on the price at which accommodations may be offered for rent or lease, or to diminish any such power which that public entity may possess, except as specifically provided in this section.

1947.10. (a) After July 1, 1990, in any city, county, or city and county which administers a system of controls on the price at which residential rental units may be offered for rent or lease and which requires the registration of rents, any owner who evicts a tenant based upon the owner's or the owner's immediate relative's intention to occupy the tenant's unit, shall be required to maintain residence in the unit for at least six continuous months. If a court determines that the eviction was based upon fraud by the owner or the owner's immediate relative to not fulfill this six-month requirement, a court may order the owner to pay treble the cost of relocating the tenant from his or her existing unit back into the previous unit and may order the owner to pay treble the amount of any increase in rent which the tenant has paid. If the tenant decides not to relocate back into the previous unit, the court may order the owner to pay treble the amount of one month's rent paid by the tenant for the unit from which he or she was evicted and treble the amount of any costs incurred in relocating to a different unit. The prevailing party shall be awarded attorney's fees and court costs.

(b) The remedy provided by this section shall not be construed to prohibit any other remedies available to a any party affected by this section.

1947.11. (a) In any city, county, or city and county which administers a system of controls on the price at which residential rental units may be offered for rent or lease and which requires the registration of rents, upon the establishment of a certified rent level, any owner who charges rent to a tenant in excess of the certified lawful rent ceiling shall refund the excess rent to the tenant upon demand. If the owner refuses to refund the excess rent and if a court determines that the owner willfully or intentionally charged the tenant rent in excess of the certified lawful rent ceiling, the court shall award the tenant a judgment for the excess amount of rent and may treble that amount. The prevailing party shall be awarded attorney's fees and court costs.

(b) The remedy provided by this section shall not be construed to prohibit any other remedies available to any party affected by this section.

(c) This section shall not be construed to extend the time within which actions are required to be brought beyond the otherwise applicable limitation set forth in the Code of Civil Procedure.

1947.15. (a) The Legislature declares the purpose of this section is to:

(1) Ensure that owners of residential rental units that are subject to a system of controls on the price at which the units may be offered for rent or lease, or controls on the adjustment of the rent level, are not precluded or discouraged from obtaining a fair return on their properties as guaranteed by the United States Constitution and California Constitution because the professional expenses reasonably required in the course of the administrative proceedings, in order to obtain the rent increases necessary to provide a fair return, are not treated as a legitimate business expense.

(2) Encourage agencies which administer a system of controls on the price at which residential rental units may be offered for rent or lease, or controls the adjustment of the rent level, to enact streamlined administrative procedures governing rent adjustment petitions which minimize, to the extent possible, the cost and expense of these administrative proceedings.

(3) Ensure that the cost of professional services reasonably incurred and required by owners of residential rental units subject to a system of controls in the price at which the units may be offered for rent or lease, or controls on the adjustments of the rent level in the course of defending rights related to the rent control system, be treated as a legitimate business expense.

(b) Any city, county, or city and county, including a charter city, which administers an ordinance, charter provision, rule, or regulation that controls or establishes a system of controls on the price at which all or any portion of the residential rental units located within the city, county, or city and county, may be offered for rent or lease, or controls the adjustment of the rent level, and which does not include a system of vacancy decontrol, as defined in subdivision (i), shall permit reasonable expenses, fees, and other costs for professional services, including, but not limited to, legal, accounting, appraisal, bookkeeping, consulting, property management, or architectural services, reasonably incurred in the course of successfully pursuing rights under or in relationship to, that ordinance, charter provision, rule, or regulation, or the right to a fair return on an owner's property as protected by the United States Constitution or California Constitution, to be included in any calculation of net operating income and operating expenses used to determine a fair return to the owner of the property. All expenses, fees, and other costs reasonably incurred by an owner of property in relation to administrative proceedings for purposes specified in this subdivision shall be included in the calculation specified in this subdivision.

(c) Reasonable fees that are incurred by the owner in successfully obtaining a judicial reversal of an adverse administrative decision regarding a petition for upward adjustment of rents shall be assessed against the respondent public agency which issued the adverse administrative decision, and shall not be included in the calculations specified in subdivisions (b) and (d).

(d) (1) Notwithstanding subdivision (b), the city, county, or city and county, on the basis of substantial evidence in the record that the expenses reasonably incurred in the underlying proceeding will not reoccur annually, may amortize the expenses for a period not to exceed five years, except that in extraordinary circumstances, the amortization period may be extended to a period of eight years. The extended amortization period shall not apply to vacant units and shall end if the unit becomes vacant during the period that the expense is being amortized. An amortization schedule shall include a reasonable rate of interest.

(2) Any determination of the reasonableness of the expenses claimed, of an appropriate amortization period, or of the award of an upward adjustment of rents to compensate the owner for expenses and costs incurred shall be made as part of, or immediately following, the decision in the underlying administrative proceeding.

(e) Any and all of the following factors shall be considered in the determination of the reasonableness of the expenses, fees, or other costs authorized by this section:

(1) The rate charged for those professional services in the relevant geographic area.

(2) The complexity of the matter.

(3) The degree of administrative burden or judicial burden, or both, imposed upon the property owner.

(4) The amount of adjustment sought or the significance of the rights defended and the results obtained.

(5) The relationship of the result obtained to the expenses, fees, and other costs incurred (that is, whether professional assistance was reasonably related to the result achieved).

(f) This section shall not be applicable to any ordinance, rule, regulation, or charter provision of any city, county, or city and county, including a charter city, to the extent that the ordinance, rule, or regulation, or charter provision places a limit on the amount of rent that an owner may charge a tenant of a mobilehome park.

(g) For purposes of this section, the rights of a property owner shall be deemed to be successfully pursued or defended if the owner obtains an upward adjustment in rents, successfully defends his or her rights in an administrative proceeding brought by the tenant or the local rent board, or prevails in a proceeding, brought pursuant to Section 1947.8 concerning certification of maximum lawful rents.

(h) (1) If it is determined that a landlord petition assisted by attorneys or consultants is wholly without merit, the tenant shall be awarded a reduction in rent to compensate for the reasonable costs of attorneys or consultants retained by the tenant to defend the petition brought by the landlord. The reasonableness of the costs of the tenant's defense of the action brought by the landlord shall be determined pursuant to the same provisions established by this section for determining the reasonableness of the landlord's costs for the professional services. The determination of the reasonableness of the expenses claimed, an appropriate amortization period, and the award of a reduction in rents to compensate the tenant for costs incurred shall be made immediately following the decision in the underlying administrative proceeding.

(2) If it is determined that a landlord's appeal of an adverse administrative decision is frivolous or solely intended to cause unnecessary delay, the public agency which defended the action shall be awarded its reasonably incurred expenses, including attorney's fees, in defending the action. As used in this paragraph, "frivolous" means either (A) totally and completely without merit; or (B) for the sole purpose of harassing an opposing party.

(i) For purposes of this section, the following terms shall have the following meanings:

(1) "Vacancy decontrol" means a system of controls on the price at which residential rental units may be offered for rent or lease which permits the rent to be increased to its market level, without restriction, each time a vacancy occurs. "Vacancy decontrol" includes systems which reimpose controls on the price at which residential rental units may be offered for rent or lease upon rerental of the unit.

(2) "Vacancy decontrol" includes circumstances where the tenant vacates the unit of his or her own volition, or where the local jurisdiction permits the rent to be raised to market rate after an eviction for cause, as specified in the ordinance, charter provision, rule, or regulation.

(j) This section shall not be construed to affect in any way the ability of a local agency to set its own fair return standards or to limit other actions under its local rent control program other than those expressly set forth in this section.

(k) This section is not operative unless the Costa-Hawkins Rental Housing Act (Chapter 2.7 (commencing with Section 1954.50) of Title 5 of Part 4 of Division 3) is repealed.

1948. The attornment of a tenant to a stranger is void, unless it is made with the consent of the landlord, or in consequence of a judgment of a Court of competent jurisdiction.

1949. Every tenant who receives notice of any proceeding to recover the real property occupied by him or her, or the possession of the real property, shall immediately inform his or her landlord of the proceeding, and also deliver to the landlord the notice, if in writing, and is responsible to the landlord for all damages which he or she may sustain by reason of any omission to inform the landlord of the notice, or to deliver it to him or her if in writing.

1950. One who hires part of a room for a dwelling is entitled to the whole of the room, notwithstanding any agreement to the contrary; and if a landlord lets a room as a dwelling for more than one family, the person to whom he first lets any part of it is entitled to the possession of the whole room for the term agreed upon, and every tenant in the building, under the same landlord, is relieved from all obligation to pay rent to him while such double letting of any room continues.

1950.5. (a) This section applies to security for a rental agreement for residential property that is used as the dwelling of the tenant.

(b) As used in this section, "security" means any payment, fee, deposit or charge, including, but not limited to, any payment, fee, deposit, or charge, except as provided in Section 1950.6, that is imposed at the beginning of the tenancy to be used to reimburse the landlord for costs associated with processing a new tenant or that is imposed as an advance payment of rent, used or to be used for any purpose, including, but not limited to, any of the following:

(1) The compensation of a landlord for a tenant's default in the payment of rent.

(2) The repair of damages to the premises, exclusive of ordinary wear and tear, caused by the tenant or by a guest or licensee of the tenant.

(3) The cleaning of the premises upon termination of the tenancy necessary to return the unit to the same level of cleanliness it was in at the inception of the tenancy. The amendments to this paragraph enacted by the act adding this sentence shall apply only to tenancies for which the tenant's right to occupy begins after January 1, 2003.

(4) To remedy future defaults by the tenant in any obligation under the rental agreement to restore, replace, or return personal property or appurtenances, exclusive of ordinary wear and tear, if the security deposit is authorized to be applied thereto by the rental agreement.

(c) A landlord may not demand or receive security, however denominated, in an amount or value in excess of an amount equal to two months' rent, in the case of unfurnished residential property, and an amount equal to three months' rent, in the case of furnished residential property, in addition to any rent for the first month paid on or before initial occupancy.

This subdivision does not prohibit an advance payment of not less than six months' rent where the term of the lease is six months or longer.

This subdivision does not preclude a landlord and a tenant from entering into a mutual agreement for the landlord, at the request of the tenant and for a specified fee or charge, to make structural, decorative, furnishing, or other similar alterations, if the alterations are other than cleaning or repairing for which the landlord may charge the previous tenant as provided by subdivision (e).

(d) Any security shall be held by the landlord for the tenant who is party to the lease or agreement. The claim of a tenant to the security shall be prior to the claim of any creditor of the landlord.

(e) The landlord may claim of the security only those amounts as are reasonably necessary for the purposes specified in subdivision (b). The landlord may not assert a claim against the tenant or the security for damages to the premises or any defective conditions that preexisted the tenancy, for ordinary wear and tear or the effects thereof, whether the wear and tear preexisted the tenancy or occurred during the tenancy, or for the cumulative effects of ordinary wear and tear occurring during any one or more tenancies.

(f) (1) Within a reasonable time after notification of either party's intention to terminate the tenancy, or before the end of the lease term, the landlord shall notify the tenant in writing of his or her option to request an initial inspection and of his or her right to be present at the inspection. The requirements of this subdivision do not apply when the tenancy is terminated pursuant to subdivision (2), (3), or (4) of Section 1161 of the Code of Civil Procedure. At a reasonable time, but no earlier than two weeks before the termination or the end of lease date, the landlord, or an agent of the landlord, shall, upon the request of the tenant, make an initial inspection of the premises prior to any final inspection the landlord makes after the tenant has vacated the premises. The purpose of the initial inspection shall be to allow the tenant an opportunity to remedy identified deficiencies, in a manner consistent with the rights and obligations of the parties under the rental agreement, in order to avoid deductions from the security. If a tenant chooses not to request an initial inspection, the duties of the landlord under this subdivision are discharged. If an inspection is requested, the parties shall attempt to schedule the inspection at a mutually acceptable date and time. The landlord shall give at least 48 hours' prior written notice of the date and time of the inspection if either a mutual time is agreed upon, or if a mutually agreed time cannot be scheduled but the tenant still wishes an inspection. The tenant and landlord may agree to forgo the 48-hour prior written notice by both signing a written waiver.

The landlord shall proceed with the inspection whether the tenant is present or not, unless the tenant previously withdrew his or her request for the inspection.

(2) Based on the inspection, the landlord shall give the tenant an itemized statement specifying repairs or cleaning that are proposed to be the basis of any deductions from the security the landlord intends to make pursuant to paragraphs (1) to (4), inclusive of subdivision (b). This statement shall also include the texts of subdivision (d) and paragraphs (1) to (4), inclusive, of subdivision (b). The statement shall be given to the tenant, if the tenant is present for the inspection, or shall be left inside the premises.

(3) The tenant shall have the opportunity during the period following the initial inspection until termination of the tenancy to remedy identified deficiencies, in a manner consistent with the rights and obligations of the parties under the rental agreement, in order to avoid deductions from the security.

(4) Nothing in this subdivision shall prevent a landlord from using the security for deductions itemized in the statement provided for in paragraph (2) that were not cured by the tenant so long as the deductions are for damages authorized by this section.

(5) Nothing in this subdivision shall prevent a landlord from using the security for any purpose specified in paragraphs (1) to (4), inclusive, of subdivision (b) that occurs between completion of the initial inspection and termination of the tenancy or was not identified during the initial inspection due to the presence of a tenant's possessions.

(g) (1) No later than 21 calendar days after the tenant has vacated the premises, but not earlier than the time that either the landlord or the tenant provides a notice to terminate the tenancy under Section 1946 or 1946.1, Section 1161 of the Code of Civil Procedure, or not earlier than 60 calendar days prior to the expiration of a fixed-term lease, the landlord shall furnish the tenant, by personal delivery or by first-class mail, postage prepaid, a copy of an itemized statement indicating the basis for, and the amount of, any security received and the disposition of the security and shall return any remaining portion of the security to the tenant.

(2) Along with the itemized statement, the landlord shall also include copies of documents showing charges incurred and deducted by the landlord to repair or clean the premises, as follows:

(A) If the landlord or landlord's employee did the work, the itemized statement shall reasonably describe the work performed. The itemized statement shall include the time spent and the reasonable hourly rate charged.

(B) If the landlord or landlord's employee did not do the work, the landlord shall provide the tenant a copy of the bill, invoice, or receipt supplied by the person or entity performing the work. The itemized statement shall provide the tenant with the name, address, and telephone number of the person or entity, if the bill, invoice, or receipt does not include that information.

(C) If a deduction is made for materials or supplies, the landlord shall provide a copy of the bill, invoice, or receipt. If a particular material or supply item is purchased by the landlord on an ongoing basis, the landlord may document the cost of the item by providing a copy of a bill, invoice, receipt, vendor price list, or other vendor document that reasonably documents the cost of the item used in the repair or cleaning of the unit.

(3) If a repair to be done by the landlord or the landlord's employee cannot reasonably be completed within 21 calendar days after the tenant has vacated the premises, or if the documents from a person or entity providing services, materials, or supplies are not in the landlord's possession within 21 calendar days after the tenant has vacated the premises, the landlord may deduct the amount of a good faith estimate of the charges that will be incurred and provide that estimate with the itemized statement. If the reason for the estimate is because the documents from a person or entity providing services, materials, or supplies are not in the landlord's possession, the itemized statement shall include the name, address, and telephone number of the person or entity. Within 14 calendar days of completing the repair or receiving the documentation, the landlord shall complete the requirements in paragraphs (1) and (2) in the manner specified.

(4) The landlord need not comply with paragraph (2) or (3) if either of the following apply:

(A) The deductions for repairs and cleaning together do not exceed one hundred twenty-five dollars ($125).

(B) The tenant waived the rights specified in paragraphs (2) and (3). The waiver shall only be effective if it is signed by the tenant at the same time or after a notice to terminate a tenancy under Section 1946 or 1946.1 has been given, a notice under Section 1161 of the Code of Civil Procedure has been given, or no earlier than 60 calendar days prior to the expiration of a fixed-term lease. The waiver shall substantially include the text of paragraph (2).

(5) Notwithstanding paragraph (4), the landlord shall comply with paragraphs (2) and (3) when a tenant makes a request for documentation within 14 calendar days after receiving the itemized statement specified in paragraph (1). The landlord shall comply within 14 calendar days after receiving the request from the tenant.

(6) Any mailings to the tenant pursuant to this subdivision shall be sent to the address provided by the tenant. If the tenant does not provide an address, mailings pursuant to this subdivision shall be sent to the unit that has been vacated.

(h) Upon termination of the landlord's interest in the premises, whether by sale, assignment, death, appointment of receiver or otherwise, the landlord or the landlord's agent shall, within a reasonable time, do one of the following acts, either of which shall relieve the landlord of further liability with respect to the security held:

(1) Transfer the portion of the security remaining after any lawful deductions made under subdivision (e) to the landlord's successor in interest. The landlord shall thereafter notify the tenant by personal delivery or by first-class mail, postage prepaid, of the transfer, of any claims made against the security, of the amount of the security deposited, and of the names of the successors in interest, their address, and their telephone number. If the notice to the tenant is made by personal delivery, the tenant shall acknowledge receipt of the notice and sign his or her name on the landlord's copy of the notice.

(2) Return the portion of the security remaining after any lawful deductions made under subdivision (e) to the tenant, together with an accounting as provided in subdivision (g).

(i) Prior to the voluntary transfer of a landlord's interest in the premises, the landlord shall deliver to the landlord's successor in interest a written statement indicating the following:

(1) The security remaining after any lawful deductions are made.

(2) An itemization of any lawful deductions from any security received.

(3) His or her election under paragraph (1) or (2) of subdivision (h). This subdivision does not affect the validity of title to the real property transferred in violation of this subdivision.

(j) In the event of noncompliance with subdivision (h), the landlord's successors in interest shall be jointly and severally liable with the landlord for repayment of the security, or that portion thereof to which the tenant is entitled, when and as provided in subdivisions (e) and (g). A successor in interest of a landlord may not require the tenant to post any security to replace that amount not transferred to the tenant or successors in interest as provided in subdivision (h), unless and until the successor in interest first makes restitution of the initial security as provided in paragraph (2) of subdivision (h) or provides the tenant with an accounting as provided in subdivision (g).

This subdivision does not preclude a successor in interest from recovering from the tenant compensatory damages that are in excess of the security received from the landlord previously paid by the tenant to the landlord.

Notwithstanding this subdivision, if, upon inquiry and reasonable investigation, a landlord's successor in interest has a good faith belief that the lawfully remaining security deposit is transferred to him or her or returned to the tenant pursuant to subdivision (h), he or she is not liable for damages as provided in subdivision (l), or any security not transferred pursuant to subdivision (h).

(k) Upon receipt of any portion of the security under paragraph (1) of subdivision (h), the landlord's successors in interest shall have all of the rights and obligations of a landlord holding the security with respect to the security.

(l) The bad faith claim or retention by a landlord or the landlord's successors in interest of the security or any portion thereof in violation of this section, or the bad faith demand of replacement security in violation of subdivision (j), may subject the landlord or the landlord's successors in interest to statutory damages of up to twice the amount of the security, in addition to actual damages. The court may award damages for bad faith whenever the facts warrant such an award, regardless of whether the injured party has specifically requested relief. In any action under this section, the landlord or the landlord's successors in interest shall have the burden of proof as to the reasonableness of the amounts claimed or the authority pursuant to this section to demand additional security deposits.

(m) No lease or rental agreement may contain any provision characterizing any security as "nonrefundable."

(n) Any action under this section may be maintained in small claims court if the damages claimed, whether actual or statutory or both, are within the jurisdictional amount allowed by Section 116.220 of the Code of Civil Procedure.

(o) Proof of the existence of and the amount of a security deposit may be established by any credible evidence, including, but not limited to, a canceled check, a receipt, a lease indicating the requirement of a deposit as well as the amount, prior consistent statements or actions of the landlord or tenant, or a statement under penalty of perjury that satisfies the credibility requirements set forth in Section 780 of the Evidence Code.

(p) The amendments to this section made during the 1985 portion of the 1985-86 Regular Session of the Legislature that are set forth in subdivision (e) are declaratory of existing law.

(q) The amendments to this section made during the 2003 portion of the 2003-04 Regular Session of the Legislature that are set forth in paragraph (1) of subdivision (f) are declaratory of existing law.

1950.6. (a) Notwithstanding Section 1950.5, when a landlord or his or her agent receives a request to rent a residential property from an applicant, the landlord or his or her agent may charge that applicant an application screening fee to cover the costs of obtaining information about the applicant. The information requested and obtained by the landlord or his or her agent may include, but is not limited to, personal reference checks and consumer credit reports produced by consumer credit reporting agencies as defined in Section 1785.3. A landlord or his or her agent may, but is not required to, accept and rely upon a consumer credit report presented by an applicant.

(b) The amount of the application screening fee shall not be greater than the actual out-of-pocket costs of gathering information concerning the applicant, including, but not limited to, the cost of using a tenant screening service or a consumer credit reporting service, and the reasonable value of time spent by the landlord or his or her agent in obtaining information on the applicant. In no case shall the amount of the application screening fee charged by the landlord or his or her agent be greater than thirty dollars ($30) per applicant. The thirty dollar ($30) application screening fee may be adjusted annually by the landlord or his or her agent commensurate with an increase in the Consumer Price Index, beginning on January 1, 1998.

(c) Unless the applicant agrees in writing, a landlord or his or her agent may not charge an applicant an application screening fee when he or she knows or should have known that no rental unit is available at that time or will be available within a reasonable period of time.

(d) The landlord or his or her agent shall provide, personally, or by mail, the applicant with a receipt for the fee paid by the applicant, which receipt shall itemize the out-of-pocket expenses and time spent by the landlord or his or her agent to obtain and process the information about the applicant.

(e) If the landlord or his or her agent does not perform a personal reference check or does not obtain a consumer credit report, the landlord or his or her agent shall return any amount of the screening fee that is not used for the purposes authorized by this section to the applicant.

(f) If an application screening fee has been paid by the applicant and if requested by the applicant, the landlord or his or her agent shall provide a copy of the consumer credit report to the applicant who is the subject of that report.

(g) As used in this section, "landlord" means an owner of residential rental property.

(h) As used in this section, "application screening fee" means any nonrefundable payment of money charged by a landlord or his or her agent to an applicant, the purpose of which is to purchase a consumer credit report and to validate, review, or otherwise process an application for the rent or lease of residential rental property.

(i) As used in this section, "applicant" means any entity or individual who makes a request to a landlord or his or her agent to rent a residential housing unit, or an entity or individual who agrees to act as a guarantor or cosignor on a rental agreement.

(j) The application screening fee shall not be considered an "advance fee" as that term is used in Section 10026 of the Business and Professions Code, and shall not be considered "security" as that term is used in Section 1950.5.

(k) This section is not intended to preempt any provisions or regulations that govern the collection of deposits and fees under federal or state housing assistance programs.

1950.7. (a) Any payment or deposit of money the primary function of which is to secure the performance of a rental agreement for other than residential property or any part of the agreement, other than a payment or deposit, including an advance payment of rent, made to secure the execution of a rental agreement, shall be governed by the provisions of this section. With respect to residential property, the provisions of Section 1950.5 shall prevail.

(b) Any such payment or deposit of money shall be held by the landlord for the tenant who is party to the agreement. The claim of a tenant to the payment or deposit shall be prior to the claim of any creditor of the landlord, except a trustee in bankruptcy.

(c) The landlord may claim of the payment or deposit only those amounts as are reasonably necessary to remedy tenant defaults in the payment of rent, to repair damages to the premises caused by the tenant, or to clean the premises upon termination of the tenancy, if the payment or deposit is made for any or all of those specific purposes.

(1) If the claim of the landlord upon the payment or deposit is only for defaults in the payment of rent and the security deposit equals no more than one month's rent plus a deposit amount clearly described as the payment of the last month's rent, then any remaining portion of the payment or deposit shall be returned to the tenant at a time as may be mutually agreed upon by landlord and tenant, but in no event later than 30 days from the date the landlord receives possession of the premises.

(2) If the claim of the landlord upon the payment or deposit is only for defaults in the payment of rent and the security deposit exceeds the amount of one month's rent plus a deposit amount clearly described as the payment of the last month's rent, then any remaining portion of the payment or deposit in excess of an amount equal to one month's rent shall be returned to the tenant no later than two weeks after the date the landlord receives possession of the premises, with the remainder to be returned or accounted for within 30 days from the date the landlord receives possession of the premises.

(3) If the claim of the landlord upon the payment or deposit includes amounts reasonably necessary to repair damages to the premises caused by the tenant or to clean the premises, then any remaining portion of the payment or deposit shall be returned to the tenant at a time as may be mutually agreed upon by landlord and tenant, but in no event later than 30 days from the date the landlord receives possession of the premises.

(d) Upon termination of the landlord's interest in the unit in question, whether by sale, assignment, death, appointment of receiver or otherwise, the landlord or the landlord's agent shall, within a reasonable time, do one of the following acts, either of which shall relieve the landlord of further liability with respect to the payment or deposit:

(1) Transfer the portion of the payment or deposit remaining after any lawful deductions made under subdivision (c) to the landlord's successor in interest, and thereafter notify the tenant by personal delivery or certified mail of the transfer, of any claims made against the payment or deposit, and of the transferee's name and address. If the notice to the tenant is made by personal delivery, the tenant shall acknowledge receipt of the notice and sign his or her name on the landlord's copy of the notice.

(2) Return the portion of the payment or deposit remaining after any lawful deductions made under subdivision (c) to the tenant.

(e) Upon receipt of any portion of the payment or deposit under paragraph (1) of subdivision (d), the transferee shall have all of the rights and obligations of a landlord holding the payment or deposit with respect to the payment or deposit.

(f) The bad faith retention by a landlord or transferee of a payment or deposit or any portion thereof, in violation of this section, may subject the landlord or the transferee to damages not to exceed two hundred dollars ($200), in addition to any actual damages.

(g) This section is declarative of existing law and therefore operative as to all tenancies, leases, or rental agreements for other than residential property created or renewed on or after January 1, 1971.

1951. As used in Sections 1951.2 to 1952.6, inclusive:

(a) "Rent" includes charges equivalent to rent.

(b) "Lease" includes a sublease.

1951.2. (a) Except as otherwise provided in Section 1951.4, if a lessee of real property breaches the lease and abandons the property before the end of the term or if his right to possession is terminated by the lessor because of a breach of the lease, the lease terminates. Upon such termination, the lessor may recover from the lessee:

(1) The worth at the time of award of the unpaid rent which had been earned at the time of termination;

(2) The worth at the time of award of the amount by which the unpaid rent which would have been earned after termination until the time of award exceeds the amount of such rental loss that the lessee proves could have been reasonably avoided;

(3) Subject to subdivision (c), the worth at the time of award of the amount by which the unpaid rent for the balance of the term after the time of award exceeds the amount of such rental loss that the lessee proves could be reasonably avoided; and

(4) Any other amount necessary to compensate the lessor for all the detriment proximately caused by the lessee's failure to perform his obligations under the lease or which in the ordinary course of things would be likely to result therefrom.

(b) The "worth at the time of award" of the amounts referred to in paragraphs (1) and (2) of subdivision (a) is computed by allowing interest at such lawful rate as may be specified in the lease or, if no such rate is specified in the lease, at the legal rate. The worth at the time of award of the amount referred to in paragraph (3) of subdivision (a) is computed by discounting such amount at the discount rate of the Federal Reserve Bank of San Francisco at the time of award plus 1 percent.

(c) The lessor may recover damages under paragraph (3) of subdivision (a) only if:

(1) The lease provides that the damages he may recover include the worth at the time of award of the amount by which the unpaid rent for the balance of the term after the time of award, or for any shorter period of time specified in the lease, exceeds the amount of such rental loss for the same period that the lessee proves could be reasonably avoided; or

(2) The lessor relet the property prior to the time of award and proves that in reletting the property he acted reasonably and in a good-faith effort to mitigate the damages, but the recovery of damages under this paragraph is subject to any limitations specified in the lease.

(d) Efforts by the lessor to mitigate the damages caused by the lessee's breach of the lease do not waive the lessor's right to recover damages under this section.

(e) Nothing in this section affects the right of the lessor under a lease of real property to indemnification for liability arising prior to the termination of the lease for personal injuries or property damage where the lease provides for such indemnification.

1951.3. (a) Real property shall be deemed abandoned by the lessee, within the meaning of Section 1951.2, and the lease shall terminate if the lessor gives written notice of his belief of abandonment as provided in this section and the lessee fails to give the lessor written notice, prior to the date of termination specified in the lessor's notice, stating that he does not intend to abandon the real property and stating an address at which the lessee may be served by certified mail in any action for unlawful detainer of the real property.

(b) The lessor may give a notice of belief of abandonment to the lessee pursuant to this section only where the rent on the property has been due and unpaid for at least 14 consecutive days and the lessor reasonably believes that the lessee has abandoned the property. The date of termination of the lease shall be specified in the lessor's notice and shall be not less than 15 days after the notice is served personally or, if mailed, not less than 18 days after the notice is deposited in the mail.

(c) The lessor's notice of belief of abandonment shall be personally delivered to the lessee or sent by first-class mail, postage prepaid, to the lessee at his last known address and, if there is reason to believe that the notice sent to that address will not be received by the lessee, also to such other address, if any, known to the lessor where the lessee may reasonably be expected to receive the notice.

(d) The notice of belief of abandonment shall be in substantially the following form:

Notice of Belief of Abandonment

To: _____

(Name of lessee/tenant)

_____

(Address of lessee/tenant)

This notice is given pursuant to Section 1951.3 of the Civil Code concerning the real property leased by you at _____ (state location of the property by address or other sufficient description). The rent on this property has been due and unpaid for 14 consecutive days and the lessor/landlord believes that you have abandoned the property. The real property will be deemed abandoned within the meaning of Section 1951.2 of the Civil Code and your lease will terminate on _____ (here insert a date not less than 15 days after this notice is served personally or, if mailed, not less than 18 days after this notice is deposited in the mail) unless before such date the undersigned receives at the address indicated below a written notice from you stating both of the following:

(1) Your intent not to abandon the real property.

(2) An address at which you may be served by certified mail in any action for unlawful detainer of the real property. You are required to pay the rent due and unpaid on this real property as required by the lease, and your failure to do so can lead to a court proceeding against you.

Dated: _____

_____

(Signature of lessor/landlord)

_____

(Type or print name of lessor/landlord)

_____

(Address to which lessee/tenant is to send notice)

(e) The real property shall not be deemed to be abandoned pursuant to this section if the lessee proves any of the following:

(1) At the time the notice of belief of abandonment was given, the rent was not due and unpaid for 14 consecutive days.

(2) At the time the notice of belief of abandonment was given, it was not reasonable for the lessor to believe that the lessee had abandoned the real property. The fact that the lessor knew that the lessee left personal property on the real property does not, of itself, justify a finding that the lessor did not reasonably believe that the lessee had abandoned the real property.

(3) Prior to the date specified in the lessor's notice, the lessee gave written notice to the lessor stating his intent not to abandon the real property and stating an address at which he may be served by certified mail in any action for unlawful detainer of the real property.

(4) During the period commencing 14 days before the time the notice of belief of abandonment was given and ending on the date the lease would have terminated pur-

suant to the notice, the lessee paid to the lessor all or a portion of the rent due and unpaid on the real property.

(f) Nothing in this section precludes the lessor or the lessee from otherwise proving that the real property has been abandoned by the lessee within the meaning of Section 1951.2.

(g) Nothing in this section precludes the lessor from serving a notice requiring the lessee to pay rent or quit as provided in Sections 1161 and 1162 of the Code of Civil Procedure at any time permitted by those sections, or affects the time and manner of giving any other notice required or permitted by law. The giving of the notice provided by this section does not satisfy the requirements of Sections 1161 and 1162 of the Code of Civil Procedure.

1951.4. (a) The remedy described in this section is available only if the lease provides for this remedy. In addition to any other type of provision used in a lease to provide for the remedy described in this section, a provision in the lease in substantially the following form satisfies this subdivision:

"The lessor has the remedy described in California Civil Code Section 1951.4 (lessor may continue lease in effect after lessee's breach and abandonment and recover rent as it becomes due, if lessee has right to sublet or assign, subject only to reasonable limitations)."

(b) Even though a lessee of real property has breached the lease and abandoned the property, the lease continues in effect for so long as the lessor does not terminate the lessee's right to possession, and the lessor may enforce all the lessor's rights and remedies under the lease, including the right to recover the rent as it becomes due under the lease, if any of the following conditions is satisfied:

(1) The lease permits the lessee, or does not prohibit or otherwise restrict the right of the lessee, to sublet the property, assign the lessee's interest in the lease, or both.

(2) The lease permits the lessee to sublet the property, assign the lessee's interest in the lease, or both, subject to express standards or conditions, provided the standards and conditions are reasonable at the time the lease is executed and the lessor does not require compliance with any standard or condition that has become unreasonable at the time the lessee seeks to sublet or assign. For purposes of this paragraph, an express standard or condition is presumed to be reasonable; this presumption is a presumption affecting the burden of proof.

(3) The lease permits the lessee to sublet the property, assign the lessee's interest in the lease, or both, with the consent of the lessor, and the lease provides that the consent shall not be unreasonably withheld or the lease includes a standard implied by law that consent shall not be unreasonably withheld.

(c) For the purposes of subdivision (b), the following do not constitute a termination of the lessee's right to possession:

(1) Acts of maintenance or preservation or efforts to relet the property.

(2) The appointment of a receiver upon initiative of the lessor to protect the lessor's interest under the lease.

(3) Withholding consent to a subletting or assignment, or terminating a subletting or assignment, if the withholding or termination does not violate the rights of the lessee specified in subdivision (b).

1951.5. Section 1671, relating to liquidated damages, applies to a lease of real property.

1951.7. (a) As used in this section, "advance payment" means moneys paid to the lessor of real property as prepayment of rent, or as a deposit to secure faithful performance of the terms of the lease, or any other payment which is the substantial equivalent of either of these. A payment that is not in excess of the amount of one month's rent is not an advance payment for the purposes of this section.

(b) The notice provided by subdivision (c) is required to be given only if:

(1) The lessee has made an advance payment;

(2) The lease is terminated pursuant to Section 1951.2; and

(3) The lessee has made a request, in writing, to the lessor that he be given notice under subdivision (c).

(c) Upon the initial reletting of the property, the lessor shall send a written notice to the lessee stating that the property has been relet, the name and address of the new lessee, and the length of the new lease and the amount of the rent. The notice shall be delivered to the lessee personally, or be sent by regular mail to the lessee at the address shown on the request, not later than 30 days after the new lessee takes possession of the property. No notice is required if the amount of the rent due and unpaid at the time of termination exceeds the amount of the advance payment.

1951.8. Nothing in Section 1951.2 or 1951.4 affects the right of the lessor under a lease of real property to equitable relief where such relief is appropriate.

1952. (a) Except as provided in subdivision (c), nothing in Sections 1951 to 1951.8, inclusive, affects the provisions of Chapter 4 (commencing with Section 1159) of Title 3 of Part 3 of the Code of Civil Procedure, relating to actions for unlawful detainer, forcible entry, and forcible detainer.

(b) Unless the lessor amends the complaint as provided in paragraph (1) of subdivision (a) of Section 1952.3 to state a claim for damages not recoverable in the unlawful detainer proceeding, the bringing of an action under the provisions of Chapter 4 (commencing with Section 1159) of Title 3 of Part 3 of the Code of Civil Procedure does not affect the lessor's right to bring a separate action for relief under Sections 1951.2, 1951.5, and 1951.8, but no damages shall be recovered in the subsequent action for any detriment for which a claim for damages was made and determined on the merits in the previous action.

(c) After the lessor obtains possession of the property under a judgment pursuant to Section 1174 of the Code of Civil Procedure, he is no longer entitled to the remedy provided under Section 1951.4 unless the lessee obtains relief under Section 1179 of the Code of Civil Procedure.

1952.2. Sections 1951 to 1952, inclusive, do not apply to:

(a) Any lease executed before July 1, 1971.

(b) Any lease executed on or after July 1, 1971, if the terms of the lease were fixed by a lease, option, or other agreement executed before July 1, 1971.

1952.3. (a) Except as provided in subdivisions (b) and (c), if the lessor brings an unlawful detainer proceeding and possession of the property is no longer in issue because possession of the property has been delivered to the lessor before trial or, if there is no trial, before judgment is entered, the case becomes an ordinary civil action in which:

(1) The lessor may obtain any relief to which he is entitled, including, where applicable, relief authorized by Section 1951.2; but, if the lessor seeks to recover damages described in paragraph (3) of subdivision (a) of Section 1951.2 or any other damages not recoverable in the unlawful detainer proceeding, the lessor shall first amend the complaint pursuant to Section 472 or 473 of the Code of Civil Procedure so that possession of the property is no longer in issue and to state a claim for such damages and shall serve a copy of the amended complaint on the defendant in the same manner as a copy of a summons and original complaint is served.

(2) The defendant may, by appropriate pleadings or amendments to pleadings, seek any affirmative relief, and assert all defenses, to which he is entitled, whether or not the lessor has amended the complaint; but subdivision (a) of Section 426.30 of the Code of Civil Procedure does not apply unless, after delivering possession of the property to the lessor, the defendant (i) files a cross-complaint or (ii) files an answer or an amended answer in response to an amended complaint filed pursuant to paragraph (1).

(b) The defendant's time to respond to a complaint for unlawful detainer is not affected by the delivery of possession of the property to the lessor; but, if the complaint is amended as provided in paragraph (1) of subdivision (a), the defendant has the same time to respond to the amended complaint as in an ordinary civil action.

(c) The case shall proceed as an unlawful detainer proceeding if the defendant's default (1) has been entered on the unlawful detainer complaint and (2) has not been opened by an amendment of the complaint or otherwise set aside.

(d) Nothing in this section affects the pleadings that may be filed, relief that may be sought, or defenses that may be asserted in an unlawful detainer proceeding that has not become an ordinary civil action as provided in subdivision (a).

1952.4. An agreement for the exploration for or the removal of natural resources is not a lease of real property within the meaning of Sections 1951 to 1952.2, inclusive.

1952.6. (a) Sections 1951 to 1952.2, inclusive, shall not apply to any lease or agreement for a lease of real property between any public entity and any nonprofit corporation whose title or interest in the property is subject to reversion to or vesting in a public entity and which issues bonds or other evidences of indebtedness, the interest on which is exempt from federal income taxes for the purpose of acquiring, constructing, or improving the property or a building or other facility thereon, or between any public entity and any other public entity, unless the lease or the agreement shall specifically provide that Sections 1951 to 1952.2, inclusive, or any portions thereof, are applicable to the lease or the agreement.

(b) Except as provided in subdivision (a), a public entity lessee in a contract for a capital lease of real property involving the payment of rents of one million dollars ($1,000,000) or more may elect to waive any of the remedies for a breach of the lease provided in Sections 1951 to 1952.2, inclusive, and contract instead for any other remedy permitted by law. As used in this subdivision, "capital lease" refers to a lease entered into for the purpose of acquiring, constructing, or improving the property or a building or other facility thereon.

(c) As used in this section, "public entity" includes the state, a county, city and county, city, district, public authority, public agency, or any other political subdivision or public corporation.

1953. (a) Any provision of a lease or rental agreement of a dwelling by which the lessee agrees to modify or waive any of the following rights shall be void as contrary to public policy:

(1) His rights or remedies under Section 1950.5 or 1954.

(2) His right to assert a cause of action against the lessor which may arise in the future.

(3) His right to a notice or hearing required by law.

(4) His procedural rights in litigation in any action involving his rights and obligations as a tenant.

(5) His right to have the landlord exercise a duty of care to prevent personal injury or personal property damage where that duty is imposed by law.

(b) Any provision of a lease or rental agreement of a dwelling by which the lessee agrees to modify or waive a statutory right, where the modification or waiver is not void under subdivision (a) or under Section 1942.1, 1942.5, or 1954, shall be void as contrary to public policy unless the lease or rental agreement is presented to the lessee before he takes actual possession of the premises. This subdivision does not apply to any provisions modifying or waiving a statutory right in agreements renewing leases or rental agreements where the same provision was also contained in the lease or rental agreement which is being renewed.

(c) This section shall apply only to leases and rental agreements executed on or after January 1, 1976.

1954. (a) A landlord may enter the dwelling unit only in the following cases:

(1) In case of emergency.

(2) To make necessary or agreed repairs, decorations, alterations or improvements, supply necessary or agreed services, or exhibit the dwelling unit to prospective or actual purchasers, mortgagees, tenants, workers, or contractors or to make an inspection pursuant to subdivision (f) of Section 1950.5.

(3) When the tenant has abandoned or surrendered the premises.

(4) Pursuant to court order.

(b) Except in cases of emergency or when the tenant has abandoned or surrendered the premises, entry may not be made during other than normal business hours unless the tenant consents to an entry during other than normal business hours at the time of entry.

(c) The landlord may not abuse the right of access or use it to harass the tenant.

(d) (1) Except as provided in subdivision (e), or as provided in paragraph (2) or (3), the landlord shall give the tenant reasonable notice in writing of his or her intent to enter and enter only during normal business hours. The notice shall include the date, approximate time, and purpose of the entry. The notice may be personally delivered to the tenant, left with someone of a suitable age and discretion at the premises, or, left on, near, or under the usual entry door of the premises in a manner in which a reasonable person would discover the notice. Twenty-four hours shall be presumed to be reasonable notice in absence of evidence to the contrary. The notice may be mailed to the tenant. Mailing of the notice at least six days prior to an intended entry is presumed reasonable notice in the absence of evidence to the contrary.

(2) If the purpose of the entry is to exhibit the dwelling unit to prospective or actual purchasers, the notice may be given orally, in person or by telephone, if the landlord or his or her agent has notified the tenant in writing within 120 days of the oral notice that the property is for sale and that the landlord or agent may contact the tenant orally for the purpose described above. Twenty-four hours is presumed reasonable notice in the absence of evidence to the contrary. The notice shall include the date, approximate time, and purpose of the entry. At the time of entry, the landlord or agent shall leave written evidence of the entry inside the unit.

(3) The tenant and the landlord may agree orally to an entry to make agreed repairs or supply agreed services. The agreement shall include the date and approximate time of the entry, which shall be within one week of the

agreement. In this case, the landlord is not required to provide the tenant a written notice.

(e) No notice of entry is required under this section:

(1) To respond to an emergency.

(2) If the tenant is present and consents to the entry at the time of entry.

(3) After the tenant has abandoned or surrendered the unit.

1954.1. In any general assignment for the benefit of creditors, as defined in Section 493.010 of the Code of Civil Procedure, the assignee shall have the right to occupy, for a period of up to 90 days after the date of the assignment, any business premises held under a lease by the assignor upon payment when due of the monthly rental reserved in the lease for the period of such occupancy, notwithstanding any provision in the lease (whether heretofore or hereafter entered into) for the termination thereof upon the making of the assignment or the insolvency of the lessee or other condition relating to the financial condition of the lessee. This section shall be construed as establishing the reasonable rental value of the premises recoverable by a landlord upon a holding-over by the tenant upon the termination of a lease under the circumstances specified herein.

1954.50. This chapter shall be known and may be cited as the Costa-Hawkins Rental Housing Act.

1954.51. As used in this chapter, the following terms have the following meanings:

(a) "Comparable units" means rental units that have approximately the same living space, have the same number of bedrooms, are located in the same or similar neighborhoods, and feature the same, similar, or equal amenities and housing services.

(b) "Owner" includes any person, acting as principal or through an agent, having the right to offer residential real property for rent, and includes a predecessor in interest to the owner, except that this term does not include the owner or operator of a mobilehome park, or the owner of a mobilehome or his or her agent.

(c) "Prevailing market rent" means the rental rate that would be authorized pursuant to 42 U.S.C.A. 1437 (f), as calculated by the United States Department of Housing and Urban Development pursuant to Part 888 of Title 24 of the Code of Federal Regulations.

(d) "Public entity" has the same meaning as set forth in Section 811.2 of the Government Code.

(e) "Residential real property" includes any dwelling or unit that is intended for human habitation.

(f) "Tenancy" includes the lawful occupation of property and includes a lease or sublease.

1954.52. (a) Notwithstanding any other provision of law, an owner of residential real property may establish the initial and all subsequent rental rates for a dwelling or a unit about which any of the following is true:

(1) It has a certificate of occupancy issued after February 1, 1995.

(2) It has already been exempt from the residential rent control ordinance of a public entity on or before February 1, 1995, pursuant to a local exemption for newly constructed units.

(3) (A) It is alienable separate from the title to any other dwelling unit or is a subdivided interest in a subdivision, as specified in subdivision (b), (d), or (f) of Section 11004.5 of the Business and Professions Code.

(B) This paragraph does not apply to either of the following:

(i) A dwelling or unit where the preceding tenancy has been terminated by the owner by notice pursuant to Section 1946 or has been terminated upon a change in the terms of the tenancy noticed pursuant to Section 827.

(ii) A condominium dwelling or unit that has not been sold separately by the subdivider to a bona fide purchaser for value. The initial rent amount of such a unit for purposes of this chapter shall be the lawful rent in effect on May 7, 2001, unless the rent amount is governed by a different provision of this chapter. However, if a condominium dwelling or unit meets the criteria of paragraph (1) or (2) of subdivision (a), or if all the dwellings or units except one have been sold separately by the subdivider to bona fide purchasers for value, and the subdivider has occupied that remaining unsold condominium dwelling or unit as his or her principal residence for at least one year after the subdivision occurred, then subparagraph (A) of paragraph (3) shall apply to that unsold condominium dwelling or unit.

(C) Where a dwelling or unit in which the initial or subsequent rental rates are controlled by an ordinance or charter provision in effect on January 1, 1995, the following shall apply:

(i) An owner of real property as described in this paragraph may establish the initial and all subsequent rental rates for all existing and new tenancies in effect on or after January 1, 1999, if the tenancy in effect on or after January 1, 1999, was created between January 1, 1996, and December 31, 1998.

(ii) Commencing on January 1, 1999, an owner of real property as described in this paragraph may establish the initial and all subsequent rental rates for all new tenancies if the previous tenancy was in effect on December 31, 1995.

(iii) The initial rental rate for a dwelling or unit as described in this paragraph in which the initial rental rate is controlled by an ordinance or charter provision in effect on January 1, 1995, may not, until January 1, 1999, exceed the amount calculated pursuant to subdivision (c) of Section 1954.53. An owner of residential real property as described in this paragraph may, until January 1, 1999, establish the initial rental rate for a dwelling or unit only where the tenant has voluntarily vacated, abandoned, or been evicted pursuant to paragraph (2) of Section 1161 of the Code of Civil Procedure.

(b) Subdivision (a) does not apply where the owner has otherwise agreed by contract with a public entity in con-sideration for a direct financial contribution or any other forms of assistance specified in Chapter 4.3 (commencing with Section 65915) of Division 1 of Title 7 of the Government Code.

(c) Nothing in this section shall be construed to affect the authority of a public entity that may otherwise exist to regulate or monitor the basis for eviction.

(d) This section does not apply to any dwelling or unit that contains serious health, safety, fire, or building code violations, excluding those caused by disasters, for which a citation has been issued by the appropriate governmental agency and which has remained unabated for six months or longer preceding the vacancy.

1954.53. (a) Notwithstanding any other provision of law, an owner of residential real property may establish the initial rental rate for a dwelling or unit, except where any of the following applies:

(1) The previous tenancy has been terminated by the owner by notice pursuant to Section 1946.1 or has been terminated upon a change in the terms of the tenancy noticed pursuant to Section 827, except a change permitted by law in the amount of rent or fees. For the purpose of this paragraph, the owner's termination or nonrenewal of a contract or recorded agreement with a governmental agency that provides for a rent limitation to a qualified tenant, shall be construed as a change in the terms of the tenancy pursuant to Section 827.

(A) In a jurisdiction that controls by ordinance or charter provision the rental rate for a dwelling or unit, an owner who terminates or fails to renew a contract or recorded agreement with a governmental agency that provides for a rent limitation to a qualified tenant shall not be eligible to set an initial rent for three years following the date of the termination or nonrenewal of the contract or agreement. For any new tenancy established during the three-year period, the rental rate for a new tenancy established in that vacated dwelling or unit shall be at the same rate as the rent under the terminated or nonrenewed contract or recorded agreement with a governmental agency that provided for a rent limitation to a qualified tenant, plus any increases authorized after the termination or cancellation of the contract or recorded agreement.

(B) Subparagraph (A) shall not apply to any new tenancy of 12 months or more duration established after January 1, 2000, pursuant to the owner's contract or recorded agreement with a governmental agency that provides for a rent limitation to a qualified tenant unless the prior vacancy in that dwelling or unit was pursuant to a nonrenewed or canceled contract or recorded agreement with a governmental agency that provides for a rent limitation to a qualified tenant as set forth in that subparagraph.

(2) The owner has otherwise agreed by contract with a public entity in consideration for a direct financial contribution or any other forms of assistance specified in

Chapter 4.3 (commencing with Section 65915) of Division 1 of Title 7 of the Government Code.

(3) The initial rental rate for a dwelling or unit whose initial rental rate is controlled by an ordinance or charter provision in effect on January 1, 1995, shall not until January 1, 1999, exceed the amount calculated pursuant to subdivision (c). (b) Subdivision (a) applies to, and includes, renewal of the initial hiring by the same tenant, lessee, authorized subtenant, or authorized sublessee for the entire period of his or her occupancy at the rental rate established for the initial hiring.

(c) The rental rate of a dwelling or unit whose initial rental rate is controlled by ordinance or charter provision in effect on January 1, 1995, shall, until January 1, 1999, be established in accordance with this subdivision. Where the previous tenant has voluntarily vacated, abandoned, or been evicted pursuant to paragraph (2) of Section 1161 of Code of Civil Procedure, an owner of residential real property may, no more than twice, establish the initial rental rate for a dwelling or unit in an amount that is no greater than 15 percent more than the rental rate in effect for the immediately preceding tenancy or in an amount that is 70 percent of the prevailing market rent for comparable units, whichever amount is greater. The initial rental rate established pursuant to this subdivision shall not be deemed to substitute for or replace increases in rental rates otherwise authorized pursuant to law.

(d) (1) Nothing in this section or any other provision of law shall be construed to preclude express establishment in a lease or rental agreement of the rental rates to be applicable in the event the rental unit subject thereto is sublet, and nothing in this section shall be construed to impair the obligations of contracts entered into prior to January 1, 1996.

(2) Where the original occupant or occupants who took possession of the dwelling or unit pursuant to the rental agreement with the owner no longer permanently reside there, an owner may increase the rent by any amount allowed by this section to a lawful sublessee or assignee who did not reside at the dwelling or unit prior to January 1, 1996.

(3) This subdivision shall not apply to partial changes in occupancy of a dwelling or unit where one or more of the occupants of the premises, pursuant to the agreement with the owner provided for above, remains an occupant in lawful possession of the dwelling or unit, or where a lawful sublessee or assignee who resided at the dwelling or unit prior to January 1, 1996, remains in possession of the dwelling or unit. Nothing contained in this section shall be construed to enlarge or diminish an owner's right to withhold consent to a sublease or assignment.

(4) Acceptance of rent by the owner shall not operate as a waiver or otherwise prevent enforcement of a covenant prohibiting sublease or assignment or as a waiver of an owner's rights to establish the initial rental rate unless the owner has received written notice from the tenant that is party to the agreement and thereafter accepted rent.

(e) Nothing in this section shall be construed to affect any authority of a public entity that may otherwise exist to regulate or monitor the grounds for eviction.

(f) This section shall not apply to any dwelling or unit if all the following conditions are met:

(1) The dwelling or unit has been cited in an inspection report by the appropriate governmental agency as containing serious health, safety, fire, or building code violations, as defined by Section 17920.3 of the Health and Safety Code, excluding any violation caused by a disaster.

(2) The citation was issued at least 60 days prior to the date of the vacancy.

(3) The cited violation had not been abated when the prior tenant vacated and had remained unabated for 60 days or for a longer period of time. However, the 60-day time period may be extended by the appropriate governmental agency that issued the citation.

1954.535. Where an owner terminates or fails to renew a contract or recorded agreement with a governmental agency that provides for rent limitations to a qualified tenant, the tenant or tenants who were the beneficiaries of the contract or recorded agreement shall be given at least 90 days' written notice of the effective date of the termination and shall not be obligated to pay more than the tenant's portion of the rent, as calculated under the contract or recorded agreement to be terminated, for 90 days following receipt of the notice of termination of nonrenewal of the contract.

SECTIONS 1961-1962

1961. This chapter shall apply to every dwelling structure containing one or more units offered to the public for rent or for lease for residential purposes.

1962. (a) Any owner of a dwelling structure specified in Section 1961 or a party signing a rental agreement or lease on behalf of the owner shall do all of the following:

(1) Disclose therein the name, telephone number, and usual street address at which personal service may be effected of each person who is:

(A) Authorized to manage the premises.

(B) An owner of the premises or a person who is authorized to act for and on behalf of the owner for the purpose of service of process and for the purpose of receiving and receipting for all notices and demands.

(2) Disclose therein the name, telephone number, and address of the person or entity to whom rent payments shall be made.

(A) If rent payments may be made personally, the usual days and hours that the person will be available to receive the payments shall also be disclosed.

(B) At the owner's option, the rental agreement or lease shall instead disclose the number of either:

(i) The account in a financial institution into which rent payments may be made, and the name and street address of the institution; provided that the institution is located within five miles of the rental property.

(ii) The information necessary to establish an electronic funds transfer procedure for paying the rent.

(3) Disclose therein the form or forms in which rent payments are to be made.

(4) Provide a copy of the rental agreement or lease to the tenant within 15 days of its execution by the tenant. Once each calendar year thereafter, upon request by the tenant, the owner or owner's agent shall provide an additional copy to the tenant within 15 days. If the owner or owner's agent does not possess the rental agreement or lease or a copy of it, the owner or owner's agent shall instead furnish the tenant with a written statement stating that fact and containing the information required by paragraphs (1), (2), and (3) of subdivision (a).

(b) In the case of an oral rental agreement, the owner, or a person acting on behalf of the owner for the receipt of rent or otherwise, shall furnish the tenant, within 15 days of the agreement, with a written statement containing the information required by paragraphs (1), (2), and (3) of subdivision (a). Once each calendar year thereafter, upon request by the tenant, the owner or owner's agent shall provide an additional copy of the statement to the tenant within 15 days.

(c) The information required by this section shall be kept current and this section shall extend to and be enforceable against any successor owner or manager, who shall comply with this section within 15 days of succeeding the previous owner or manager.

(d) A party who enters into a rental agreement on behalf of the owner who fails to comply with this section is deemed an agent of each person who is an owner:

(1) For the purpose of service of process and receiving and receipting for notices and demands.

(2) For the purpose of performing the obligations of the owner under law and under the rental agreement.

(3) For the purpose of receiving rental payments, which may be made in cash, by check, by money order, or in any form previously accepted by the owner or owner's agent, unless the form of payment has been specified in the oral or written agreement, or the tenant has been notified by the owner in writing that a particular form of payment is unacceptable.

(e) Nothing in this section limits or excludes the liability of any undisclosed owner.

(f) If the address provided by the owner does not allow for personal delivery, then it shall be conclusively presumed that upon the mailing of any rent or notice to the owner by the tenant to the name and address provided, the notice or rent is deemed receivable by the owner on the date posted, if the tenant can show proof of mailing to the name and address provided by the owner.

1962.5. (a) Notwithstanding subdivisions (a) and (b) of Section 1962, the information required by paragraph (1) of subdivision (a) of Section 1962 to be disclosed to a tenant may, instead of being disclosed in the manner described in subdivisions (a) and (b) of Section 1962, be disclosed by the following method:

(1) In each dwelling structure containing an elevator a printed or typewritten notice containing the information required by paragraph (1) of subdivision (a) of Section 1962 shall be placed in every elevator and in one other conspicuous place.

(2) In each structure not containing an elevator, a printed or typewritten notice containing the information required by paragraph (1) of subdivision (a) of Section 1962 shall be placed in at least two conspicuous places.

(3) In the case of a single unit dwelling structure, the information to be disclosed under this section may be disclosed by complying with either paragraph (1) or (2).

(b) Except as provided in subdivision (a), all the provisions of Section 1962 shall be applicable.

1962.7. In the event an owner, successor owner, manager, or agent specified in Section 1961 fails to comply with the requirements of this chapter, service of process by a tenant with respect to a dispute arising out of the tenancy may be made by registered or certified mail sent to the address at which rent is paid, in which case the provisions of Section 1013 of the Code of Civil Procedure shall apply.

SECTIONS 1980-1991

1980. As used in this chapter:

(a) "Landlord" means any operator, keeper, lessor, or sublessor of any furnished or unfurnished premises for hire, or his agent or successor in interest.

(b) "Owner" means any person other than the landlord who has any right, title, or interest in personal property.

(c) "Premises" includes any common areas associated therewith.

(d) "Reasonable belief" means the actual knowledge or belief a prudent person would have without making an investigation (including any investigation of public records) except that, where the landlord has specific information indicating that such an investigation would more probably than not reveal pertinent information and the cost of such an investigation would be reasonable in relation to the probable value of the personal property involved, "reasonable belief" includes the actual knowledge or belief a prudent person would have if such an investigation were made.

(e) "Tenant" includes any paying guest, lessee, or sublessee of any premises for hire.

1981. (a) This chapter provides an optional procedure for the disposition of personal property that remains on the premises after a tenancy has terminated and the premises have been vacated by the tenant.

(b) This chapter does not apply whenever Section 1862.5, 2080.8, 2080.9, or 2081 to 2081.6, inclusive, applies. This chapter does not apply to property that exists for the purpose of providing utility services and is owned by a public utility, whether or not that property is actually in operation to provide those utility services.

(c) This chapter does not apply to any manufactured home as defined in Section 18007 of the Health and Safety Code, any mobilehome as defined in Section 18008 of the Health and Safety Code, or to any commercial coach as defined in Section 18001.8 of the Health and Safety Code, including attachments thereto or contents thereof, whether or not the manufactured home, mobilehome, or commercial coach is subject to registration under the Health and Safety Code.

(d) This chapter does not apply to the disposition of an animal to which Chapter 7 (commencing with Section 17001) of Part 1 of Division 9 of the Food and Agricultural Code applies, and those animals shall be disposed of in accordance with those provisions.

(e) If the requirements of this chapter are not satisfied, nothing in this chapter affects the rights and liabilities of the landlord, former tenant, or any other person.

1982. (a) Personal property which the landlord reasonably believes to have been lost shall be disposed of pursuant to Article 1 (commencing with Section 2080) of Chapter 4 of Title 6. The landlord is not liable to the owner of the property if he complies with this subdivision.

(b) If the appropriate police or sheriff's department refuses to accept property pursuant to subdivision (a), the landlord may dispose of the property pursuant to this chapter.

1983. (a) Where personal property remains on the premises after a tenancy has terminated and the premises have been vacated by the tenant, the landlord shall give written notice to such tenant and to any other person the landlord reasonably believes to be the owner of the property.

(b) The notice shall describe the property in a manner reasonably adequate to permit the owner of the property to identify it. The notice may describe all or a portion of the property, but the limitation of liability provided by Section 1989 does not protect the landlord from any liability arising from the disposition of property not described in the notice except that a trunk, valise, box, or other container which is locked, fastened, or tied in a manner which deters immediate access to its contents may be described as such without describing its contents. The notice shall advise the person to be notified that reasonable costs of storage may be charged before the property is returned, where the property may be claimed, and the date before which the claim must be made. The date specified in the notice shall be a date not less than 15 days after the notice

is personally delivered or, if mailed, not less than 18 days after the notice is deposited in the mail.

(c) The notice shall be personally delivered to the person to be notified or sent by first-class mail, postage prepaid, to the person to be notified at his last known address and, if there is reason to believe that the notice sent to that address will not be received by that person, also to such other address, if any, known to the landlord where such person may reasonably be expected to receive the notice. If the notice is sent by mail to the former tenant, one copy shall be sent to the premises vacated by such tenant.

1984. (a) A notice given to the former tenant which is in substantially the following form satisfies the requirements of Section 1983:

Notice of Right to Reclaim Abandoned Property

To: _____
(Name of former tenant)

_____
_____
(Address of former tenant)

When you vacated the premises at

_____
_____
(Address of premises, including room or apartment number, if any)
the following personal property remained: _____
_____
_____
(Insert description of the personal property)
You may claim this property at _____
_____.
(Address where property may be claimed)
Unless you pay the reasonable cost of storage for all the above-described property, and take possession of the property which you claim, not later than _____ (insert date not less than 15 days after notice is personally delivered or, if mailed, not less than 18 days after notice is deposited in the mail) this property may be disposed of pursuant to Civil Code Section 1988.

(Insert here the statement required by subdivision (b) of this section)

Dated: _____

_____
(Signature of landlord)
_____
(Type or print name of landlord)
_____
(Telephone number)
_____
_____
(Address)

(b) The notice set forth in subdivision (a) shall also contain one of the following statements:

(1) "If you fail to reclaim the property, it will be sold at a public sale after notice of the sale has been given by publication. You have the right to bid on the property at this sale. After the property is sold and the cost of storage, advertising, and sale is deducted, the remaining money will be paid over to the county. You may claim the remaining money at any time within one year after the county receives the money."

(2) "Because this property is believed to be worth less than $300, it may be kept, sold, or destroyed without further notice if you fail to reclaim it within the time indicated above."

1985. A notice which is in substantially the following form given to a person (other than the former tenant) the landlord reasonably believes to be the owner of personal property satisfies the requirements of Section 1983:

Notice of Right to Reclaim Abandoned Property

To: _____

(Name of former tenant)

_____

_____

(Address of former tenant)

When you vacated the premises at

_____

_____

(Address of premises, including room or apartment number, if any)

the following personal property remained: _____

_____

_____

(Insert description of the personal property)

You may claim this property at _____

_____.

(Address where property may be claimed)

Unless you pay the reasonable cost of storage for all the above-described property, and take possession of the property which you claim, not later than _____ (insert date not less than 15 days after notice is personally delivered or, if mailed, not less than 18 days after notice is deposited in the mail) this property may be disposed of pursuant to Civil Code Section 1988.

(Insert here the statement required by subdivision (b) of this section)

Dated: _____

_____

(Signature of landlord)

_____

(Type or print name of landlord)

_____

(Telephone number)

_____

_____

(Address)

1986. The personal property described in the notice shall either be left on the vacated premises or be stored by the landlord in a place of safekeeping until the landlord either releases the property pursuant to Section 1987 or disposes of the property pursuant to Section 1988. The landlord shall exercise reasonable care in storing the property, but he is not liable to the tenant or any other owner for any loss not caused by his deliberate or negligent act.

1987. (a) The personal property described in the notice shall be released by the landlord to the former tenant or, at the landlord's option, to any person reasonably believed by the landlord to be its owner if such tenant or other person pays the reasonable cost of storage and takes possession of the property not later than the date specified in the notice for taking possession.

(b) Where personal property is not released pursuant to subdivision (a) and the notice stated that the personal property would be sold at a public sale, the landlord shall release the personal property to the former tenant if he claims it prior to the time it is sold and pays the reasonable cost of storage, advertising, and sale incurred prior to the time the property is withdrawn from sale.

1988. (a) If the personal property described in the notice is not released pursuant to Section 1987, it shall be sold at public sale by competitive bidding. However, if the landlord reasonably believes that the total resale value of the property not released is less than three hundred dollars ($300), the landlord may retain such property for his or her own use or dispose of it in any manner. Nothing in this section shall be construed to preclude the landlord or tenant from bidding on the property at the public sale.

(b) Notice of the time and place of the public sale shall be given by publication pursuant to Section 6066 of the Government Code in a newspaper of general circulation published in the county where the sale is to be held. The last publication shall be not less than five days before the sale is to be held. The notice of the sale shall not be published before the last of the dates specified for taking possession of the property in any notice given pursuant to Section 1983. The notice of the sale shall describe the property to be sold in a manner reasonably adequate to permit the owner of the property to identify it. The notice may describe all or a portion of the property, but the limitation of liability provided by Section 1989 does not protect the landlord from any liability arising from the disposition of property not described in the notice, except that a trunk, valise, box, or other container which is locked, fastened, or tied in a manner which deters immediate access to its contents may be described as such without describing its contents.

(c) After deduction of the costs of storage, advertising, and sale, any balance of the proceeds of the sale which is not claimed by the former tenant or an owner other than such tenant shall be paid into the treasury of the county in which the sale took place not later than 30 days after the date of sale. The former tenant or other owner may claim the balance within one year from the date of payment to the county by making application to the county treasurer or other official designated by the county. If the county pays the balance or any part thereof to a claimant, neither the county nor any officer or employee thereof is liable to any other claimant as to the amount paid.

1989. (a) Notwithstanding subdivision (c) of Section 1981, where the landlord releases to the former tenant property which remains on the premises after a tenancy is terminated, the landlord is not liable with respect to that property to any person.

(b) Where the landlord releases property pursuant to Section 1987 to a person (other than the former tenant) reasonably believed by the landlord to be the owner of the property, the landlord is not liable with respect to that property to:

(1) Any person to whom notice was given pursuant to Section 1983; or

(2) Any person to whom notice was not given pursuant to Section 1983 unless such person proves that, prior to releasing the property, the landlord believed or reasonably should have believed that such person had an interest in the property and also that the landlord knew or should have known upon reasonable investigation the address of such person.

(c) Where property is disposed of pursuant to Section 1988, the landlord is not liable with respect to that property to:

(1) Any person to whom notice was given pursuant to Section 1983; or

(2) Any person to whom notice was not given pursuant to Section 1983 unless such person proves that, prior to disposing of the property pursuant to Section 1988, the landlord believed or reasonably should have believed that such person had an interest in the property and also that the landlord knew or should have known upon reasonable investigation the address of such person.

1990. (a) Costs of storage which may be required to be paid under this chapter shall be assessed in the following manner:

(1) Where a former tenant claims property pursuant to Section 1987, he may be required to pay the reasonable costs of storage for all the personal property remaining on the premises at the termination of the tenancy which are unpaid at the time the claim is made.

(2) Where an owner other than the former tenant claims property pursuant to Section 1987, he may be required to pay the reasonable costs of storage for only the property in which he claims an interest.

(b) In determining the costs to be assessed under subdivision (a), the landlord shall not charge more than one person for the same costs.

(c) If the landlord stores the personal property on the premises, the cost of storage shall be the fair rental value of the space reasonably required for such storage for the term of the storage.

1991. Where a notice of belief of abandonment is given to a lessee pursuant to Section 1951.3, the notice to the former tenant given pursuant to Section 1983 may, but need not, be given at the same time as the notice of belief of abandonment even though the tenancy is not terminated until the end of the period specified in the notice of belief of abandonment. If the notices are so given, the notices may, but need not, be combined in one notice that contains all the information required by the sections under which the notices are given.

CALIFORNIA CODE OF CIVIL PROCEDURE SECTION 1013–1013a

1013. (a) In case of service by mail, the notice or other paper shall be deposited in a post office, mailbox, subpost office, substation, or mail chute, or other like facility regularly maintained by the United States Postal Service, in a sealed envelope, with postage paid, addressed to the person on whom it is to be served, at the office address as last given by that person on any document filed in the cause and served on the party making service by mail; otherwise at that party's place of residence. The service is complete at the time of the deposit, but any period of notice and any right or duty to do any act or make any response within any period or on a date certain after the service of the document, which time period or date is prescribed by statute or rule of court, shall be extended five calendar days, upon service by mail, if the place of address and the place of mailing is within the State of California, 10 calendar days if either the place of mailing or the place of address is outside the State of California but within the United States, and 20 calendar days if either the place of mailing or the place of address is outside the United States, but the extension shall not apply to extend the time for filing notice of intention to move for new trial, notice of intention to move to vacate judgment pursuant to Section 663a, or notice of appeal. This extension applies in the absence of a specific exception provided for by this section or other statute or rule of court.

(b) The copy of the notice or other paper served by mail pursuant to this chapter shall bear a notation of the date and place of mailing or be accompanied by an unsigned copy of the affidavit or certificate of mailing.

(c) In case of service by Express Mail, the notice or other paper must be deposited in a post office, mailbox, subpost office, substation, or mail chute, or other like facility regularly maintained by the United States Postal Service for receipt of Express Mail, in a sealed envelope, with Express

Mail postage paid, addressed to the person on whom it is to be served, at the office address as last given by that person on any document filed in the cause and served on the party making service by Express Mail; otherwise at that party's place of residence. In case of service by another method of delivery providing for overnight delivery, the notice or other paper must be deposited in a box or other facility regularly maintained by the express service carrier, or delivered to an authorized courier or driver authorized by the express service carrier to receive documents, in an envelope or package designated by the express service carrier with delivery fees paid or provided for, addressed to the person on whom it is to be served, at the office address as last given by that person on any document filed in the cause and served on the party making service; otherwise at that party' s place of residence. The service is complete at the time of the deposit, but any period of notice and any right or duty to do any act or make any response within any period or on a date certain after the service of the document served by Express Mail or other method of delivery providing for overnight delivery shall be extended by two court days, but the extension shall not apply to extend the time for filing notice of intention to move for new trial, notice of intention to move to vacate judgment pursuant to Section 663a, or notice of appeal. This extension applies in the absence of a specific exception provided for by this section or other statute or rule of court.

(d) The copy of the notice or other paper served by Express Mail or another means of delivery providing for overnight delivery pursuant to this chapter shall bear a notation of the date and place of deposit or be accompanied by an unsigned copy of the affidavit or certificate of deposit.

(e) Service by facsimile transmission shall be permitted only where the parties agree and a written confirmation of that agreement is made. The Judicial Council may adopt rules implementing the service of documents by facsimile transmission and may provide a form for the confirmation of the agreement required by this subdivision. In case of service by facsimile transmission, the notice or other paper must be transmitted to a facsimile machine maintained by the person on whom it is served at the facsimile machine telephone number as last given by that person on any document which he or she has filed in the cause and served on the party making the service. The service is complete at the time of transmission, but any period of notice and any right or duty to do any act or make any response within any period or on a date certain after the service of the document, which time period or date is prescribed by statute or rule of court, shall be extended, after service by facsimile transmission, by two court days, but the extension shall not apply to extend the time for filing notice of intention to move for new trial, notice of inten-

tion to move to vacate judgment pursuant to Section 663a, or notice of appeal. This extension applies in the absence of a specific exception provided for by this section or other statute or rule of court.

(f) The copy of the notice or other paper served by facsimile transmission pursuant to this chapter shall bear a notation of the date and place of transmission and the facsimile telephone number to which transmitted or be accompanied by an unsigned copy of the affidavit or certificate of transmission which shall contain the facsimile telephone number to which the notice or other paper was transmitted.

(g) Subdivisions (b), (d), and (f) are directory.

1013a. Proof of service by mail may be made by one of the following methods:

(1) An affidavit setting forth the exact title of the document served and filed in the cause, showing the name and residence or business address of the person making the service, showing that he or she is a resident of or employed in the county where the mailing occurs, that he or she is over the age of 18 years and not a party to the cause, and showing the date and place of deposit in the mail, the name and address of the person served as shown on the envelope, and also showing that the envelope was sealed and deposited in the mail with the postage thereon fully prepaid.

(2) A certificate setting forth the exact title of the document served and filed in the cause, showing the name and business address of the person making the service, showing that he or she is an active member of the State Bar of California and is not a party to the cause, and showing the date and place of deposit in the mail, the name and address of the person served as shown on the envelope, and also showing that the envelope was sealed and deposited in the mail with the postage thereon fully prepaid.

(3) An affidavit setting forth the exact title of the document served and filed in the cause, showing (A) the name and residence or business address of the person making the service, (B) that he or she is a resident of, or employed in, the county where the mailing occurs, (C) that he or she is over the age of 18 years and not a party to the cause, (D) that he or she is readily familiar with the business' practice for collection and processing of correspondence for mailing with the United States Postal Service, (E) that the correspondence would be deposited with the United States Postal Service that same day in the ordinary course of business, (F) the name and address of the person served as shown on the envelope, and the date and place of business where the correspondence was placed for deposit in the United States Postal Service, and (G) that the envelope was sealed and placed for collection and mailing on that date following ordinary business practices. Service made pursuant to this paragraph, upon motion of a party served, shall be presumed invalid if the postal can-

cellation date or postage meter date on the envelope is more than one day after the date of deposit for mailing contained in the affidavit.

(4) In case of service by the clerk of a court of record, a certificate by that clerk setting forth the exact title of the document served and filed in the cause, showing the name of the clerk and the name of the court of which he or she is the clerk, and that he or she is not a party to the cause, and showing the date and place of deposit in the mail, the name and address of the person served as shown on the envelope, and also showing that the envelope was sealed and deposited in the mail with the postage thereon fully prepaid. This form of proof is sufficient for service of process in which the clerk or deputy clerk signing the certificate places the document for collection and mailing on the date shown thereon, so as to cause it to be mailed in an envelope so sealed and so addressed on that date following standard court practices. Service made pursuant to this paragraph, upon motion of a party served and a finding of good cause by the court, shall be deemed to have occurred on the date of postage cancellation or postage meter imprint as shown on the envelope if that date is more than one day after the date of deposit for mailing contained in the certificate.

SECTION 1162

1162. The notices required by Sections 1161 and 1161a may be served, either:

1. By delivering a copy to the tenant personally; or,

2. If he or she is absent from his or her place of residence, and from his or her usual place of business, by leaving a copy with some person of suitable age and discretion at either place, and sending a copy through the mail addressed to the tenant at his or her place of residence; or,

3. If such place of residence and business can not be ascertained, or a person of suitable age or discretion there can not be found, then by affixing a copy in a conspicuous place on the property, and also delivering a copy to a person there residing, if such person can be found; and also sending a copy through the mail addressed to the tenant at the place where the property is situated. Service upon a subtenant may be made in the same manner.

Appendix B:
Eviction Flowchart and Legal Holidays

On the next page is a flowchart showing each step in the eviction process for nonpayment of rent or the tenant's breach of some clause of the lease.

Page 145 contains a list of the legal holidays in California. It is important to keep these dates in mind when calculating the three-day notices.

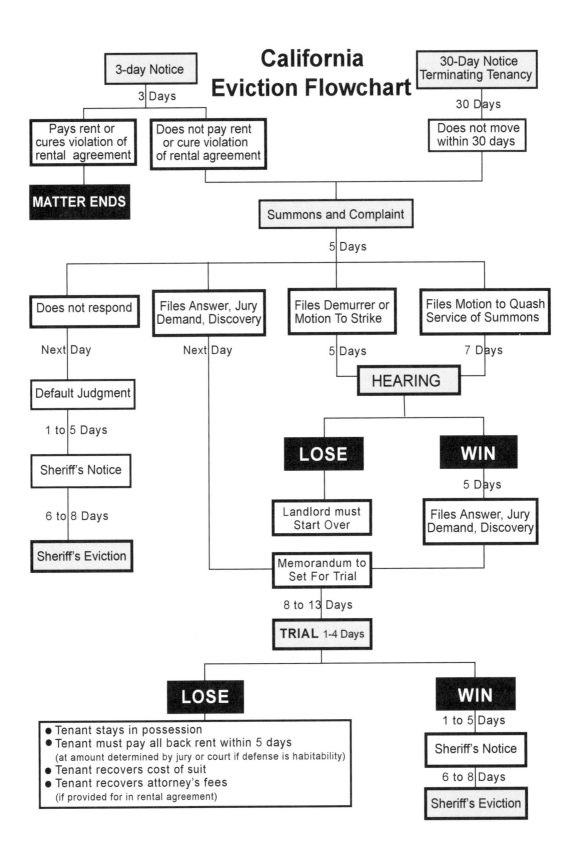

Legal Holidays in California

New Year's Day	January 1
Martin Luther King, Jr.'s Birthday	January 15
Abraham Lincoln's Birthday	February 12
George Washington's Birthday	Third Monday in February
Good Friday	(varies)
Memorial Day	Last Monday in May
Independence Day	July 4
Labor Day	First Monday In September
Admissions Day	September 9
Columbus Day	Second Monday in October
Veterans' Day	November 11
General Election Day	(varies)
Thanksgiving Day	Fourth Thursday in November
Christmas Day	December 25

NOTE: *When a legal holiday falls on a Sunday, the next day is considered a legal holiday. Not all California counties observe the same holidays, such as Good Friday, Admissions Day, and Columbus Day. Check your county to be sure you are not filing too soon after serving a notice.*

Appendix C:
The California Association of Realtors® (CAR) Sample Forms

The forms contained in the appendix are provided with the permission of the *California Association of Realtors®*. Contact the association for further information or to find a local realtor.

To purchase these and other CAR authorized products, contact your local association or CAR Customer Service at 213-739-8227, **www.car.org/mall**, or fax 213-480-7724.

CALIFORNIA ASSOCIATION OF REALTORS®

APPLICATION TO RENT/SCREENING FEE
(C.A.R. Form LRA, Revised 4/03)

I. APPLICATION TO RENT

THIS SECTION TO BE COMPLETED BY APPLICANT. A SEPARATE APPLICATION TO RENT IS REQUIRED FOR EACH OCCUPANT 18 YEARS OF AGE OR OVER, OR AN EMANCIPATED MINOR.

Applicant is completing Application as a (check one) ☐ tenant, ☐ tenant with co-tenant(s) or ☐ guarantor/co-signor.
Total number of applicants _____.

PREMISES INFORMATION

Application to rent property at _____ ("Premises")
Rent: $_____ per _____ Proposed move-in date _____

PERSONAL INFORMATION

FULL NAME OF APPLICANT _____
Social security No. _____ Driver's license No. _____ State _____ Expires _____
Phone number: Home _____ Work _____ Other _____
Email _____
Name(s) of all other proposed occupant(s) and relationship to applicant _____
_____
Pet(s) or service animals (number and type) _____
Auto: Make _____ Model _____ Year _____ License No. _____ State _____ Color _____
Other vehicle(s): _____
In case of emergency, person to notify _____ Relationship _____
Address _____ Phone _____
Does applicant or any proposed occupant plan to use liquid-filled furniture? ☐ No ☐ Yes Type _____
Has applicant been a party to an unlawful detainer action or filed bankruptcy within the last seven years? ☐ No ☐ Yes
If yes, explain _____
Has applicant or any proposed occupant ever been convicted of or pleaded no contest to a felony? ☐ No ☐ Yes
If yes, explain _____
Has applicant or any proposed occupant ever been asked to move out of a residence? ☐ No ☐ Yes
If yes, explain _____

RESIDENCE HISTORY

Current address _____	Previous address _____
City/State/Zip _____	City/State/Zip _____
From _____ to _____	From _____ to _____
Name of Landlord/Manager _____	Name of Landlord/Manager _____
Landlord/Manager's phone _____	Landlord/Manager's phone _____
Do you own this property? ☐ No ☐ Yes	Did you own this property? ☐ No ☐ Yes
Reason for leaving current address _____	Reason for leaving this address _____

EMPLOYMENT AND INCOME HISTORY

Current employer _____ Supervisor _____ From _____ To _____
Employer's address _____ Supervisor's phone _____
Position or title _____ Phone number to verify employment _____
Employment gross income $_____ per _____ Other $_____ per _____ Source _____
Previous employer _____ Supervisor _____ From _____ To _____
Employer's address _____ Supervisor's phone _____
Position or title _____ Employment gross income $_____ per _____

LRA REVISED 4/03 (PAGE 1 OF 2) Print Date

Applicant's Initials (_____)(_____)
Reviewed by _____ Date _____

EQUAL HOUSING OPPORTUNITY

APPLICATION TO RENT/SCREENING FEE (LRA PAGE 1 OF 2)

150

Property Address: _____ Date: _____

CREDIT INFORMATION

Name of creditor	Account number	Monthly payment	Balance due

Name of bank/branch	Account number	Type of account	Account balance

PERSONAL REFERENCES

Name _____ Address _____
Phone _____ Length of acquaintance _____ Occupation _____
Name _____ Address _____
Phone _____ Length of acquaintance _____ Occupation _____

NEAREST RELATIVE(S)

Name _____ Address _____
Phone _____ Relationship _____
Name _____ Address _____
Phone _____ Relationship _____

Applicant understands and agrees: **(i)** this is an application to rent only and does not guarantee that applicant will be offered the Premises; and **(ii)** Landlord or Manager or Agent may accept more than one application for the Premises and, using their sole discretion, will select the best qualified applicant.

Applicant represents the above information to be true and complete, and hereby authorizes Landlord or Manager or Agent to: **(i)** verify the information provided; and **(ii)** obtain credit report on applicant.

If application is not fully completed, or received without the screening fee: (i) the application will not be processed, and (ii) the application and any screening fee will be returned.

Applicant _____ Date _____ Time _____

Return your completed application and any applicable fee not already paid to: _____
Address _____ City _____ State _____ Zip _____

II. SCREENING FEE

THIS SECTION TO BE COMPLETED BY LANDLORD, MANAGER OR AGENT.

Applicant has paid a **nonrefundable** screening fee of $ _____, applied as follows: (The screening fee may not exceed $30.00 (adjusted annually from 1-1-98 commensurate with the increase in the Consumer Price Index).)

$ _____ for credit reports prepared by _____;
$ _____ for _____ (other out-of-pocket expenses); and
$ _____ for processing.
The undersigned has read the foregoing and acknowledges receipt of a copy.

_____   _____
Applicant Signature   Date

The undersigned has received the screening fee indicated above.

_____   _____
Landlord or Manager or Agent Signature   Date

SURE TRAC
The System for Success®
Published and Distributed by:
REAL ESTATE BUSINESS SERVICES, INC.
a subsidiary of the California Association of REALTORS®
525 South Virgil Avenue, Los Angeles, California 90020

Reviewed by _____ Date _____

EQUAL HOUSING OPPORTUNITY

LRA REVISED 4/03 (PAGE 2 OF 2) Print Date

APPLICATION TO RENT/SCREENING FEE (LRA PAGE 2 OF 2)

Displayed / Reprinted with permission, CALIFORNIA ASSOCIATION OF REALTORS®. Endorsement not implied.

CALIFORNIA ASSOCIATION OF REALTORS®

RESIDENTIAL LEASE OR MONTH-TO-MONTH RENTAL AGREEMENT
(C.A.R. Form LR, Revised 1/06)

_____ ("Landlord") and
_____ ("Tenant") agree as follows:

1. PROPERTY:
  A. Landlord rents to Tenant and Tenant rents from Landlord, the real property and improvements described as: _____
_____ ("Premises").
  B. The Premises are for the sole use as a personal residence by the following named person(s) **only:** _____
_____.
  C. The following personal property, maintained pursuant to paragraph 11, is included: _____
_____ or ☐ (if checked) the personal property on the attached addendum.
2. TERM: The term begins on (date) _____ ("Commencement Date"), **(Check A or B):**
  ☐ **A. Month-to-Month:** and continues as a month-to-month tenancy. Tenant may terminate the tenancy by giving written notice at least 30 days prior to the intended termination date. Landlord may terminate the tenancy by giving written notice as provided by law. Such notices may be given on any date.
  ☐ **B. Lease:** and shall terminate on (date) _____ at _____ ☐ AM/☐ PM.
  Tenant shall vacate the Premises upon termination of the Agreement, unless: **(i)** Landlord and Tenant have extended this agreement in writing or signed a new agreement; **(ii)** mandated by local rent control law; or **(iii)** Landlord accepts Rent from Tenant (other than past due Rent), in which case a month-to-month tenancy shall be created which either party may terminate as specified in paragraph 2A. Rent shall be at a rate agreed to by Landlord and Tenant, or as allowed by law. All other terms and conditions of this Agreement shall remain in full force and effect.
3. RENT: "Rent" shall mean all monetary obligations of Tenant to Landlord under the terms of the Agreement, except security deposit.
  A. Tenant agrees to pay $ _____ per month for the term of the Agreement.
  B. Rent is payable in advance on the **1st (or ☐ _____) day** of each calendar month, and is delinquent on the next day.
  C. If Commencement Date falls on any day other than the day Rent is payable under paragraph 3B, and Tenant has paid one full month's Rent in advance of Commencement Date, Rent for the second calendar month shall be prorated based on a 30-day period.
  D. PAYMENT: Rent shall be paid by ☐ personal check, ☐ money order, ☐ cashier's check, or ☐ other _____, to (name) _____ (phone) _____ at (address) _____, (or at any other location subsequently specified by Landlord in writing to Tenant) between the hours of _____ and _____ on the following days _____. If any payment is returned for non-sufficient funds ("NSF") or because tenant stops payment, then, after that: (i) Landlord may, in writing, require Tenant to pay Rent in cash for three months and (ii) all future Rent shall be paid by ☐ money order, or ☐ cashier's check.
4. SECURITY DEPOSIT:
  A. Tenant agrees to pay $ _____ as a security deposit. Security deposit will be ☐ transferred to and held by the Owner of the Premises, or ☐ held in Owner's Broker's trust account.
  B. All or any portion of the security deposit may be used, as reasonably necessary, to: **(i)** cure Tenant's default in payment of Rent (which includes Late Charges, NSF fees or other sums due); **(ii)** repair damage, excluding ordinary wear and tear, caused by Tenant or by a guest or licensee of Tenant; **(iii)** clean Premises, if necessary, upon termination of the tenancy; and **(iv)** replace or return personal property or appurtenances. **SECURITY DEPOSIT SHALL NOT BE USED BY TENANT IN LIEU OF PAYMENT OF LAST MONTH'S RENT.** If all or any portion of the security deposit is used during the tenancy, Tenant agrees to reinstate the total security deposit within five days after written notice is delivered to Tenant. Within 21 days after Tenant vacates the Premises, Landlord shall: **(1)** furnish Tenant an itemized statement indicating the amount of any security deposit received and the basis for its disposition and supporting documentation as required by California Civil Code § 1950.5(g); and **(2)** return any remaining portion of the security deposit to Tenant.
  C. Security deposit will not be returned until all Tenants have vacated the Premises and all keys returned. **Any security deposit returned by check shall be made out to all Tenants named on this Agreement, or as subsequently modified.**
  D. No interest will be paid on security deposit unless required by local law.
  E. If the security deposit is held by Owner, Tenant agrees not to hold Broker responsible for its return. If the security deposit is held in Owner's Broker's trust account, **and** Broker's authority is terminated before expiration of this Agreement, **and** security deposit is released to someone other than Tenant, **then** Broker shall notify Tenant, in writing, where and to whom security deposit has been released. Once Tenant has been provided such notice, Tenant agrees not to hold Broker responsible for the security deposit.
5. MOVE-IN COSTS RECEIVED/DUE: Move-in funds made payable to _____ shall be paid by ☐ personal check, ☐ money order, or ☐ cashier's check.

Category	Total Due	Payment Received	Balance Due	Date Due
Rent from _____ to _____ (date)				
*Security Deposit				
Other _____				
Other _____				
Total				

*The maximum amount Landlord may receive as security deposit, however designated, cannot exceed two months' Rent for unfurnished premises, or three months' Rent for furnished premises.

Tenant's Initials (_____)(_____)
Landlord's Initials (_____)(_____)

Reviewed by _____ Date _____

EQUAL HOUSING OPPORTUNITY

LR REVISED 1/06 (PAGE 1 OF 6) Print Date

RESIDENTIAL LEASE OR MONTH-TO-MONTH RENTAL AGREEMENT (LR PAGE 1 OF 6)

152

Premises: _____ Date: _____

6. **LATE CHARGE; RETURNED CHECKS:**
   A. Tenant acknowledges either late payment of Rent or issuance of a returned check may cause Landlord to incur costs and expenses, the exact amounts of which are extremely difficult and impractical to determine. These costs may include, but are not limited to, processing, enforcement and accounting expenses, and late charges imposed on Landlord. If any installment of Rent due from Tenant is not received by Landlord within **5 (or ☐ _____) calendar days** after the date due, or if a check is returned, Tenant shall pay to Landlord, respectively, an additional sum of $ _____ or _____% of the Rent due as a Late Charge and $25.00 as a NSF fee for the first returned check and $35.00 as a NSF fee for each additional returned check, either or both of which shall be deemed additional Rent.
   B. Landlord and Tenant agree that these charges represent a fair and reasonable estimate of the costs Landlord may incur by reason of Tenant's late or NSF payment. Any Late Charge or NSF fee due shall be paid with the current installment of Rent. Landlord's acceptance of any Late Charge or NSF fee shall not constitute a waiver as to any default of Tenant. Landlord's right to collect a Late Charge or NSF fee shall not be deemed an extension of the date Rent is due under paragraph 3 or prevent Landlord from exercising any other rights and remedies under this Agreement and as provided by law.

7. **PARKING: (Check A or B)**
   ☐ A. Parking is permitted as follows: _____
   _____.
   The right to parking ☐ is ☐ is not included in the Rent charged pursuant to paragraph 3. If not included in the Rent, the parking rental fee shall be an additional $ _____ per month. Parking space(s) are to be used for parking properly licensed and operable motor vehicles, except for trailers, boats, campers, buses or trucks (other than pick-up trucks). Tenant shall park in assigned space(s) only. Parking space(s) are to be kept clean. Vehicles leaking oil, gas or other motor vehicle fluids shall not be parked on the Premises. Mechanical work or storage of inoperable vehicles is not permitted in parking space(s) or elsewhere on the Premises.
   OR ☐ B. Parking is not permitted on the Premises.

8. **STORAGE: (Check A or B)**
   ☐ A. Storage is permitted as follows: _____
   The right to storage space ☐ is, ☐ is not, included in the Rent charged pursuant to paragraph 3. If not included in the Rent, storage space fee shall be an additional $ _____ per month. Tenant shall store only personal property Tenant owns, and shall not store property claimed by another or in which another has any right, title or interest. Tenant shall not store any improperly packaged food or perishable goods, flammable materials, explosives, hazardous waste or other inherently dangerous material, or illegal substances.
   OR ☐ B. Storage is not permitted on the Premises.

9. **UTILITIES:** Tenant agrees to pay for all utilities and services, and the following charges: _____
   except _____, which shall be paid for by Landlord. If any utilities are not separately metered, Tenant shall pay Tenant's proportional share, as reasonably determined and directed by Landlord. If utilities are separately metered, Tenant shall place utilities in Tenant's name as of the Commencement Date. Landlord is only responsible for installing and maintaining one usable telephone jack and one telephone line to the Premises. Tenant shall pay any cost for conversion from existing utilities service provider.

10. **CONDITION OF PREMISES:** Tenant has examined Premises and, if any, all furniture, furnishings, appliances, landscaping and fixtures, including smoke detector(s).
    (Check all that apply:)
    ☐ A. Tenant acknowledges these items are clean and in operable condition, with the following exceptions: _____
    _____.
    ☐ B. Tenant's acknowledgment of the condition of these items is contained in an attached statement of condition (C.A.R. Form MIMO).
    ☐ C. Tenant will provide Landlord a list of items that are damaged or not in operable condition within **3 (or ☐ _____) days** after Commencement Date, not as a contingency of this Agreement but rather as an acknowledgment of the condition of the Premises.
    ☐ D. Other: _____.

11. **MAINTENANCE:**
    A. Tenant shall properly use, operate and safeguard Premises, including if applicable, any landscaping, furniture, furnishings and appliances, and all mechanical, electrical, gas and plumbing fixtures, and keep them and the Premises clean, sanitary and well ventilated. Tenant shall be responsible for checking and maintaining all smoke detectors and any additional phone lines beyond the one line and jack that Landlord shall provide and maintain. Tenant shall immediately notify Landlord, in writing, of any problem, malfunction or damage. Tenant shall be charged for all repairs or replacements caused by Tenant, pets, guests or licensees of Tenant, excluding ordinary wear and tear. Tenant shall be charged for all damage to Premises as a result of failure to report a problem in a timely manner. Tenant shall be charged for repair of drain blockages or stoppages, unless caused by defective plumbing parts or tree roots invading sewer lines.
    B. ☐ Landlord ☐ Tenant shall water the garden, landscaping, trees and shrubs, except: _____
    _____.
    C. ☐ Landlord ☐ Tenant shall maintain the garden, landscaping, trees and shrubs, except: _____
    _____.
    D. ☐ Landlord ☐ Tenant shall maintain _____.
    E. Tenant's failure to maintain any item for which Tenant is responsible shall give Landlord the right to hire someone to perform such maintenance and charge Tenant to cover the cost of such maintenance.
    F. The following items of personal property are included in the Premises without warranty and Landlord will not maintain, repair or replace them: _____.

Tenant's Initials (_____)(_____)
Landlord's Initials (_____)(_____)

Reviewed by _____ Date _____

EQUAL HOUSING OPPORTUNITY

RESIDENTIAL LEASE OR MONTH-TO-MONTH RENTAL AGREEMENT (LR PAGE 2 OF 6)
Displayed/Reprinted with permission, CALIFORNIA ASSOCIATION OF REALTORS®. Endorsement not implied.

Premises: _____ Date: _____

12. NEIGHBORHOOD CONDITIONS: Tenant is advised to satisfy him or herself as to neighborhood or area conditions, including schools, proximity and adequacy of law enforcement, crime statistics, proximity of registered felons or offenders, fire protection, other governmental services, availability, adequacy and cost of any speed-wired, wireless internet connections or other telecommunications or other technology services and installations, proximity to commercial, industrial or agricultural activities, existing and proposed transportation, construction and development that may affect noise, view, or traffic, airport noise, noise or odor from any source, wild and domestic animals, other nuisances, hazards, or circumstances, cemeteries, facilities and condition of common areas, conditions and influences of significance to certain cultures and/or religions, and personal needs, requirements and preferences of Tenant.

13. PETS: Unless otherwise provided in California Civil Code § 54.2, no animal or pet shall be kept on or about the Premises without Landlord's prior written consent, except: _____.

14. RULES/REGULATIONS:

  A. Tenant agrees to comply with all Landlord rules and regulations that are at any time posted on the Premises or delivered to Tenant. Tenant shall not, and shall ensure that guests and licensees of Tenant shall not, disturb, annoy, endanger or interfere with other tenants of the building or neighbors, or use the Premises for any unlawful purposes, including, but not limited to, using, manufacturing, selling, storing or transporting illicit drugs or other contraband, or violate any law or ordinance, or commit a waste or nuisance on or about the Premises.

  B. (If applicable, check one)
  ☐ **1.** Landlord shall provide Tenant with a copy of the rules and regulations within _____ days
       or _____.
  OR ☐ **2.** Tenant has been provided with, and acknowledges receipt of, a copy of the rules and regulations.

15. ☐ **(If checked) CONDOMINIUM;PLANNED UNIT DEVELOPMENT:**

  A. The Premises is a unit in a condominium, planned unit development, common interest subdivision or other development governed by a homeowners' association ("HOA"). The name of the HOA is _____. Tenant agrees to comply with all HOA covenants, conditions and restrictions, bylaws, rules and regulations and decisions. Landlord shall provide Tenant copies of rules and regulations, if any. Tenant shall reimburse Landlord for any fines or charges imposed by HOA or other authorities, due to any violation by Tenant, or the guests or licensees of Tenant.

  B. (Check one)
  ☐ **1.** Landlord shall provide Tenant with a copy of the HOA rules and regulations within _____ days
       or _____.
  OR ☐ **2.** Tenant has been provided with, and acknowledges receipt of, a copy of the HOA rules and regulations.

16. ALTERATIONS; REPAIRS: Unless otherwise specified by law or paragraph 27C, without Landlord's prior written consent, **(i)** Tenant shall not make any repairs, alterations or improvements in or about the Premises including: painting, wallpapering, adding or changing locks, installing antenna or satellite dish(es), placing signs, displays or exhibits, or using screws, fastening devices, large nails or adhesive materials; **(ii)** Landlord shall not be responsible for the costs of alterations or repairs made by Tenant; **(iii)** Tenant shall not deduct from Rent the costs of any repairs, alterations or improvements; and **(iv)** any deduction made by Tenant shall be considered unpaid Rent.

17. KEYS; LOCKS:

  A. Tenant acknowledges receipt of (or Tenant will receive ☐ prior to the Commencement Date, or ☐ _____):
  ☐ _____ key(s) to Premises,   ☐ _____ remote control device(s) for garage door/gate opener(s),
  ☐ _____ key(s) to mailbox,   ☐ _____,
  ☐ _____ key(s) to common area(s),   ☐ _____.

  B. Tenant acknowledges that locks to the Premises ☐ have, ☐ have not, been re-keyed.

  C. If Tenant re-keys existing locks or opening devices, Tenant shall immediately deliver copies of all keys to Landlord. Tenant shall pay all costs and charges related to loss of any keys or opening devices. Tenant may not remove locks, even if installed by Tenant.

18. ENTRY:

  A. Tenant shall make Premises available to Landlord or Landlord's representative for the purpose of entering to make necessary or agreed repairs, decorations, alterations, or improvements, or to supply necessary or agreed services, or to show Premises to prospective or actual purchasers, tenants, mortgagees, lenders, appraisers, or contractors.

  B. Landlord and Tenant agree that 24-hour written notice shall be reasonable and sufficient notice, except as follows. 48-hour written notice is required to conduct an inspection of the Premises prior to the Tenant moving out, unless the Tenant waives the right to such notice. Notice may be given orally to show the Premises to actual or prospective purchasers provided Tenant has been notified in writing within 120 days preceding the oral notice that the Premises are for sale and that oral notice may be given to show the Premises. No notice is required: **(i)** to enter in case of an emergency; **(ii)** if the Tenant is present and consents at the time of entry or **(iii)** if the Tenant has abandoned or surrendered the Premises. No written notice is required if Landlord and Tenant orally agree to an entry for agreed services or repairs if the date and time of entry are within one week of the oral agreement.

  C. ☐ (If checked) Tenant authorizes the use of a keysafe/lockbox to allow entry into the Premises and agrees to sign a keysafe/lockbox addendum (C.A.R. Form KLA).

19. SIGNS: Tenant authorizes Landlord to place FOR SALE/LEASE signs on the Premises.

20. ASSIGNMENT; SUBLETTING: Tenant shall not sublet all or any part of Premises, or assign or transfer this Agreement or any interest in it, without Landlord's prior written consent. Unless such consent is obtained, any assignment, transfer or subletting of Premises or this Agreement or tenancy, by voluntary act of Tenant, operation of law or otherwise, shall, at the option of Landlord, terminate this Agreement. Any proposed assignee, transferee or sublessee shall submit to Landlord an application and credit information for Landlord's approval and, if approved, sign a separate written agreement with Landlord and Tenant. Landlord's consent to any one assignment, transfer or sublease, shall not be construed as consent to any subsequent assignment, transfer or sublease and does not release Tenant of Tenant's obligations under this Agreement.

21. JOINT AND INDIVIDUAL OBLIGATIONS: If there is more than one Tenant, each one shall be individually and completely responsible for the performance of all obligations of Tenant under this Agreement, jointly with every other Tenant, and individually, whether or not in possession.

Tenant's Initials (_____)(_____)
Landlord's Initials (_____)(_____)

LR REVISED 1/06 (PAGE 3 OF 6)

| Reviewed by _____ Date _____ |

EQUAL HOUSING OPPORTUNITY

RESIDENTIAL LEASE OR MONTH-TO-MONTH RENTAL AGREEMENT (LR PAGE 3 OF 6)
Displayed / Reprinted with permission, CALIFORNIA ASSOCIATION OF REALTORS®. Endorsement not implied.

Premises: _____ Date: _____

22. ☐ **LEAD-BASED PAINT (If checked):** Premises was constructed prior to 1978. In accordance with federal law, Landlord gives and Tenant acknowledges receipt of the disclosures on the attached form (C.A.R. Form FLD) and a federally approved lead pamphlet.

23. ☐ **MILITARY ORDNANCE DISCLOSURE:** (If applicable and known to Landlord) Premises is located within one mile of an area once used for military training, and may contain potentially explosive munitions.

24. ☐ **PERIODIC PEST CONTROL:** Landlord has entered into a contract for periodic pest control treatment of the Premises and shall give Tenant a copy of the notice originally given to Landlord by the pest control company.

25. ☐ **METHAMPHETAMINE CONTAMINATION:** Prior to signing this Agreement, Landlord has given Tenant a notice that a health official has issued an order prohibiting occupancy of the property because of methamphetamine contamination. A copy of the notice and order are attached.

26. **DATABASE DISCLOSURE:** Notice: Pursuant to Section 290.46 of the Penal Code, information about specified registered sex offenders is made available to the public via an Internet Web site maintained by the Department of Justice at www.meganslaw.ca.gov. Depending on an offender's criminal history, this information will include either the address at which the offender resides or the community of residence and ZIP Code in which he or she resides. (Neither Landlord nor Brokers, if any, are required to check this website. If Tenant wants further information, Tenant should obtain information directly from this website.)

27. **POSSESSION:**
   A. Tenant is not in possession of the premises. If Landlord is unable to deliver possession of Premises on Commencement Date, such Date shall be extended to the date on which possession is made available to Tenant. If Landlord is unable to deliver possession within **5 (or ☐ _____) calendar days** after agreed Commencement Date, Tenant may terminate this Agreement by giving written notice to Landlord, and shall be refunded all Rent and security deposit paid. Possession is deemed terminated when Tenant has returned all keys to the Premises to Landlord.
   B. ☐ Tenant is already in possession of the Premises.

28. **TENANT'S OBLIGATIONS UPON VACATING PREMISES:**
   A. Upon termination of the Agreement, Tenant shall: **(i)** give Landlord all copies of all keys or opening devices to Premises, including any common areas; **(ii)** vacate and surrender Premises to Landlord, empty of all persons; **(iii)** vacate any/all parking and/or storage space; **(iv)** clean and deliver Premises, as specified in paragraph C below, to Landlord in the same condition as referenced in paragraph 10; **(v)** remove all debris; **(vi)** give written notice to Landlord of Tenant's forwarding address; and **(vii)** _____.
   B. All alterations/improvements made by or caused to be made by Tenant, with or without Landlord's consent, become the property of Landlord upon termination. Landlord may charge Tenant for restoration of the Premises to the condition it was in prior to any alterations/improvements.
   C. **Right to Pre-Move-Out Inspection and Repairs as follows: (i)** After giving or receiving notice of termination of a tenancy (C.A.R. Form NTT), or before the end of a lease, Tenant has the right to request that an inspection of the Premises take place prior to termination of the lease or rental (C.A.R. Form NRI). If Tenant requests such an inspection, Tenant shall be given an opportunity to remedy identified deficiencies prior to termination, consistent with the terms of this Agreement. **(ii)** Any repairs or alterations made to the Premises as a result of this inspection (collectively, "Repairs") shall be made at Tenant's expense. Repairs may be performed by Tenant or through others, who have adequate insurance and licenses and are approved by Landlord. The work shall comply with applicable law, including governmental permit, inspection and approval requirements. Repairs shall be performed in a good, skillful manner with materials of quality and appearance comparable to existing materials. It is understood that exact restoration of appearance or cosmetic items following all Repairs may not be possible. **(iii)** Tenant shall: **(a)** obtain receipts for Repairs performed by others; **(b)** prepare a written statement indicating the Repairs performed by Tenant and the date of such Repairs; and **(c)** provide copies of receipts and statements to Landlord prior to termination. Paragraph 28C does not apply when the tenancy is terminated pursuant to California Code of Civil Procedure § 1161(2), (3) or (4).

29. **BREACH OF CONTRACT; EARLY TERMINATION:** In addition to any obligations established by paragraph 28, in the event of termination by Tenant prior to completion of the original term of the Agreement, Tenant shall also be responsible for lost Rent, rental commissions, advertising expenses and painting costs necessary to ready Premises for re-rental. Landlord may withhold any such amounts from Tenant's security deposit.

30. **TEMPORARY RELOCATION:** Subject to local law, Tenant agrees, upon demand of Landlord, to temporarily vacate Premises for a reasonable period, to allow for fumigation (or other methods) to control wood destroying pests or organisms, or other repairs to Premises. Tenant agrees to comply with all instructions and requirements necessary to prepare Premises to accommodate pest control, fumigation or other work, including bagging or storage of food and medicine, and removal of perishables and valuables. Tenant shall only be entitled to a credit of Rent equal to the per diem Rent for the period of time Tenant is required to vacate Premises.

31. **DAMAGE TO PREMISES:** If, by no fault of Tenant, Premises are totally or partially damaged or destroyed by fire, earthquake, accident or other casualty that render Premises totally or partially uninhabitable, either Landlord or Tenant may terminate this Agreement by giving the other written notice. Rent shall be abated as of the date Premises become totally or partially uninhabitable. The abated amount shall be the current monthly Rent prorated on a 30-day period. If the Agreement is not terminated, Landlord shall promptly repair the damage, and Rent shall be reduced based on the extent to which the damage interferes with Tenant's reasonable use of Premises. If damage occurs as a result of an act of Tenant or Tenant's guests, only Landlord shall have the right of termination, and no reduction in Rent shall be made.

32. **INSURANCE:** Tenant's or guest's personal property and vehicles are not insured by Landlord, manager or, if applicable, HOA, against loss or damage due to fire, theft, vandalism, rain, water, criminal or negligent acts of others, or any other cause. **Tenant is advised to carry Tenant's own insurance (renter's insurance) to protect Tenant from any such loss or damage.** Tenant shall comply with any requirement imposed on Tenant by Landlord's insurer to avoid: **(i)** an increase in Landlord's insurance premium (or Tenant shall pay for the increase in premium); or **(ii)** loss of insurance.

Tenant's Initials (_____)(_____)
Landlord's Initials (_____)(_____)

| Reviewed by _____ Date _____ |

LR REVISED 1/06 (PAGE 4 OF 6)

RESIDENTIAL LEASE OR MONTH-TO-MONTH RENTAL AGREEMENT (LR PAGE 4 OF 6)
Displayed/Reprinted with permission, CALIFORNIA ASSOCIATION OF REALTORS®. Endorsement not implied.

Premises: _____ Date: _____

33. **WATERBEDS:** Tenant shall not use or have waterbeds on the Premises unless: **(i)** Tenant obtains a valid waterbed insurance policy; **(ii)** Tenant increases the security deposit in an amount equal to one-half of one month's Rent; and **(iii)** the bed conforms to the floor load capacity of Premises.

34. **WAIVER:** The waiver of any breach shall not be construed as a continuing waiver of the same or any subsequent breach.

35. **NOTICE:** Notices may be served at the following address, or at any other location subsequently designated:
Landlord: _____ Tenant: _____
_____ _____
_____ _____

36. **TENANT ESTOPPEL CERTIFICATE:** Tenant shall execute and return a tenant estoppel certificate delivered to Tenant by Landlord or Landlord's agent within 3 days after its receipt. Failure to comply with this requirement shall be deemed Tenant's acknowledgment that the tenant estoppel certificate is true and correct, and may be relied upon by a lender or purchaser.

37. **TENANT REPRESENTATIONS; CREDIT:** Tenant warrants that all statements in Tenant's rental application are accurate. Tenant authorizes Landlord and Broker(s) to obtain Tenant's credit report periodically during the tenancy in connection with the modification or enforcement of this Agreement. Landlord may cancel this Agreement: **(i)** before occupancy begins; **(ii)** upon disapproval of the credit report(s); or **(iii)** at any time, upon discovering that information in Tenant's application is false. A negative credit report reflecting on Tenant's record may be submitted to a credit reporting agency if Tenant fails to fulfill the terms of payment and other obligations under this Agreement.

38. **MEDIATION:**
   A. Consistent with paragraphs B and C below, Landlord and Tenant agree to mediate any dispute or claim arising between them out of this Agreement, or any resulting transaction, before resorting to court action. Mediation fees, if any, shall be divided equally among the parties involved. If, for any dispute or claim to which this paragraph applies, any party commences an action without first attempting to resolve the matter through mediation, or refuses to mediate after a request has been made, then that party shall not be entitled to recover attorney fees, even if they would otherwise be available to that party in any such action.
   B. The following matters are excluded from mediation: **(i)** an unlawful detainer action; **(ii)** the filing or enforcement of a mechanic's lien; and **(iii)** any matter within the jurisdiction of a probate, small claims or bankruptcy court. The filing of a court action to enable the recording of a notice of pending action, for order of attachment, receivership, injunction, or other provisional remedies, shall not constitute a waiver of the mediation provision.
   C. Landlord and Tenant agree to mediate disputes or claims involving Listing Agent, Leasing Agent or property manager ("Broker"), provided Broker shall have agreed to such mediation prior to, or within a reasonable time after, the dispute or claim is presented to such Broker. Any election by Broker to participate in mediation shall not result in Broker being deemed a party to this Agreement.

39. **ATTORNEY FEES:** In any action or proceeding arising out of this Agreement, the prevailing party between Landlord and Tenant shall be entitled to reasonable attorney fees and costs, except as provided in paragraph 37A.

40. **C.A.R. FORM:** C.A.R. Form means the specific form referenced or another comparable from agreed to by the parties.

41. **OTHER TERMS AND CONDITIONS;SUPPLEMENTS:** ☐ Interpreter/Translator Agreement (C.A.R. Form ITA); ☐ Keysafe/Lockbox Addendum (C.A.R. Form KLA); ☐ Lead-Based Paint and Lead-Based Paint Hazards Disclosure (C.A.R. Form FLD)
_____
The following ATTACHED supplements are incorporated in this Agreement: _____
_____
_____

42. **TIME OF ESSENCE; ENTIRE CONTRACT; CHANGES:** Time is of the essence. All understandings between the parties are incorporated in this Agreement. Its terms are intended by the parties as a final, complete and exclusive expression of their Agreement with respect to its subject matter, and may not be contradicted by evidence of any prior agreement or contemporaneous oral agreement. If any provision of this Agreement is held to be ineffective or invalid, the remaining provisions will nevertheless be given full force and effect. Neither this Agreement nor any provision in it may be extended, amended, modified, altered or changed except in writing. This Agreement is subject to California landlord-tenant law and shall incorporate all changes required by amendment or successors to such law. This Agreement and any supplement, addendum or modification, including any copy, may be signed in two or more counterparts, all of which shall constitute one and the same writing.

43. **AGENCY:**
   A. CONFIRMATION: The following agency relationship(s) are hereby confirmed for this transaction:
   Listing Agent: (Print firm name) _____ is the agent of (check one): ☐ the Landlord exclusively; or ☐ both the Landlord and Tenant.
   Leasing Agent: (Print firm name) _____ (if not same as Listing Agent) is the agent of (check one): ☐ the Tenant exclusively; or ☐ the Landlord exclusively; or ☐ both the Tenant and Landlord.
   B. DISCLOSURE: ☐ (If checked): The term of this lease exceeds one year. A disclosure regarding real estate agency relationships (C.A.R. Form AD) has been provided to Landlord and Tenant, who each acknowledge its receipt.

44. ☐ **TENANT COMPENSATION TO BROKER:** Upon execution of this Agreement, Tenant agrees to pay compensation to Broker as specified in a separate written agreement between Tenant and Broker.

45. ☐ **INTERPRETER/TRANSLATOR:** The terms of this Agreement have been interpreted for Tenant into the following language: _____. Landlord and Tenant acknowledge receipt of the attached interpretor/translator agreement (C.A.R. Form ITA).

46. **FOREIGN LANGUAGE NEGOTIATION:** If this Agreement has been negotiated by Landlord and Tenant primarily in Spanish,

Tenant's Initials (_____)(_____)
Landlord's Initials (_____)(_____)

LR REVISED 1/06 (PAGE 5 OF 6)

| Reviewed by _____ Date _____ |

EQUAL HOUSING OPPORTUNITY

RESIDENTIAL LEASE OR MONTH-TO-MONTH RENTAL AGREEMENT (LR PAGE 5 OF 6)
Displayed / Reprinted with permission, CALIFORNIA ASSOCIATION OF REALTORS®. Endorsement not implied.

156

Premises: _____ Date: _____

47. OWNER COMPENSATION TO BROKER: Upon execution of this Agreement, Owner agrees to pay compensation to Broker as specified in a separate written agreement between Owner and Broker (C.A.R. Form LCA).

48. RECEIPT: If specified in paragraph 5, Landlord or Broker, acknowledges receipt of move-in funds.

Landlord and Tenant acknowledge and agree Brokers: **(a)** do not guarantee the condition of the Premises; **(b)** cannot verify representations made by others; **(c)** cannot provide legal or tax advice; **(d)** will not provide other advice or information that exceeds the knowledge, education or experience required to obtain a real estate license. Furthermore, if Brokers are not also acting as Landlord in this Agreement, Brokers: **(e)** do not decide what rental rate a Tenant should pay or Landlord should accept; and **(f)** do not decide upon the length or other terms of tenancy. Landlord and Tenant agree that they will seek legal, tax, insurance and other desired assistance from appropriate professionals.

Chinese, Tagalog, Korean or Vietnamese. Pursuant to the California Civil Code Tenant shall be provided a translation of this Agreement inthe language used for the negotiation.

Tenant agrees to rent the premises on the above terms and conditions.

Tenant _____ Date _____
Address _____ City _____ State _____ Zip _____
Telephone _____ Fax _____ E-mail_____
Tenant _____ Date _____
Address _____ City _____ State _____ Zip _____
Telephone _____ Fax _____ E-mail_____

☐ **GUARANTEE:** In consideration of the execution of the Agreement by and between Landlord and Tenant and for valuable consideration, receipt of which is hereby acknowledged, the undersigned ("Guarantor") does hereby: **(i)** guarantee unconditionally to Landlord and Landlord's agents, successors and assigns, the prompt payment of Rent or other sums that become due pursuant to this Agreement, including any and all court costs and attorney fees included in enforcing the Agreement; **(ii)** consent to any changes, modifications or alterations of any term in this Agreement agreed to by Landlord and Tenant; and **(iii)** waive any right to require Landlord and/or Landlord's agents to proceed against Tenant for any default occurring under this Agreement before seeking to enforce this Guarantee.

Guarantor (Print Name) _____
Guarantor _____ Date _____
Address _____ City _____ State _____ Zip _____
Telephone _____ Fax _____ E-mail_____

Landlord agrees to rent the premises on the above terms and conditions.

Landlord _____ Date _____
(Owner or Agent with authority to enter into this Agreement)
Landlord _____ Date _____
(Owner or Agent with authority to enter into this Agreement)

REAL ESTATE BROKERS:
A. Real estate brokers who are not also Landlord under the Agreement are not parties to the Agreement between Landlord and Tenant.
B. Agency relationships are confirmed in paragraph 42.
C. **COOPERATING BROKER COMPENSATION:** Listing Broker agrees to pay Cooperating Broker (Leasing Firm) and Cooperating Broker agrees to accept: **(i)** the amount specified in the MLS, provided Cooperating Broker is a Participant of the MLS in which the Property is offered for sale or a reciprocal MLS; or **(ii)** ☐ (if checked) the amount specified in a separate written agreement between Listing Broker and Cooperating Broker.

Landlord Address _____ City _____ State _____ Zip _____
Telephone _____ Fax _____ E-mail_____

Real Estate Broker (Listing Firm) _____ License # _____
By (Agent) _____ License # _____ Date _____
Address _____ City _____ State _____ Zip _____
Telephone _____ Fax _____ E-mail_____

Real Estate Broker (Leasing Firm) _____ License # _____
By (Agent) _____ License # _____ Date _____
Address _____ City _____ State _____ Zip _____
Telephone _____ Fax _____ E-mail_____

THIS FORM HAS BEEN APPROVED BY THE CALIFORNIA ASSOCIATION OF REALTORS® (C.A.R.). NO REPRESENTATION IS MADE AS TO THE LEGAL VALIDITY OR ADEQUACY OF ANY PROVISION IN ANY SPECIFIC TRANSACTION. A REAL ESTATE BROKER IS THE PERSON QUALIFIED TO ADVISE ON REAL ESTATE TRANSACTIONS. IF YOU DESIRE LEGAL OR TAX ADVICE, CONSULT AN APPROPRIATE PROFESSIONAL.
This form is available for use by the entire real estate industry. It is not intended to identify the user as a REALTOR®. REALTOR® is a registered collective membership mark which may be used only by members of the NATIONAL ASSOCIATION OF REALTORS® who subscribe to its Code of Ethics.

Published and Distributed by:
REAL ESTATE BUSINESS SERVICES, INC.
a subsidiary of the California Association of REALTORS®
525 South Virgil Avenue, Los Angeles, California 90020

LR REVISED 1/06 (PAGE 6 OF 6)

Reviewed by _____ Date _____

EQUAL HOUSING
OPPORTUNITY

RESIDENTIAL LEASE OR MONTH-TO-MONTH RENTAL AGREEMENT (LR PAGE 6 OF 6)
Displayed / Reprinted with permission, CALIFORNIA ASSOCIATION OF REALTORS®. Endorsement not implied.

CALIFORNIA ASSOCIATION OF REALTORS®

NOTICE OF CHANGE IN TERMS OF TENANCY
(C.A.R. Form CTT, Revised 4/03)

To: _____ ("Tenant")
and any other occupant(s) in possession of the premises located at:
(Street Address) _____ (Unit/Apartment #) _____
(City) _____ (State) _____ (Zip Code) _____ ("Premises")

YOUR TENANCY IN THE PREMISES IS CHANGED AS FOLLOWS: Unless otherwise provided, the change shall take effect 30 days from service of this Notice or on _____, whichever is later.
All other terms and conditions of your tenancy shall remain unchanged.

1. **Rent shall be $** _____ **per month.**

    (NOTE: Pursuant to California Civil Code § 827, if the change increases the rent to an amount that exceeds any rental payment charged during the last 12 months by more than 10%, then the change shall take effect 60 days from service of this Notice or on _____, whichever is later.)

2. **Security deposit shall be increased by $**_____.

3. **Other:** _____
    _____
    _____
    _____
    _____
    _____
    _____
    _____.

If this Notice increases the rent charged, and is served by mailing, it was mailed on _____ (Date)
at _____ (Location)

Landlord _____ Date _____
(Owner or Agent)

TENANT CONSENT TO EXTENSION OR RENEWAL OF LEASE
If this Notice extends or renews an existing lease term, by signing below, Tenant acknowledges and agrees to such extension or renewal.

Tenant _____ Date _____
Tenant _____ Date _____

By signing below, Landlord acknowledges Tenant's consent to extension or renewal of lease.

Landlord _____ Date _____
(Owner or Agent)
Landlord _____
(Print Name)

(Keep a copy for your records.)

SURE TRAC
The System for Success®

Published and Distributed by:
REAL ESTATE BUSINESS SERVICES, INC.
a subsidiary of the California Association of REALTORS®
525 South Virgil Avenue, Los Angeles, California 90020

CTT REVISED 4/03 (PAGE 1 OF 1)   Print Date

Reviewed by _____ Date _____

EQUAL HOUSING OPPORTUNITY

NOTICE OF CHANGE IN TERMS OF TENANCY (CTT PAGE 1 OF 1)

Displayed / Reprinted with permission, CALIFORNIA ASSOCIATION OF REALTORS®. Endorsement not implied.

This page intentionally left blank.

NOTICE OF TERMINATION OF TENANCY

(C.A.R. Form NTT, Revised 1/06)

CALIFORNIA ASSOCIATION OF REALTORS®

To: _____ ("Tenant")

and any other occupant(s) in possession of the premises located at:

(Street Address) _____ (Unit/Apartment #) _____

(City) _____ (State) _____ (Zip Code) _____ ("Premises").

Your tenancy, if any, in the Premises is terminated **30 days** from service of this Notice, or on

_____ (whichever is later).

If you fail to give up possession by the specified date, a legal action will be filed seeking possession and damages that could result in a judgment being awarded against you.

Landlord (Owner or Agent) _____

Date _____

Address _____

City _____ **State** _____ **Zip** _____

Telephone _____

Fax _____

E-mail _____

(Keep a copy for your records.)

SURE•TRAC
The System for Success®

Published and Distributed by:
REAL ESTATE BUSINESS SERVICES, INC.
a subsidiary of the California Association of REALTORS®
525 South Virgil Avenue, Los Angeles, California 90020

EQUAL HOUSING OPPORTUNITY

NTT REVISED 1/06 (PAGE 1 OF 1)   Print Date

Reviewed by _____ Date _____

NOTICE OF TERMINATION OF TENANCY (NTT PAGE 1 OF 1)

Displayed / Reprinted with permission, CALIFORNIA ASSOCIATION OF REALTORS®. Endorsement not implied.

This page intentionally left blank.

NOTICE TO PAY RENT OR QUIT

CALIFORNIA ASSOCIATION OF REALTORS®

(C.A.R. Form PRQ, Revised 4/03)

To: _____ ("Tenant")
_____ (Street Address)
_____ (Street Address), (Unit/Apartment #)
_____, ____ _____ (City), (State) (Zip Code) ("Premises").

Other notice address if different from Premises above: _____
_____.

Notice to the above-named person(s) and any other occupants of the above-referenced Premises:

WITHIN 3 (OR ☐ _____ (BUT NOT LESS THAN 3)) DAYS from service of this Notice you are required to either:

   1. Pay rent for the Premises in the following amount, which is past due, to _____
_____ (Name) _____ (Phone)

    at _____
_____ (Address)

    between the hours of _____ on the following days: _____.

    Past Due Rent: $ _____ for the period _____ to _____
              $ _____ for the period _____ to _____
              $ _____ for the period _____ to _____
    Total Due: $ _____.

OR 2. Vacate the Premises and surrender possession.

If you do not pay the past due amount or give up possession by the required time, a legal action will be filed seeking not only damages and possession, but also a statutory damage penalty of up to $600.00 (California Code of Civil Procedure § 1174). Landlord declares a forfeiture of the lease if past due rent is not paid and you continue to occupy the Premises. As required by law, you are hereby notified that a negative credit report reflecting on your credit record may be submitted to a credit reporting agency if you fail to pay your rent.

Landlord _____ Date _____
(Owner or Agent)

Address _____ City _____ State _____ Zip _____

Telephone _____ Fax _____ E-mail _____

(Keep a copy for your records.)

This Notice was served by:

1. ☐ **Personal service.** A copy of the Notice was personally delivered to the above named Tenant.

2. ☐ **Substituted service.** A copy of the Notice was left with a person of suitable age and discretion at the Tenant's residence or usual place of business and a copy was mailed to the Tenant at Tenant's residence.

3. ☐ **Post and mail.** A copy of the Notice was affixed to a conspicuous place on the Premises and a copy was mailed to the Tenant at the Premises.

SURE TRAC
The System for Success®

Published and Distributed by:
REAL ESTATE BUSINESS SERVICES, INC.
a subsidiary of the California Association of REALTORS®
525 South Virgil Avenue, Los Angeles, California 90020

PRQ REVISED 4/03 (PAGE 1 OF 1) Print Date

Reviewed by _____ Date _____

EQUAL HOUSING OPPORTUNITY

NOTICE TO PAY RENT OR QUIT (PRQ PAGE 1 OF 1)

This page intentionally left blank.

CALIFORNIA
ASSOCIATION
OF REALTORS®

LEASE/RENTAL COMMISSION AGREEMENT
(C.A.R. Form LCA, Revised 10/98)

COMPENSATION:

Notice: The amount or rate of real estate commissions is not fixed by law. They are set by each broker individually and may be negotiable between the Landlord/Tenant and Broker.

For services in arranging the lease or month-to-month rental agreement dated _____, between
_____, ("Landlord"), and
_____, ("Tenant")
I agree to pay to _____, ("Broker"),
compensation equal to _____
_____.
Broker may retain said compensation from any first monies (advance rentals and security deposits) collected by Broker from Tenant. If the Lease or Rental Agreement is extended or renewed, or Tenant holds over in possession beyond the initial period (collectively, "extension period"), I agree to pay to Broker additional compensation equal to _____
_____, within 5 days of the commencement of each such extension period. If the Tenant directly or indirectly acquires, or enters into an agreement to acquire, title to the Property or any part of it, whether by sale, exchange, or otherwise, during the term of the tenancy or any extension period, I agree to pay to Broker compensation equal to _____ percent of the selling price or total consideration in said transfer, whichever is greater. Said sum shall be payable upon close of escrow, or if there is no escrow then upon Tenant's direct or indirect acquisition of any legal or equitable interest in the Property. If there is more than one Landlord, by my signature below I agree and represent that I am authorized to obligate all and that the other Landlord(s) and I shall be jointly and individually responsible for payment of the sums due as above.

The undersigned has read and acknowledges receipt of a copy of this Agreement and agrees to pay compensation as stated above.

Date _____ Telephone _____

LANDLORD/TENANT_____

LANDLORD/TENANT_____

Address _____

Real Estate Broker(s) agree(s) to the foregoing.

Broker _____

By _____ Date _____

Broker _____

By _____ Date _____

THIS FORM HAS BEEN APPROVED BY THE CALIFORNIA ASSOCIATION OF REALTORS® (C.A.R.). NO REPRESENTATION IS MADE AS TO THE LEGAL VALIDITY OR ADEQUACY OF ANY PROVISION IN ANY SPECIFIC TRANSACTION. A REAL ESTATE BROKER IS THE PERSON QUALIFIED TO ADVISE ON REAL ESTATE TRANSACTIONS. IF YOU DESIRE LEGAL OR TAX ADVICE, CONSULT AN APPROPRIATE PROFESSIONAL.
This form is available for use by the entire real estate industry. It is not intended to identify the user as a REALTOR®. REALTOR® is a registered collective membership mark which may be used only by members of the NATIONAL ASSOCIATION OF REALTORS® who subscribe to its Code of Ethics.
The copyright laws of the United States (Title 17 U.S. Code) forbid the unauthorized reproduction of this form, or any portion thereof, by photocopy machine or any other means, including facsimile or computerized formats. Copyright © 1994-1998, CALIFORNIA ASSOCIATION OF REALTORS®, INC. ALL RIGHTS RESERVED.

SURE TRAC
The System for Success®

Published and Distributed by:
REAL ESTATE BUSINESS SERVICES, INC.
a subsidiary of the California Association of REALTORS®
525 South Virgil Avenue, Los Angeles, California 90020

LCA REVISED 10/98 (PAGE 1 OF 1) Print Date

Reviewed by _____ Date _____

EQUAL HOUSING
OPPORTUNITY

LEASE/RENTAL COMMISSION AGREEMENT (LCA PAGE 1 OF 1)

Displayed / Reprinted with permission, CALIFORNIA ASSOCIATION OF REALTORS®. Endorsement not implied.

This page intentionally left blank.

CALIFORNIA ASSOCIATION OF REALTORS®

MOVE IN / MOVE OUT INSPECTION
(C.A.R. Form MIMO, Revised 4/03)

Property Address _____ Unit No. _____
Inspection: Move In _____ (Date) Move Out _____ (Date)
Tenant(s) _____

When completing this form, check the Premises carefully and be specific in all items noted. Check the appropriate box:
N - NEW   S - SATISFACTORY/CLEAN   O - OTHER   D - DEPOSIT DEDUCTION

	MOVE IN				MOVE OUT			
	N	S	O	Comments	S	O	D	Comments
Front Yard/Exterior								
Landscaping	☐	☐	☐	_____	☐	☐	☐	_____
Fences/Gates	☐	☐	☐	_____	☐	☐	☐	_____
Sprinklers/Timers	☐	☐	☐	_____	☐	☐	☐	_____
Walks/Driveway	☐	☐	☐	_____	☐	☐	☐	_____
Porches/Stairs	☐	☐	☐	_____	☐	☐	☐	_____
Mailbox	☐	☐	☐	_____	☐	☐	☐	_____
Light Fixtures	☐	☐	☐	_____	☐	☐	☐	_____
Building Exterior	☐	☐	☐	_____	☐	☐	☐	_____
Entry								
Security/Screen Doors	☐	☐	☐	_____	☐	☐	☐	_____
Doors/Knobs/Locks	☐	☐	☐	_____	☐	☐	☐	_____
Flooring/Baseboards	☐	☐	☐	_____	☐	☐	☐	_____
Walls/ Ceilings	☐	☐	☐	_____	☐	☐	☐	_____
Light Fixtures/Fans	☐	☐	☐	_____	☐	☐	☐	_____
Switches/Outlets	☐	☐	☐	_____	☐	☐	☐	_____
Living Room								
Doors/Knobs/Locks	☐	☐	☐	_____	☐	☐	☐	_____
Flooring/Baseboards	☐	☐	☐	_____	☐	☐	☐	_____
Walls/Ceilings	☐	☐	☐	_____	☐	☐	☐	_____
Window Coverings	☐	☐	☐	_____	☐	☐	☐	_____
Windows/Locks/Screens	☐	☐	☐	_____	☐	☐	☐	_____
Light Fixtures/Fans	☐	☐	☐	_____	☐	☐	☐	_____
Switches/Outlets	☐	☐	☐	_____	☐	☐	☐	_____
Fireplace/Equipment	☐	☐	☐	_____	☐	☐	☐	_____
Dining Room								
Flooring/Baseboards	☐	☐	☐	_____	☐	☐	☐	_____
Walls/Ceilings	☐	☐	☐	_____	☐	☐	☐	_____
Window Coverings	☐	☐	☐	_____	☐	☐	☐	_____
Windows/Locks/Screens	☐	☐	☐	_____	☐	☐	☐	_____
Light Fixtures/Fans	☐	☐	☐	_____	☐	☐	☐	_____
Switches/Outlets	☐	☐	☐	_____	☐	☐	☐	_____

Tenant's Initials (_____)(_____)   Tenant's Initials (_____)(_____)

MIMO REVISED 4/03 (PAGE 1 OF 5) Print Date

Reviewed by _____ Date _____

EQUAL HOUSING OPPORTUNITY

MOVE IN / MOVE OUT INSPECTION (MIMO PAGE 1 OF 5)

166

Property Address: _____ Date: _____

	MOVE IN				**MOVE OUT**			
	N	S	O	Comments	S	O	D	Comments

Other Room _____
Doors/Knobs/Locks ☐ ☐ ☐ _____ ☐ ☐ ☐ _____
Flooring/Baseboards ☐ ☐ ☐ _____ ☐ ☐ ☐ _____
Walls/Ceilings ☐ ☐ ☐ _____ ☐ ☐ ☐ _____
Window Coverings ☐ ☐ ☐ _____ ☐ ☐ ☐ _____
Windows/Locks/Screens ☐ ☐ ☐ _____ ☐ ☐ ☐ _____
Light Fixtures/Fans ☐ ☐ ☐ _____ ☐ ☐ ☐ _____
Switches/Outlets ☐ ☐ ☐ _____ ☐ ☐ ☐ _____

Bedroom # _____
Doors/Knobs/Locks ☐ ☐ ☐ _____ ☐ ☐ ☐ _____
Flooring/Baseboards ☐ ☐ ☐ _____ ☐ ☐ ☐ _____
Walls/Ceilings ☐ ☐ ☐ _____ ☐ ☐ ☐ _____
Window Coverings ☐ ☐ ☐ _____ ☐ ☐ ☐ _____
Windows/Locks/Screens ☐ ☐ ☐ _____ ☐ ☐ ☐ _____
Light Fixtures/Fans ☐ ☐ ☐ _____ ☐ ☐ ☐ _____
Switches/Outlets ☐ ☐ ☐ _____ ☐ ☐ ☐ _____
Closets/Doors/Tracks ☐ ☐ ☐ _____ ☐ ☐ ☐ _____

Bedroom # _____
Doors/Knobs/Locks ☐ ☐ ☐ _____ ☐ ☐ ☐ _____
Flooring/Baseboards ☐ ☐ ☐ _____ ☐ ☐ ☐ _____
Walls/Ceilings ☐ ☐ ☐ _____ ☐ ☐ ☐ _____
Window Coverings ☐ ☐ ☐ _____ ☐ ☐ ☐ _____
Windows/Locks/Screens ☐ ☐ ☐ _____ ☐ ☐ ☐ _____
Light Fixtures/Fans ☐ ☐ ☐ _____ ☐ ☐ ☐ _____
Switches/Outlets ☐ ☐ ☐ _____ ☐ ☐ ☐ _____
Closets/Doors/Tracks ☐ ☐ ☐ _____ ☐ ☐ ☐ _____

Bedroom # _____
Doors/Knobs/Locks ☐ ☐ ☐ _____ ☐ ☐ ☐ _____
Flooring/Baseboards ☐ ☐ ☐ _____ ☐ ☐ ☐ _____
Walls/Ceilings ☐ ☐ ☐ _____ ☐ ☐ ☐ _____
Window Coverings ☐ ☐ ☐ _____ ☐ ☐ ☐ _____
Windows/Locks/Screens ☐ ☐ ☐ _____ ☐ ☐ ☐ _____
Light Fixtures/Fans ☐ ☐ ☐ _____ ☐ ☐ ☐ _____
Switches/Outlets ☐ ☐ ☐ _____ ☐ ☐ ☐ _____
Closets/Doors/Tracks ☐ ☐ ☐ _____ ☐ ☐ ☐ _____

Bedroom # _____
Doors/Knobs/Locks ☐ ☐ ☐ _____ ☐ ☐ ☐ _____
Flooring/Baseboards ☐ ☐ ☐ _____ ☐ ☐ ☐ _____
Walls/Ceilings ☐ ☐ ☐ _____ ☐ ☐ ☐ _____
Window Coverings ☐ ☐ ☐ _____ ☐ ☐ ☐ _____
Windows/Locks/Screens ☐ ☐ ☐ _____ ☐ ☐ ☐ _____
Light Fixtures/Fans ☐ ☐ ☐ _____ ☐ ☐ ☐ _____
Switches/Outlets ☐ ☐ ☐ _____ ☐ ☐ ☐ _____
Closets/Doors/Tracks ☐ ☐ ☐ _____ ☐ ☐ ☐ _____

Tenant's Initials (_____)(_____)   Tenant's Initials (_____)(_____)

Copyright © 1982-2003, CALIFORNIA ASSOCIATION OF REALTORS®, INC.
MIMO REVISED 4/03 (PAGE 2 OF 5)

Reviewed by _____ Date _____

EQUAL HOUSING OPPORTUNITY

MOVE IN / MOVE OUT INSPECTION (MIMO PAGE 2 OF 5)
Displayed / Reprinted with permission, CALIFORNIA ASSOCIATION OF REALTORS®. Endorsement not implied.

Property Address: _____ Date: _____

	MOVE IN					**MOVE OUT**			
	N	**S**	**O**	**Comments**		**S**	**O**	**D**	**Comments**
Bath #_____									
Doors/Knobs/Locks	☐	☐	☐	_____		☐	☐	☐	_____
Flooring/Baseboards	☐	☐	☐	_____		☐	☐	☐	_____
Walls/Ceilings	☐	☐	☐	_____		☐	☐	☐	_____
Window Coverings	☐	☐	☐	_____		☐	☐	☐	_____
Windows/Locks/Screens	☐	☐	☐	_____		☐	☐	☐	_____
Light Fixtures	☐	☐	☐	_____		☐	☐	☐	_____
Switches/Outlets	☐	☐	☐	_____		☐	☐	☐	_____
Toilet	☐	☐	☐	_____		☐	☐	☐	_____
Tub/Shower	☐	☐	☐	_____		☐	☐	☐	_____
Shower Door/Rail/Curtain	☐	☐	☐	_____		☐	☐	☐	_____
Sink/Faucets	☐	☐	☐	_____		☐	☐	☐	_____
Plumbing/Drains	☐	☐	☐	_____		☐	☐	☐	_____
Exhaust Fan	☐	☐	☐	_____		☐	☐	☐	_____
Towel Rack(s)	☐	☐	☐	_____		☐	☐	☐	_____
Toilet Paper Holder	☐	☐	☐	_____		☐	☐	☐	_____
Cabinets/Counters	☐	☐	☐	_____		☐	☐	☐	_____
Bath #_____									
Doors/Knobs/Locks	☐	☐	☐	_____		☐	☐	☐	_____
Flooring/Baseboards	☐	☐	☐	_____		☐	☐	☐	_____
Walls/Ceilings	☐	☐	☐	_____		☐	☐	☐	_____
Window Coverings	☐	☐	☐	_____		☐	☐	☐	_____
Windows/Locks/Screens	☐	☐	☐	_____		☐	☐	☐	_____
Light Fixtures	☐	☐	☐	_____		☐	☐	☐	_____
Switches/Outlets	☐	☐	☐	_____		☐	☐	☐	_____
Toilet	☐	☐	☐	_____		☐	☐	☐	_____
Tub/Shower	☐	☐	☐	_____		☐	☐	☐	_____
Shower Door/Rail/Curtain	☐	☐	☐	_____		☐	☐	☐	_____
Sink/Faucets	☐	☐	☐	_____		☐	☐	☐	_____
Plumbing/Drains	☐	☐	☐	_____		☐	☐	☐	_____
Exhaust Fan	☐	☐	☐	_____		☐	☐	☐	_____
Towel Rack(s)	☐	☐	☐	_____		☐	☐	☐	_____
Toilet Paper Holder	☐	☐	☐	_____		☐	☐	☐	_____
Cabinets/Counters	☐	☐	☐	_____		☐	☐	☐	_____
Bath #_____									
Doors/Knobs/Locks	☐	☐	☐	_____		☐	☐	☐	_____
Flooring/Baseboards	☐	☐	☐	_____		☐	☐	☐	_____
Walls/Ceilings	☐	☐	☐	_____		☐	☐	☐	_____
Window Coverings	☐	☐	☐	_____		☐	☐	☐	_____
Windows/Locks/Screens	☐	☐	☐	_____		☐	☐	☐	_____
Light Fixtures	☐	☐	☐	_____		☐	☐	☐	_____
Switches/Outlets	☐	☐	☐	_____		☐	☐	☐	_____
Toilet	☐	☐	☐	_____		☐	☐	☐	_____
Tub/Shower	☐	☐	☐	_____		☐	☐	☐	_____
Shower Door/Rail/Curtain	☐	☐	☐	_____		☐	☐	☐	_____
Sink/Faucets	☐	☐	☐	_____		☐	☐	☐	_____
Plumbing/Drains	☐	☐	☐	_____		☐	☐	☐	_____
Exhaust Fan	☐	☐	☐	_____		☐	☐	☐	_____
Towel Rack(s)	☐	☐	☐	_____		☐	☐	☐	_____
Toilet Paper Holder	☐	☐	☐	_____		☐	☐	☐	_____
Cabinets/Counters	☐	☐	☐	_____		☐	☐	☐	_____

Tenant's Initials (_____)(_____)   Tenant's Initials (_____)(_____)

MIMO REVISED 4/03 (PAGE 3 OF 5)

Reviewed by _____ Date _____

EQUAL HOUSING OPPORTUNITY

MOVE IN / MOVE OUT INSPECTION (MIMO PAGE 3 OF 5)
Displayed/Reprinted with permission, CALIFORNIA ASSOCIATION OF REALTORS®. Endorsement not implied.

168

Property Address: _____ Date: _____

	MOVE IN				**MOVE OUT**			
	N	**S**	**O**	**Comments**	**S**	**O**	**D**	**Comments**
Kitchen								
Flooring/Baseboards	☐	☐	☐	_____	☐	☐	☐	_____
Walls/Ceilings	☐	☐	☐	_____	☐	☐	☐	_____
Window Coverings	☐	☐	☐	_____	☐	☐	☐	_____
Windows/Locks/Screens	☐	☐	☐	_____	☐	☐	☐	_____
Light Fixtures	☐	☐	☐	_____	☐	☐	☐	_____
Switches/Outlets	☐	☐	☐	_____	☐	☐	☐	_____
Range/Fan/Hood	☐	☐	☐	_____	☐	☐	☐	_____
Oven(s)/Microwave	☐	☐	☐	_____	☐	☐	☐	_____
Refrigerator	☐	☐	☐	_____	☐	☐	☐	_____
Dishwasher	☐	☐	☐	_____	☐	☐	☐	_____
Sink/Disposal	☐	☐	☐	_____	☐	☐	☐	_____
Faucet(s)/Plumbing	☐	☐	☐	_____	☐	☐	☐	_____
Cabinets	☐	☐	☐	_____	☐	☐	☐	_____
Counters	☐	☐	☐	_____	☐	☐	☐	_____

_____   _____
_____   _____
_____   _____

Hall/Stairs								
Flooring/Baseboards	☐	☐	☐	_____	☐	☐	☐	_____
Walls/Ceilings	☐	☐	☐	_____	☐	☐	☐	_____
Light Fixtures	☐	☐	☐	_____	☐	☐	☐	_____
Switches/Outlets	☐	☐	☐	_____	☐	☐	☐	_____
Closets/Cabinets	☐	☐	☐	_____	☐	☐	☐	_____
Railings/Banisters	☐	☐	☐	_____	☐	☐	☐	_____

_____   _____
_____   _____
_____   _____

Laundry _____

Faucets/Valves	☐	☐	☐	_____	☐	☐	☐	_____
Plumbing/Drains	☐	☐	☐	_____	☐	☐	☐	_____
Cabinets/Counters	☐	☐	☐	_____	☐	☐	☐	_____

_____   _____
_____   _____
_____   _____

Systems								
Furnace/Thermostat	☐	☐	☐	_____	☐	☐	☐	_____
Air Conditioning	☐	☐	☐	_____	☐	☐	☐	_____
Water Heater	☐	☐	☐	_____	☐	☐	☐	_____
Water Softener	☐	☐	☐	_____	☐	☐	☐	_____

_____   _____
_____   _____

Other _____

_____   _____
_____   _____
_____   _____
_____   _____
_____   _____
_____   _____
_____   _____
_____   _____
_____   _____

Tenant's Initials (_____)(_____)   Tenant's Initials (_____)(_____)

MIMO REVISED 4/03 (PAGE 4 OF 5)

Reviewed by _____ Date _____

EQUAL HOUSING OPPORTUNITY

MOVE IN / MOVE OUT INSPECTION (MIMO PAGE 4 OF 5)

Property Address: _____ Date: _____

	MOVE IN				**MOVE OUT**			
	N	S	O	Comments	S	O	D	Comments
Garage/Parking								
Garage Door	☐	☐	☐	_____	☐	☐	☐	_____
Other Door(s)	☐	☐	☐	_____	☐	☐	☐	_____
Driveway/Floor	☐	☐	☐	_____	☐	☐	☐	_____
Cabinets/Counters	☐	☐	☐	_____	☐	☐	☐	_____
Light Fixtures	☐	☐	☐	_____	☐	☐	☐	_____
Switches/Outlets	☐	☐	☐	_____	☐	☐	☐	_____
Electrical/Exposed Wiring	☐	☐	☐	_____	☐	☐	☐	_____
Window(s)	☐	☐	☐	_____	☐	☐	☐	_____
Other Storage/Shelving	☐	☐	☐	_____	☐	☐	☐	_____
				_____				_____

Back/Side/Yard								
Patio/Deck/Balcony	☐	☐		_____	☐	☐	☐	_____
Patio Cover(s)	☐	☐	☐	_____	☐	☐	☐	_____
Landscaping	☐	☐	☐	_____	☐	☐	☐	_____
Sprinklers/Timers	☐	☐	☐	_____	☐	☐	☐	_____
Pool/Heater/Equipment	☐	☐	☐	_____	☐	☐	☐	_____
Spa/Cover/Equipment	☐	☐	☐	_____	☐	☐	☐	_____
Fences/Gates	☐	☐	☐	_____	☐	☐	☐	_____
				_____				_____

Safety/Security								
Smoke/CO Detector(s)	☐	☐	☐	_____	☐	☐	☐	_____
Security System	☐	☐	☐	_____	☐	☐	☐	_____
Security Window Bars	☐	☐	☐	_____	☐	☐	☐	_____
				_____				_____

Personal Property

_____
_____

Keys/Remotes/Devices
Keys _____
Remotes/Devices _____

☐ **Attached Supplement(s)** _____

THIS SECTION TO BE COMPLETED AT MOVE IN: Receipt of a copy of this form is acknowledged by:
Tenant _____ Date _____
Tenant _____ Date _____
New Phone Service Established? ☐ Yes ☐ No   New Phone Number _____
Landlord (Owner or Agent) _____ Date _____
Landlord _____
    (Print Name)

THIS SECTION TO BE COMPLETED AT MOVE OUT: Receipt of a copy of this form is acknowledged by:
Tenant _____ Date _____
Tenant _____ Date _____
Tenant Forwarding Address _____

Landlord (Owner or Agent) _____ Date _____
Landlord _____
    (Print Name)

SURE·TRAC The System for Success®

Published and Distributed by:
REAL ESTATE BUSINESS SERVICES, INC.
a subsidiary of the California Association of REALTORS®
525 South Virgil Avenue, Los Angeles, California 90020

Reviewed by _____ Date _____

EQUAL HOUSING OPPORTUNITY

MIMO REVISED 4/03 (PAGE 5 OF 5)

MOVE IN / MOVE OUT INSPECTION (MIMO PAGE 5 OF 5)

Displayed / Reprinted with permission, CALIFORNIA ASSOCIATION OF REALTORS®. Endorsement not implied.

This page intentionally left blank.

CALIFORNIA ASSOCIATION OF REALTORS®

LEASE LISTING AGREEMENT
EXCLUSIVE AUTHORIZATION TO LEASE OR RENT
(C.A.R. Form LL, Revised 4/06)

1. **EXCLUSIVE RIGHT TO LEASE:** _____ ("Owner")
hereby employs and grants _____ ("Broker")
beginning (date) _____ and ending at 11:59 P.M. on (date) _____ ("Listing Period")
the exclusive and irrevocable right to lease or rent the real property in the City of _____,
County of _____, California, described as _____
_____ ("Premises").

2. **LISTING TERMS:**
   A. **RENT AMOUNT:** _____ Dollars $ _____ per _____.
   B. **SECURITY DEPOSIT** _____.
   C. **TYPE OF TENANCY:** (Check all that apply): ☐ Month-to-month; ☐ One year ☐ Other _____.
   D. **ITEMS INCLUDED IN LEASE/RENTAL:** All fixtures and fittings attached to the Premises and the following items of personal property: _____
   E. **ITEMS EXCLUDED FROM LEASE/RENTAL:** ☐ Garage/Carport; ☐ _____
   F. **ADDITIONAL TERMS:** _____
   _____

3. **COMPENSATION:** _____
   Notice: The amount or rate of real estate commissions is not fixed by law. They are set by each Broker individually and may be negotiable between Owner and Broker (real estate commissions include all compensation and fees to Broker).
   A. Owner agrees to pay to Broker as compensation for services, irrespective of agency relationship(s):
   (1) **For fixed-term leases:**
   (a) Either **(i)** ☐ _____ percent of the total rent for the term specified in paragraph 2 (or if a fixed term lease is executed, of the total base payments due under the lease); or **(ii)** ☐ _____;
   (b) Owner agrees to pay Broker additional compensation of _____, if a fixed term lease is executed and is extended or renewed. Payment is due upon such extension or renewal.
   (2) **For month-to-month rental:** either **(i)** ☐ _____ percent of _____; or **(ii)** ☐ _____.
   (3) **The following terms apply whether the tenancy is for a fixed term or month-to-month:**
   (a) If during the Listing Period, or any extension Broker, cooperating broker or any other person procures a Tenant who offers to lease/rent the Premises on the above amount and terms, or on any amount and terms acceptable to Owner. (Broker is entitled to compensation whether any tenancy resulting from such offer begins during or after the expiration of the Listing Period.)
   (b) If Owner, within _____ **calendar days** after the end of the Listing Period or any extension thereof, enters into a contract to transfer, lease or rent the Premises to anyone ("Prospective Transferee") or that person's related entity: **(i)** who physically entered and was shown the Premises during the Listing Period or any extension thereof by Broker or a cooperating broker; or **(ii)** for whom Broker or any cooperating broker submitted to Owner a signed, written offer to lease or rent the Premises. Owner, however, shall have no obligation to Broker under this subparagraph 3A(3)(b) unless, not later than **5 calendar days** after the end of the Listing Period or any extension, Broker has given Owner a written notice of the names of such Prospective Transferees.
   (c) If, without Broker's prior written consent, the Premises are withdrawn from lease/rental, are leased, rented, or otherwise transferred, or made unmarketable by a voluntary act of Owner during the Listing Period, or any extension.
   B. If commencement of the lease or rental is prevented by a party to the transaction other than Owner, then compensation due under paragraph 3A shall be payable only if and when Owner collects damages by suit, arbitration, settlement or otherwise, and then in an amount equal to the lesser of one-half of the damages recovered or the above compensation, after first deducting title and escrow expenses and the expenses of collection, if any.
   C. In addition, Owner agrees to pay: _____
   _____.
   D. Broker may retain compensation due from any Tenant payments collected by Broker.
   E. Owner agrees to pay Broker if Tenant directly or indirectly acquires, or enters into an agreement to acquire title to Premises or any part thereof, whether by sale, exchange or otherwise, during the term or any extension of tenancy, compensation equal to _____ percent of the selling price or total consideration in said transfer, whichever is greater. Payment is due upon Tenant's direct or indirect acquisition of any legal or equitable interest in the Premises and, if there is an escrow, shall be through escrow.
   F. Broker is authorized to cooperate with and compensate other brokers in any manner acceptable to Broker.
   G. **(1)** Owner warrants that Owner has no obligation to pay compensation to any other broker regarding the lease or rental of Premises unless the Premises are leased or rented to: _____
   (2) If Premises are leased or rented to anyone listed in 3G(1) during the time Owner is obligated to compensate another broker: **(i)** Broker is not entitled to compensation under this Agreement; and **(ii)** Broker is not obligated to represent Owner with respect to such transaction.

4. **TENANT PAYMENTS:** Broker is authorized to accept and hold from a prospective Tenant, a deposit to be ☐ held uncashed or ☐ placed in Broker's trust account. Upon execution of a fixed term or month-to-month lease, payments received from Tenant shall be given to Owner or ☐ _____.

Owner acknowledges receipt of a copy of this page.
Owner's Initials (_____)(_____)

LL REVISED 4/06 (PAGE 1 OF 3) **Print Date**

Reviewed by _____ Date _____

EQUAL HOUSING OPPORTUNITY

LEASE LISTING AGREEMENT (LL PAGE 1 OF 3)

Property Address: _____ Date: _____

5. **KEYSAFE/LOCKBOX:** ☐ (If checked) Owner authorizes the use of a keysafe/lockbox to allow entry into the Premises and agrees to sign a keysafe/lockbox addendum (C.A.R. Form KLA).

6. **SIGN:** (If checked) ☐ Owner authorizes Broker to install a FOR LEASE sign on the Premises.

7. **MULTIPLE LISTING SERVICE:** Information about this listing will (or ☐ will not) be provided to a multiple listing service(s) ("MLS") of Broker's selection. All terms of the transaction will be provided to the selected MLS for publication, dissemination and use by persons and entities on terms approved by the MLS. Seller authorizes Broker to comply with all applicable MLS rules. MLS rules allow MLS data to be made available by the MLS to additional Internet sites unless Broker gives the MLS instructions to the contrary.

8. **SECURITY AND INSURANCE:** Owner agrees: **(i)** Broker is not responsible for loss of or damage to personal or real property or person, whether attributable to use of a keysafe/lockbox, a showing of the Premises, or use of the Premises during any resulting tenancy; **(ii)** to take reasonable precautions to safeguard, protect or insure valuables that might be accessible during showings of the Premises; and **(iii)** to obtain insurance to protect against these risks. **Broker does not maintain insurance to protect Owner.**

9. **OWNERSHIP, TITLE AND AUTHORITY:** Owner warrants that: **(i)** Owner is the legal owner of the Property; **(ii)** no other persons or entities have title to the Property; and **(iii)** Owner has the authority to both execute this contract and lease or rent the Property. Exceptions to ownership, title and authority: _____.

10. **LEAD-BASED PAINT DISCLOSURE:** The Premises ☐ were ☐ were not constructed prior to 1978. If the Premises were constructed prior to 1978, Owner is required to complete a federally mandated and approved lead-based paint disclosure form and pamphlet, which shall be given to Tenant prior to or upon execution of a lease or rental agreement.

11. **OWNER REPRESENTATIONS:** Owner represents that Owner is unaware of: **(i)** any recorded Notice of Default affecting the Premises; **(ii)** any delinquent amounts due under any loan secured by, or other obligation affecting, the Premises; **(iii)** any bankruptcy, insolvency or similar proceeding affecting the Premises; **(iv)** any litigation, arbitration, administrative action, government investigation, or other pending or threatened action that does or may affect the Premises or Owner's ability to transfer it; and **(v)** any current, pending or proposed special assessments affecting the Premises. Owner shall promptly notify Broker in writing if Owner becomes aware of any of these items during the Listing Period or any extension thereof.

12. **BROKER'S AND OWNER'S DUTIES:** Broker agrees to exercise reasonable effort and due diligence to achieve the purposes of this Agreement. Unless Owner gives Broker written instructions to the contrary, Broker is authorized to advertise and market the Premises in any medium, selected by Broker including MLS and the Internet and, to the extent permitted by these media, including MLS, control the dissemination of the information submitted to any medium. Owner agrees to consider offers presented by Broker and to act in good faith to accomplish the lease or rental of the Premises by, among other things, making the Premises available for showing at reasonable times and referring to Broker all inquiries of any party interested in the Premises. Owner is responsible for determining at what price and terms to list and lease or rent the Premises. **Owner further agrees, regardless of responsibility, to indemnify, defend and hold Broker harmless from all claims, disputes, litigation, judgments and attorney's fees arising from any incorrect information supplied by Owner, whether contained in any document, omitted therefrom or otherwise, or from any material facts that Owner knows but fails to disclose.**

13. **AGENCY RELATIONSHIPS:**

    A. **Disclosure:** If the Premises includes residential property with one to four dwelling units, and the listing is for a tenancy in excess of one year, Owner acknowledges receipt of the "Disclosure Regarding Agency Relationships" form (C.A.R. Form AD).

    B. **Owner Representation:** Broker shall represent Owner in any resulting transaction, except as specified in paragraph 3G.

    C. **Possible Dual Agency With Tenant:** Depending upon the circumstances, it may be necessary or appropriate for Broker to act as an agent for both Owner and Tenant. Broker shall, as soon as practicable, disclose to Owner any election to act as a dual agent representing both Owner and Tenant. If a Tenant is procured directly by Broker or an associate licensee in Broker's firm, Owner hereby consents to Broker acting as a dual agent for Owner and such Tenant.

    D. **Other Owners:** Owner understands that Broker may have or obtain listings on other properties and that potential tenants may consider, make offers on, or lease or rent through Broker, premises the same as or similar to Owner's Premises. Owner consents to Broker's representation of owners and tenants of other properties before, during and after the end of this Agreement.

    E. **Confirmation:** If the Premises includes residential property with one to four dwelling units, and the agreed-upon lease is for a tenancy in excess of one year, Broker shall confirm the agency relationship described above, or as modified, in writing, prior to or coincident with Owner's execution of such lease.

14. **EQUAL HOUSING OPPORTUNITY:** The Premises is offered in compliance with federal, state and local anti-discrimination laws.

15. **ATTORNEY'S FEES:** In any action, proceeding or arbitration between Owner and Broker regarding the obligation to pay compensation under this Agreement, the prevailing Owner or Broker shall be entitled to reasonable attorney's fees and costs from the non-prevailing Owner or Broker, except as provided in paragraph 19A.

16. **ADDITIONAL TERMS:** _____
    _____
    _____
    _____

17. **MANAGEMENT APPROVAL:** If a salesperson or broker-associate enters this Agreement on Broker's behalf, and Broker/Manager does not approve of its terms, Broker/Manager has the right to cancel this Agreement, in writing, within **5 calendar Days** After its execution.

18. **SUCCESSORS AND ASSIGNS:** This Agreement shall be binding upon Owner and Owner's successors and assigns.

19. **DISPUTE RESOLUTION:**

    A. **MEDIATION:** Owner and Broker agree to mediate any dispute or claim arising between them out of this Agreement, or any resulting transaction, before resorting to arbitration or court action. Paragraph 19B(2) below applies whether or not the Arbitration provision is initialed. Mediation fees, if any, shall be divided equally among the parties involved. If, for any dispute or claim to which this paragraph applies, any party commences an action without first attempting to resolve the matter through mediation, or refuses to mediate after a request has been made, then that party shall not be entitled to recover attorney's fees, even if they would otherwise be available to that party in any such action. THIS MEDIATION PROVISION APPLIES WHETHER OR NOT THE ARBITRATION PROVISION IS INITIALED.

Owner acknowledges receipt of a copy of this page.

Owner's Initials (_____)(_____)

Reviewed by _____ Date _____

LL REVISED 4/06 (PAGE 2 OF 3)

LEASE LISTING AGREEMENT (LL PAGE 2 OF 3)

Property Address: _____ Date: _____

B. **ARBITRATION OF DISPUTES:** (1) Owner and Broker agree that any dispute or claim in law or equity arising between them regarding the obligation to pay compensation under this Agreement, which is not settled through mediation, shall be decided by neutral, binding arbitration, including and subject to paragraph 19B(2) below. The arbitrator shall be a retired judge or justice, or an attorney with at least 5 years of residential real estate law experience, unless the parties mutually agree to a different arbitrator, who shall render an award in accordance with substantive California law. The parties shall have the right to discovery in accordance with Code of Civil Procedure §1283.05. In all other respects, the arbitration shall be conducted in accordance with Title 9 of Part III of the California Code of Civil Procedure. Judgment upon the award of the arbitrator(s) may be entered in any court having jurisdiction. Interpretation of this agreement to arbitrate shall be governed by the Federal Arbitration Act.
(2) **EXCLUSIONS FROM MEDIATION AND ARBITRATION:** The following matters are excluded from mediation and arbitration: (i) a judicial or non-judicial foreclosure or other action or proceeding to enforce a deed of trust, mortgage, or installment land sale contract as defined in Civil Code §2985; (ii) an unlawful detainer action; (iii) the filing or enforcement of a mechanic's lien; and (iv) any matter that is within the jurisdiction of a probate, small claims, or bankruptcy court. The filing of a court action to enable the recording of a notice of pending action, for order of attachment, receivership, injunction, or other provisional remedies, shall not constitute a waiver of the mediation and arbitration provisions.

"**NOTICE: BY INITIALING IN THE SPACE BELOW YOU ARE AGREEING TO HAVE ANY DISPUTE ARISING OUT OF THE MATTERS INCLUDED IN THE 'ARBITRATION OF DISPUTES' PROVISION DECIDED BY NEUTRAL ARBITRATION AS PROVIDED BY CALIFORNIA LAW AND YOU ARE GIVING UP ANY RIGHTS YOU MIGHT POSSESS TO HAVE THE DISPUTE LITIGATED IN A COURT OR JURY TRIAL. BY INITIALING IN THE SPACE BELOW YOU ARE GIVING UP YOUR JUDICIAL RIGHTS TO DISCOVERY AND APPEAL, UNLESS THOSE RIGHTS ARE SPECIFICALLY INCLUDED IN THE 'ARBITRATION OF DISPUTES' PROVISION. IF YOU REFUSE TO SUBMIT TO ARBITRATION AFTER AGREEING TO THIS PROVISION, YOU MAY BE COMPELLED TO ARBITRATE UNDER THE AUTHORITY OF THE CALIFORNIA CODE OF CIVIL PROCEDURE. YOUR AGREEMENT TO THIS ARBITRATION PROVISION IS VOLUNTARY.**"

"**WE HAVE READ AND UNDERSTAND THE FOREGOING AND AGREE TO SUBMIT DISPUTES ARISING OUT OF THE MATTERS INCLUDED IN THE 'ARBITRATION OF DISPUTES' PROVISION TO NEUTRAL ARBITRATION.**"

Owner's Initials _____/_____	Broker's Initials _____/_____

20. **TIME OF ESSENCE; ENTIRE CONTRACT; CHANGES:** Time is of the essence. All understandings between the parties are incorporated in this Agreement. Its terms are intended by the parties as a final, complete and exclusive expression of their Agreement with respect to its subject matter, and may not be contradicted by evidence of any prior agreement or contemporaneous oral agreement. If any provision of this Agreement is held to be ineffective or invalid, the remaining provisions will nevertheless be given full force and effect. Neither this Agreement nor any provision in it may be extended, amended, modified, altered or changed except in writing. This Agreement and any supplement, addendum or modification, including any copy, may be signed in two or more counterparts, all of which shall constitute one and the same writing.

Owner acknowledges Owner has read, understands, received a copy of and agrees to the terms of this Agreement.

Owner _____ Date _____
Owner _____
　　　　Print Name
Address _____ City _____ State _____ Zip _____
Telephone _____ Fax _____ E-mail _____

Owner _____ Date _____
Owner _____
　　　　Print Name
Address _____ City _____ State _____ Zip _____
Telephone _____ Fax _____ E-mail _____

Real Estate Broker (Firm) _____ DRE Lic. # _____
By (Agent) _____ DRE Lic. # _____ Date _____
Address _____ City _____ State _____ Zip _____
Telephone _____ Fax _____ E-mail _____

THIS FORM HAS BEEN APPROVED BY THE CALIFORNIA ASSOCIATION OF REALTORS® (C.A.R.). NO REPRESENTATION IS MADE AS TO THE LEGAL VALIDITY OR ADEQUACY OF ANY PROVISION IN ANY SPECIFIC TRANSACTION. A REAL ESTATE BROKER IS THE PERSON QUALIFIED TO ADVISE ON REAL ESTATE TRANSACTIONS. IF YOU DESIRE LEGAL OR TAX ADVICE, CONSULT AN APPROPRIATE PROFESSIONAL.
This form is available for use by the entire real estate industry. It is not intended to identify the user as a REALTOR®. REALTOR® is a registered collective membership mark which may be used only by members of the NATIONAL ASSOCIATION OF REALTORS® who subscribe to its Code of Ethics.

Published and Distributed by:
REAL ESTATE BUSINESS SERVICES, INC.
a subsidiary of the California Association of REALTORS®
525 South Virgil Avenue, Los Angeles, California 90020

LL REVISED 4/06 (PAGE 3 OF 3)

Reviewed by _____ Date _____

LEASE LISTING AGREEMENT (LL PAGE 3 OF 3)

Displayed / Reprinted with permission, CALIFORNIA ASSOCIATION OF REALTORS®. Endorsement not implied.

This page intentionally left blank.

CALIFORNIA ASSOCIATION OF REALTORS®

EXCLUSIVE AUTHORIZATION TO LEASE OR RENT
LEASE LISTING AGREEMENT
(C.A.R. Form LL-11, Revised 4/01)

1. **EXCLUSIVE RIGHT TO LEASE:** _____ ("Owner") hereby employs and grants
_____ ("Broker") the exclusive and irrevocable right
to lease or rent the real property in the City of _____, County of _____,
California described as _____ ("Premises"),
beginning (date) _____ and ending at 11:59 P.M. on (date) _____ ("Listing Period").

2. **LISTING TERMS:** -
   A. **RENT AMOUNT:** _____ Dollars $_____ Per _____.
   B. **TYPE OF TENANCY:** (Check all that apply): ☐ Month-to-Month; ☐ One year ☐ Other_____
   C. **ITEMS INCLUDED IN LEASE/RENTAL:** All fixtures and fittings that are attached to the Premises and the following items of personal property:
   _____
   _____
   D. **ITEMS EXCLUDED FROM LEASE/RENTAL:** ☐ Garage/Carport _____
   _____
   E. **ADDITIONAL TERMS:** _____
   _____

3. **COMPENSATION:**
   Notice: The amount or rate of real estate commissions is not fixed by law. They are set by each Broker individually and may be negotiable between Owner and Broker.
   A. Owner agrees to pay to Broker as compensation for services, irrespective of agency relationships:
      For fixed term leases, either ☐ _____ percent of the total rent for the term specified in paragraph 2 (or if a lease is entered into, of the total base payments due under the lease), or ☐ $_____ ;
      For month-to-month rental, either ☐ _____ percent of _____, or ☐ $_____.
      (The following terms apply whether the lease is for a fixed term or month-to-month):
      (1) If Broker, cooperating broker, or any other person produces a Tenant who offers to lease/rent the Premises on the above amount and terms, or on any price and terms acceptable to Owner during the Listing Period or any extension thereof;
      (2) If Owner, within _____ calendar days after the end of the Listing Period or any extension thereof, enters into a contract to transfer, lease or rent the Premises to anyone ("Prospective Transferee") or that person's related entity **(i)** who physically entered and was shown the Property during the Listing Period or any extension thereof by Broker or a cooperating broker, or **(ii)** for whom Broker or any cooperating broker submitted to Owner a signed, written offer to lease or rent the Premises. Owner shall have no obligation to Broker under this subparagraph (3A(2)) unless, not later than **5 calendar days** after the end of the Listing Period or any extension, Broker has given Owner a written notice of the names of such Prospective Transferees.
      (3) If, without Broker's prior written consent, the Premises are withdrawn from lease/rental, are leased, rented, or otherwise transferred, or made unmarketable by a voluntary act of Owner during the Listing Period, or any extension.
   B. If commencement of the lease or rental is prevented by a party to the transaction other than Owner, then compensation due under paragraph 3A shall be payable only if and when Owner collects damages by suit, arbitration, settlement, or otherwise, and then in an amount equal to the lesser of one-half of the damages recovered or the above compensation, after first deducting title and escrow expenses and the expenses of collection, if any.
   C. In addition, Owner agrees to pay: _____
   _____
   D. Broker may retain said compensation from any Tenant payments collected by Broker.
   E. Owner agrees to pay Broker additional compensation of _____,
   if a fixed term lease is executed and is extended or renewed. Payment is due upon such extension or renewal.
   F. Owner agrees to pay Broker if Tenant directly or indirectly acquires or enters into an agreement to acquire title to Premises or any part of it, whether by sale, exchange, or otherwise, during the term or any extension of tenancy, as follows: Compensation shall be equal to _____ percent of selling price or total consideration in said transfer, whichever is greater. Payment is due upon Tenant's direct or indirect acquisition of any legal or equitable interest in Premises and, if there is an escrow, shall be through escrow.
   G. Broker is authorized to cooperate with and compensate other brokers in any manner acceptable to Broker.
   H. **(1)** Owner warrants that Owner has no obligation to pay compensation to any other broker regarding the lease or rental of Premises except if the Premises are leased or rented to: _____
      (2) If Premises are leased or rented to anyone listed in 3H(1) during the time Owner is obligated to compensate another broker: **(a)** Broker is not entitled to compensation under this Agreement and **(b)** Broker is not obligated to represent Owner with respect to such transaction.

4. **TENANT PAYMENTS:** Broker is authorized to accept and hold from a prospective Tenant, a deposit to be ☐ held uncashed, or ☐ placed in Broker's trust account. Upon execution of a fixed term or month-to-month lease, payments received from Tenant shall be: ☐ given to Owner, ☐ held in Broker's Trust Account, or ☐ _____.

LL-11 (PAGE 1 OF 3)   Print Date

Owner and Broker acknowledge receipt of a copy of this page.
Owner's Initials (_____)(_____)
Broker's Initials (_____)(_____)

Reviewed by
Broker or Designee _____ Date _____

EQUAL HOUSING OPPORTUNITY

EXCLUSIVE AUTHORIZATION TO LEASE OR RENT (LL-11 PAGE 1 OF 3)

Displayed / Reprinted with permission, CALIFORNIA ASSOCIATION OF REALTORS®. Endorsement not implied.

Property Address: _____ Date: _____

5. KEYSAFE/LOCKBOX:

    A. A lockbox is designed to hold a key to the Premises to permit access to the Premises by Broker, cooperating brokers, MLS participants, their authorized licensees and representatives, and accompanied prospective Tenants. Broker, cooperating brokers, MLS and Associations/Boards of REALTORS® are **not** insurers against theft, loss, vandalism, or damage attributed to the use of a lockbox. Owner is advised to verify the existence of, or obtain appropriate insurance through Owner's own insurance broker.

    B. (If checked) ☐ Owner authorizes Broker to install a lockbox. If Premises are occupied by someone other than Owner, Owner shall be responsible for obtaining occupant(s)' written permission for use of a lockbox.

6. SIGN: (If checked) ☐ Owner authorizes Broker to install a FOR LEASE sign on the Premises.

7. MULTIPLE LISTING SERVICE: Information about this listing will (or ☐ will not) be provided to a multiple listing service(s) ("MLS") of Broker's selection. All terms of the transaction, including financing, if applicable, will be provided to the selected MLS for publication, dissemination and use by persons and entities on terms approved by the MLS. Seller authorizes Broker to comply with all applicable MLS rules. MLS rules allow MLS data to be made available by the MLS to additional Internet sites unless Broker gives the MLS instructions to the contrary.

8. SECURITY AND INSURANCE: Owner agrees: **(i)** that Broker is not responsible for loss of or damage to personal or real property or person, whether attributable to use of a keysafe/lockbox or a showing of the Premises; **(ii)** to take reasonable precautions to safeguard, protect, or insure valuables that might be accessible during showings of the Premises; and **(iii)** to obtain insurance to protect against these risks. **Broker does not maintain insurance to protect Owner.**

9. OWNERSHIP, TITLE AND AUTHORITY: Owner warrants that **(i)** Owner is the legal owner of the Property; **(ii)** no other persons or entities have title to the Property; and **(iii)** Owner has the authority to both execute this contract and lease or rent the Property. Exceptions to ownership, title and authority: _____

10. LEAD-BASED PAINT DISCLOSURE: The Premises ☐ were, ☐ were not, constructed prior to 1978. If the Premises were constructed prior to 1978, Owner is required to complete a federally mandated and approved lead-based paint disclosure form and pamphlet, which shall be given to Tenant prior to or upon execution of a lease or rental agreement.

11. OWNER REPRESENTATIONS: Owner represents that Owner is unaware of: **(i)** any recorded Notice of Default affecting the Premises; **(ii)** any delinquent amounts due under any loan secured by, or other obligation affecting the Premises; **(iii)** any bankruptcy, insolvency or similar proceeding affecting the Premises; **(iv)** any litigation, arbitration, administrative action, government investigation, or other pending or threatened action that does or may affect the Premises or Owner's ability to transfer it; and **(v)** any current, pending or proposed special assessments affecting the Premises. Exceptions: _____

12. BROKER'S AND OWNER'S DUTIES: Broker agrees to exercise reasonable effort and due diligence to achieve the purposes of this Agreement. Unless Owner gives Broker written instructions to the contrary, Broker is authorized to advertise and market the Property in any medium, including the Internet (e-commerce), selected by Broker and, to the extent permitted by these media, including MLS, control the dissemination of the information submitted to any medium. Owner agrees to consider offers presented by Broker, and to act in good faith to accomplish the lease or rental of the Premises by, among others things, making the Premises available for showing at reasonable times and referring to Broker all inquiries of any party interested in the Premises. Owner is responsible for determining at what price to list and lease or rent the Premises. **Owner further agrees, regardless of responsibility, to indemnify, defend and hold Broker harmless from all claims, disputes, litigation, judgments and attorney fees arising from any incorrect information supplied by Owner, whether contained in any document, omitted therefrom, or otherwise, or from any material facts that Owner knows but fails to disclose.**

13. AGENCY RELATIONSHIPS:

    A. **Disclosure:** If the Premises includes residential property with one-to-four dwelling units, and the listing is for a tenancy in excess of one year, Owner acknowledges receipt of the "Disclosure Regarding Agency Relationships" form. (C.A.R. FORM AD-11)

    B. **Owner Representation:** Broker shall represent Owner in any resulting transaction, except as specified in paragraph 3H.

    C. **Possible Dual Agency With Tenant:** Depending upon the circumstances, it may be necessary or appropriate for Broker to act as an agent for both Owner and Tenant. Broker shall, as soon as practicable, disclose to Owner any election to act as a dual agent representing both Owner and Tenant. If a Tenant is procured directly by Broker or an associate licensee in Broker's firm, Owner hereby consents to Broker acting as a dual agent for Owner and such Tenant.

    D. **Other Owners:** Owner understands that Broker may have or obtain listings on other properties, and that potential tenants may consider, make offers on, or lease or rent through Broker, Premises the same as or similar to Owner's Premises. Owner consents to Broker's representation of owners and tenants of other properties before, during and after the end of this Agreement.

    E. **Confirmation:** If the Premises includes residential property with one-to-four dwelling units, and the agreed-upon lease is for a tenancy in excess of one year, Broker shall confirm the agency relationship described above, or as modified, in writing, prior to or coincident with Owner's execution of such a lease.

14. EQUAL HOUSING OPPORTUNITY: The Premises is offered in compliance with federal, state, and local anti-discrimination laws.

15. ATTORNEY FEES: In any action, proceeding, or arbitration between Owner and Broker regarding the obligation to pay compensation under this Agreement, the prevailing Owner or Broker shall be entitled to reasonable attorney fees and costs, except as provided in paragraph 19A.

16. ADDITIONAL TERMS: _____
_____
_____

17. MANAGEMENT APPROVAL: If a salesperson or broker-associate enters this agreement on Broker's behalf, and Broker/Manager does not approve of its terms, Broker/Manager has the right to cancel this agreement, in writing, within 5 days after its execution.

Owner and Broker acknowledge receipt of a copy of this page.

Owner's Initials (_____)(_____)
Broker's Initials (_____)(_____)

EQUAL HOUSING OPPORTUNITY

LL-11 (PAGE 2 OF 3)

Reviewed by _____
Broker or Designee _____ Date _____

EXCLUSIVE AUTHORIZATION TO LEASE OR RENT (LL-11 PAGE 2 OF 3)

Displayed/Reprinted with permission, CALIFORNIA ASSOCIATION OF REALTORS®. Endorsement not implied.

Property Address: _____ Date: _____

18. SUCCESSORS AND ASSIGNS: This agreement shall be binding upon Owner, and Owner's successors and assigns.

19. DISPUTE RESOLUTION:

    A. MEDIATION: Owner and Broker agree to mediate any dispute or claim arising between them out of this Agreement, or any resulting transaction, before resorting to arbitration or court action. Paragraph 19B(2) below applies whether or not the Arbitration provision is initialed. Mediation fees, if any, shall be divided equally among the parties involved. If, for any dispute or claim to which this paragraph applies, any party commences an action without first attempting to resolve the matter through mediation, or refuses to mediate after a request has been made, then that party shall not be entitled to recover attorney fees, even if they would otherwise be available to that party in any such action. THIS MEDIATION PROVISION APPLIES WHETHER OR NOT THE ARBITRATION PROVISION IS INITIALED.

    B. ARBITRATION OF DISPUTES: (1) Owner and Broker agree that any dispute or claim in Law or equity arising between them out of this Agreement or any resulting transaction, which is not settled through mediation, shall be decided by neutral, binding arbitration, including and subject to paragraph 19B(2) below. The arbitrator shall be a retired judge or justice, or an attorney with at least 5 years of residential real estate Law experience, unless the parties mutually agree to a different arbitrator, who shall render an award in accordance with substantive California Law. In all other respects, the arbitration shall be conducted in accordance with Part III, Title 9 of the California Code of Civil Procedure. Judgment upon the award of the arbitrator(s) may be entered in any court having jurisdiction. The parties shall have the right to discovery in accordance with Code of Civil Procedure §1283.05.

    (2) EXCLUSIONS FROM MEDIATION AND ARBITRATION: The following matters are excluded from mediation and arbitration: **(i)** a judicial or non-judicial foreclosure or other action or proceeding to enforce a deed of trust, mortgage, or installment land sale contract as defined in Civil Code §2985; **(ii)** an unlawful detainer action; **(iii)** the filing or enforcement of a mechanic's lien; **(iv)** any matter that is within the jurisdiction of a probate, small claims, or bankruptcy court; and **(v)** an action for bodily injury or wrongful death, or any right of action to which Code of Civil Procedure §337.1 or §337.15 applies. The filing of a court action to enable the recording of a notice of pending action, for order of attachment, receivership, injunction, or other provisional remedies, shall not constitute a violation of the mediation and arbitration provisions.

    "NOTICE: BY INITIALING IN THE SPACE BELOW YOU ARE AGREEING TO HAVE ANY DISPUTE ARISING OUT OF THE MATTERS INCLUDED IN THE 'ARBITRATION OF DISPUTES' PROVISION DECIDED BY NEUTRAL ARBITRATION AS PROVIDED BY CALIFORNIA LAW AND YOU ARE GIVING UP ANY RIGHTS YOU MIGHT POSSESS TO HAVE THE DISPUTE LITIGATED IN A COURT OR JURY TRIAL. BY INITIALING IN THE SPACE BELOW YOU ARE GIVING UP YOUR JUDICIAL RIGHTS TO DISCOVERY AND APPEAL, UNLESS THOSE RIGHTS ARE SPECIFICALLY INCLUDED IN THE 'ARBITRATION OF DISPUTES' PROVISION. IF YOU REFUSE TO SUBMIT TO ARBITRATION AFTER AGREEING TO THIS PROVISION, YOU MAY BE COMPELLED TO ARBITRATE UNDER THE AUTHORITY OF THE CALIFORNIA CODE OF CIVIL PROCEDURE. YOUR AGREEMENT TO THIS ARBITRATION PROVISION IS VOLUNTARY."

    "WE HAVE READ AND UNDERSTAND THE FOREGOING AND AGREE TO SUBMIT DISPUTES ARISING OUT OF THE MATTERS INCLUDED IN THE 'ARBITRATION OF DISPUTES' PROVISION TO NEUTRAL ARBITRATION."

| Owner's Initials _____ / _____ | Broker's Initials _____ / _____ |

20. ENTIRE CONTRACT: All prior discussions, negotiations, and agreements between the parties concerning the subject matter of this Agreement are superseded by this Agreement, which constitutes the entire contract and a complete and exclusive expression of their agreement, and may not be contradicted by evidence of any prior agreement or contemporaneous oral agreement. This Agreement and any supplement, addendum, or modification, including any photocopy or facsimile, may be executed in counterparts.

Owner acknowledges that Owner has read and understands this Agreement, and has received a copy.

Owner _____ Date _____   Owner _____ Date _____

Address _____   Address _____

City _____ State _____ Zip _____   City _____ State _____ Zip _____

Real Estate Broker (Firm) _____   By (Agent) _____ Date _____

Address _____   Telephone _____

City _____ State _____ Zip _____   Fax _____

EXCLUSIVE AUTHORIZATION TO LEASE OR RENT (LL-11 PAGE 3 OF 3)

Displayed/Reprinted with permission, CALIFORNIA ASSOCIATION OF REALTORS®. Endorsement not implied.

This page intentionally left blank.

CALIFORNIA ASSOCIATION OF REALTORS®

PROPERTY MANAGEMENT AGREEMENT
(C.A.R. Form PMA, Revised 4/03)

_____ ("Owner"), and
_____ ("Broker"), agree as follows:

1. **APPOINTMENT OF BROKER:** Owner hereby appoints and grants Broker the exclusive right to rent, lease, operate and manage the property(ies) known as _____
_____,
_____ and any additional property that may later be added to this Agreement ("Property"), upon the terms below, for the period beginning (date) _____ and ending (date) _____, at 11:59 PM.
(If checked:) ☐ Either party may terminate this Property Management Agreement ("Agreement") on at least 30 days written notice _____ months after the original commencement date of this Agreement. After the exclusive term expires, this Agreement shall continue as a non-exclusive agreement that either party may terminate by giving at least 30 days written notice to the other.

2. **BROKER ACCEPTANCE:** Broker accepts the appointment and grant, and agrees to:
   A. Use due diligence in the performance of this Agreement.
   B. Furnish the services of its firm for the rental, leasing, operation and management of the Property.

3. **AUTHORITY AND POWERS:** Owner grants Broker the authority and power, at Owner's expense, to:
   A. **ADVERTISING:** Display FOR RENT/LEASE and similar signs on the Property and advertise the availability of the Property, or any part thereof, for rental or lease.
   B. **RENTAL;LEASING:** Initiate, sign, renew, modify or cancel rental agreements and leases for the Property, or any part thereof; collect and give receipts for rents, other fees, charges and security deposits. Any lease or rental agreement executed by Broker for Owner shall not exceed _____ year(s) or ☐ shall be month-to-month. Unless Owner authorizes a lower amount, rent shall be: ☐ at market rate; OR ☐ a minimum of $ _____ per _____; OR ☐ see attachment.
   C. **TENANCY TERMINATION:** Sign and serve in Owner's name notices that are required or appropriate; commence and prosecute actions to evict tenants; recover possession of the Property in Owner's name; recover rents and other sums due; and, when expedient, settle, compromise and release claims, actions and suits and/or reinstate tenancies.
   D. **REPAIR;MAINTENANCE:** Make, cause to be made, and/or supervise repairs, improvements, alterations and decorations to the Property; purchase, and pay bills for, services and supplies. Broker shall obtain prior approval of Owner for all expenditures over $ _____ for any one item. Prior approval shall not be required for monthly or recurring operating charges or, if in Broker's opinion, emergency expenditures over the maximum are needed to protect the Property or other property(ies) from damage, prevent injury to persons, avoid suspension of necessary services, avoid penalties or fines, or suspension of services to tenants required by a lease or rental agreement or by law, including, but not limited to, maintaining the Property in a condition fit for human habitation as required by Civil Code §§ 1941 and 1941.1 and Health and Safety Code §§ 17920.3 and 17920.10.
   E. **REPORTS, NOTICES AND SIGNS:** Comply with federal, state or local law requiring delivery of reports or notices and/or posting of signs or notices.
   F. **CONTRACTS;SERVICES:** Contract, hire, supervise and/or discharge firms and persons, including utilities, required for the operation and maintenance of the Property. Broker may perform any of Broker's duties through attorneys, agents, employees, or independent contractors and, except for persons working in Broker's firm, shall not be responsible for their acts, omissions, defaults, negligence and/or costs of same.
   G. **EXPENSE PAYMENTS:** Pay expenses and costs for the Property from Owner's funds held by Broker, unless otherwise directed by Owner. Expenses and costs may include, but are not limited to, property management compensation, fees and charges, expenses for goods and services, property taxes and other taxes, Owner's Association dues, assessments, loan payments and insurance premiums.
   H. **SECURITY DEPOSITS:** Receive security deposits from tenants, which deposits shall be ☐ given to Owner, or ☐ placed in Broker's trust account and, if held in Broker's trust account, pay from Owner's funds all interest on tenants' security deposits if required by local law or ordinance. Owner shall be responsible to tenants for return of security deposits and all interest due on security deposits held by Owner.
   I. **TRUST FUNDS:** Deposit all receipts collected for Owner, less any sums properly deducted or disbursed, in a financial institution whose deposits are insured by an agency of the United States government. The funds shall be held in a trust account separate from Broker's personal accounts. Broker shall not be liable in event of bankruptcy or failure of a financial institution.
   J. **RESERVES:** Maintain a reserve in Broker's trust account of $_____.
   K. **DISBURSEMENTS:** Disburse Owner's funds held in Broker's trust account in the following order:
   (1) Compensation due Broker under paragraph 6.
   (2) All other operating expenses, costs and disbursements payable from Owner's funds held by Broker.
   (3) Reserves and security deposits held by Broker.
   (4) Balance to Owner.
   L. **OWNER DISTRIBUTION:** Remit funds, if any are available, monthly (or ☐ _____), to Owner.
   M. **OWNER STATEMENTS:** Render monthly (or ☐ _____), statements of receipts, expenses and charges for each Property.
   N. **BROKER FUNDS:** Broker shall not advance Broker's own funds in connection with the Property or this Agreement.
   O. **KEYSAFE/LOCKBOX:** ☐ (If checked) Owner authorizes the use of a keysafe/lockbox to allow entry into the Propery and agrees to sign a keysafe/ lockbox addendum (C.A.R. Form KLA).

PMA REVISED 4/03 (PAGE 1 OF 3) Print Date

Owner's Initials (_____)(_____)
Broker's Initials (_____)(_____)

Reviewed by _____ Date _____

EQUAL HOUSING OPPORTUNITY

PROPERTY MANAGEMENT AGREEMENT (PMA PAGE 1 OF 3)

Owner Name: _____   Date: _____

4. **OWNER RESPONSIBILITIES:** Owner shall:
   A. Provide all documentation, records and disclosures as required by law or required by Broker to manage and operate the Property, and immediately notify Broker if Owner becomes aware of any change in such documentation, records or disclosures, or any matter affecting the habitability of the Property.
   B. Indemnify, defend and hold harmless Broker, and all persons in Broker's firm, regardless of responsibility, from all costs, expenses, suits, liabilities, damages, attorney fees and claims of every type, including but not limited to those arising out of injury or death of any person, or damage to any real or personal property of any person, including Owner, for: **(i)** any repairs performed by Owner or by others hired directly by Owner; or **(ii)** those relating to the management, leasing, rental, security deposits, or operation of the Property by Broker, or any person in Broker's firm, or the performance or exercise of any of the duties, powers or authorities granted to Broker.
   C. Maintain the Property in a condition fit for human habitation as required by Civil Code §§ 1941 and 1941.1 and Health and Safety Code §§ 17920.3 and 17920.10 and other applicable law.
   D. Pay all interest on tenants' security deposits if required by local law or ordinance.
   E. Carry and pay for: **(i)** public and premises liability insurance in an amount of no less than $1,000,000; and **(ii)** property damage and worker's compensation insurance adequate to protect the interests of Owner and Broker. Broker shall be, and Owner authorizes Broker to be, named as an additional insured party on Owner's policies.
   F. Pay any late charges, penalties and/or interest imposed by lenders or other parties for failure to make payment to those parties, if the failure is due to insufficient funds in Broker's trust account available for such payment.
   G. Immediately replace any funds required if there are insufficient funds in Broker's trust account to cover Owner's responsibilities.

5. **LEAD-BASED PAINT DISCLOSURE:**
   A. ☐ The Property was constructed on or after January 1, 1978.
   OR B. ☐ The Property was constructed prior to 1978.
      (1) Owner has no knowledge of lead-based paint or lead-based paint hazards in the housing except: _____
         _____.
      (2) Owner has no reports or records pertaining to lead-based paint or lead-based paint hazards in the housing, except the following, which Owner shall provide to Broker: _____.

6. **COMPENSATION:**
   A. Owner agrees to pay Broker fees in the amounts indicated below for:
      (1) Management: _____.
      (2) Renting or Leasing: _____.
      (3) Evictions: _____.
      (4) Preparing Property for rental or lease: _____.
      (5) Managing Property during extended periods of vacancy: _____.
      (6) An overhead and service fee added to the cost of all work performed by, or at the direction of, Broker: _____.
      (7) Other: _____
   B. This Agreement does not include providing on-site management services, property sales, refinancing, preparing Property for sale or refinancing, modernization, fire or major damage restoration, rehabilitation, obtaining income tax, accounting or legal advice, representation before public agencies, advising on proposed new construction, debt collection, counseling, attending Owner's Association meetings or _____
   _____.
   If Owner requests Broker to perform services not included in this Agreement, a fee shall be agreed upon before these services are performed.
   C. Broker may divide compensation, fees and charges due under this Agreement in any manner acceptable to Broker.
   D. Owner further agrees that:
      (1) Broker may receive and keep fees and charges from tenants for: **(i)** requesting an assignment of lease or sublease of the Property; **(ii)** processing credit applications; **(iii)** any returned checks and/or (☐ if checked) late payments; and **(iv)** any other services that are not in conflict with this Agreement.
      (2) Broker may perform any of Broker's duties, and obtain necessary products and services, through affiliated companies or organizations in which Broker may own an interest. Broker may receive fees, commissions and/or profits from these affiliated companies or organizations. Broker has an ownership interest in the following affiliated companies or organizations: _____
   _____.
   Broker shall disclose to Owner any other such relationships as they occur. Broker shall not receive any fees, commissions or profits from unaffiliated companies or organizations in the performance of this Agreement, without prior disclosure to Owner.
      (3) Other: _____.

7. **AGENCY RELATIONSHIPS:** Broker shall act, and Owner hereby consents to Broker acting, as dual agent for Owner and tenant(s) in any resulting transaction. If the Property includes residential property with one-to-four dwelling units and this Agreement permits a tenancy in excess of one year, Owner acknowledges receipt of the "Disclosure Regarding Agency Relationships" (C.A.R. Form AD). Owner understands that Broker may have or obtain property management agreements on other property, and that potential tenants may consider, make offers on, or lease through Broker, property the same as or similar to Owner's Property. Owner consents to Broker's representation of other owners' properties before, during and after the expiration of this Agreement.

8. **NOTICES:** Any written notice to Owner or Broker required under this Agreement shall be served by sending such notice by first class mail or other agreed-to delivery method to that party at the address below, or at any different address the parties may later designate for this purpose. Notice shall be deemed received three (3) calendar days after deposit into the United States mail OR ☐ _____.

Owner's Initials (_____)(_____)
Broker's Initials (_____)(_____)

Reviewed by _____ Date _____

PMA REVISED 4/03 (PAGE 2 OF 3)

EQUAL HOUSING OPPORTUNITY

PROPERTY MANAGEMENT AGREEMENT (PMA PAGE 2 OF 3)
Displayed / Reprinted with permission, CALIFORNIA ASSOCIATION OF REALTORS®. Endorsement not implied.

Owner Name: _____   Date: _____

9.   DISPUTE RESOLUTION

    A.   MEDIATION: Owner and Broker agree to mediate any dispute or claim arising between them out of this Agreement, or any resulting transaction before resorting to arbitration or court action, subject to paragraph 9B(2) below. Paragraph 9B(2) below applies whether or not the arbitration provision is initialed. Mediation fees, if any, shall be divided equally among the parties involved. If, for any dispute or claim to which this paragraph applies, any party commences an action based on a dispute or claim to which this paragraph applies, without first attempting to resolve the matter through mediation, or refuses to mediate after a request has been made, then that party shall not be entitled to recover attorney fees, even if they would otherwise be available to that party in any such action. THIS MEDIATION PROVISION APPLIES WHETHER OR NOT THE ARBITRATION PROVISION IS INITIALED.

    B.   ARBITRATION OF DISPUTES: (1) Owner and Broker agree that any dispute or claim in law or equity arising between them regarding the obligation to pay compensation under this agreement, which is not settled through mediation, shall be decided by neutral, binding arbitration, including and subject to paragraph 9B(2) below. The arbitrator shall be a retired judge or justice, or an attorney with at least 5 years of residential real estate law experience, unless the parties mutually agree to a different arbitrator, who shall render an award in accordance with substantive California Law. The parties shall have the right to discovery in accordance with Code of Civil Procedure § 1283.05. In all other respects, the arbitration shall be conducted in accordance with Title 9 of Part III of the California Code of Civil Procedure. Judgment upon the award of the arbitrator(s) may be entered in any court having jurisdiction. Interpretation of this agreement to arbitrate shall be governed by the Federal Arbitration Act.

       (2) EXCLUSIONS FROM MEDIATION AND ARBITRATION: The following matters are excluded from mediation and arbitration hereunder: **(i)** a judicial or non-judicial foreclosure or other action or proceeding to enforce a deed of trust, mortgage, or installment land sale contract as defined in Civil Code § 2985; **(ii)** an unlawful detainer action; **(iii)** the filing or enforcement of a mechanic's lien; and **(iv)** any matter that is within the jurisdiction of a probate, small claims, or bankruptcy court. The filing of a court action to enable the recording of a notice of pending action, for order of attachment, receivership, injunction, or other provisional remedies, shall not constitute a waiver of the mediation and arbitration provisions.

       "NOTICE: BY INITIALING IN THE SPACE BELOW YOU ARE AGREEING TO HAVE ANY DISPUTE ARISING OUT OF THE MATTERS INCLUDED IN THE 'ARBITRATION OF DISPUTES' PROVISION DECIDED BY NEUTRAL ARBITRATION AS PROVIDED BY CALIFORNIA LAW AND YOU ARE GIVING UP ANY RIGHTS YOU MIGHT POSSESS TO HAVE THE DISPUTE LITIGATED IN A COURT OR JURY TRIAL. BY INITIALING IN THE SPACE BELOW YOU ARE GIVING UP YOUR JUDICIAL RIGHTS TO DISCOVERY AND APPEAL, UNLESS THOSE RIGHTS ARE SPECIFICALLY INCLUDED IN THE 'ARBITRATION OF DISPUTES' PROVISION. IF YOU REFUSE TO SUBMIT TO ARBITRATION AFTER AGREEING TO THIS PROVISION, YOU MAY BE COMPELLED TO ARBITRATE UNDER THE AUTHORITY OF THE CALIFORNIA CODE OF CIVIL PROCEDURE. YOUR AGREEMENT TO THIS ARBITRATION PROVISION IS VOLUNTARY."

       "WE HAVE READ AND UNDERSTAND THE FOREGOING AND AGREE TO SUBMIT DISPUTES ARISING OUT OF THE MATTERS INCLUDED IN THE 'ARBITRATION OF DISPUTES' PROVISION TO NEUTRAL ARBITRATION."

Owner's Initials _____ / _____		**Broker's Initials** _____ / _____	

10. EQUAL HOUSING OPPORTUNITY: The Property is offered in compliance with federal, state and local anti-discrimination laws.

11. ATTORNEY FEES: In any action, proceeding or arbitration between Owner and Broker regarding the obligation to pay compensation under this Agreement, the prevailing Owner or Broker shall be entitled to reasonable attorney fees and costs from the non-prevailing Owner or Broker, except as provided in paragraph 9A.

12. ADDITIONAL TERMS: ☐ Keysafe/Lockbox Addendum (C.A.R. Form KLA); ☐ Lead-Based Paint and Lead-Based Paint Hazards Disclosure (C.A.R. Form FLD)
_____

13. TIME OF ESSENCE; ENTIRE CONTRACT; CHANGES: Time is of the essence. All understandings between the parties are incorporated in this Agreement. Its terms are intended by the parties as a final, complete and exclusive expression of their Agreement with respect to its subject matter, and may not be contradicted by evidence of any prior agreement or contemporaneous oral agreement. If any provision of this Agreement is held to be ineffective or invalid, the remaining provisions will nevertheless be given full force and effect. Neither this Agreement nor any provision in it may be extended, amended, modified, altered or changed except in writing. This Agreement and any supplement, addendum or modification, including any copy, may be signed in two or more counterparts, all of which shall constitute one and the same writing.

Owner warrants that Owner is the owner of the Property or has the authority to execute this contract. Owner acknowledges Owner has read, understands, accepts and has received a copy of the Agreement.

Owner _____ Date _____
Owner _____
      Print Name   Social Security/Tax ID # (for tax reporting purposes)
Address _____ City _____ State _____ Zip _____
Telephone _____ Fax _____ E-mail _____

Owner _____ Date _____
Owner _____
      Print Name   Social Security/Tax ID # (for tax reporting purposes)
Address _____ City _____ State _____ Zip _____
Telephone _____ Fax _____ E-mail _____

Real Estate Broker (Firm) _____ Date _____
By (Agent) _____
Address _____ City _____ State _____ Zip _____
Telephone _____ Fax _____ E-mail _____

THIS FORM HAS BEEN APPROVED BY THE CALIFORNIA ASSOCIATION OF REALTORS® (C.A.R.). NO REPRESENTATION IS MADE AS TO THE LEGAL VALIDITY OR ADEQUACY OF ANY PROVISION IN ANY SPECIFIC TRANSACTION. A REAL ESTATE BROKER IS THE PERSON QUALIFIED TO ADVISE ON REAL ESTATE TRANSACTIONS. IF YOU DESIRE LEGAL OR TAX ADVICE, CONSULT AN APPROPRIATE PROFESSIONAL.

This form is available for use by the entire real estate industry. It is not intended to identify the user as a REALTOR®. REALTOR® is a registered collective membership mark which may be used only by members of the NATIONAL ASSOCIATION OF REALTORS® who subscribe to its Code of Ethics.

SURE TRAC The System for Success®

Published and Distributed by:
REAL ESTATE BUSINESS SERVICES, INC.
a subsidiary of the California Association of REALTORS®
525 South Virgil Avenue, Los Angeles, California 90020

| Reviewed by _____ Date _____ |

EQUAL HOUSING
OPPORTUNITY

Appendix D:
Blank Forms

Use of the following forms is described in the text or should be self-explanatory. If you do not understand any aspect of a form you should seek advice from an attorney. Some forms appear with the second page upside-down. California courts require this, and you should file the form that way. Before you write on any form, it is best to make copies in case you make a mistake. These forms can be torn out for use. (None of these forms are from the *California Association of Realtors®*.)

License: Although this book is copyrighted, purchasers of the book are granted permission to copy the forms created by the author for their own personal use or use in their law practice.

Tenant Application

Name: _____
        First   *Last*   *Middle*

Date of Birth _____   Dr. Lic. No. _____

Name: _____
        First   *Last*   *Middle*

Date of Birth _____   Dr. Lic. No. _____

Names of all other occupants (all adult occupants must sign the lease). Include ages of any minor children.

Names: _____   _____

           _____   _____

Name(s) of anyone who will stay with you more than one week.

1. _____   2. _____

Your present address _____   _____

                      _____   how long?

                      _____

                      _____

Reason for leaving? _____

Present landlord _____ phone: _____

Address _____

Second previous landlord _____ phone: _____

Address _____ how long? _____

Have you ever been evicted or asked to move? _____

Have you ever filed for bankruptcy? _____

Have you ever been convicted of selling, manufacturing, or distributing illegal drugs?

_____

Employer _____ phone: _____

Address _____ how long? _____

Job title _____ Supervisor _____

Current gross monthly income (before deductions) $ _____

Other incomes $_____ Sources _____

Credit reference _____ Acct. no. _____

Balance owed _____ Monthly payment _____

Number of vehicles to be kept at rental property? _____

_____
make   *model*   *year*   *license no.*

_____
make   *model*   *year*   *license no.*

Any pet(s)? _____ Describe _____

Waterbed(s) or water-filled furniture? _____ Describe _____

Emergency contact _____
                            name   *phone*

_____
                   address

The undersigned hereby attest(s) that the above information is true and authorize(s) verification of any and all information given, as well as authorizing the obtaining of a credit report.

Application Fee $ _____   Deposited $ _____

Property to be rented is _____ Unit _____

The rental amount is $ _____ per month plus a security deposit of $ _____
Signature(s) of applicant(s)

_____ Date _____

_____ Date _____

Denial of Application to Rent

Your application to rent the property located at _____
_____

has been denied based in whole or in part on information supplied by the following credit reporting companies:

Company Name: _____
Address: _____
Phone: _____

Company Name: _____
Address: _____
Phone: _____

Company Name: _____
Address: _____
Phone: _____

You have the right to obtain a free copy of this report by contacting, within 60 days, the credit reporting agency indicated above and from any other consumer credit reporting agency that compiles and maintains files on a national basis.

You have the right to dispute the accuracy and completeness of any information in a consumer credit report furnished by a consumer credit reporting agency.

Date: _____

This page intentionally left blank.

Inspection Report

Date: _____

Unit: _____

AREA	CONDITION			
	Move-In		Move-Out	
	Good	Poor	Good	Poor
Yard/garden				
Driveway				
Patio/porch				
Exterior				
Entry light/bell				
Living room/Dining room/Halls:				
Floors/carpets				
Walls/ceiling				
Doors/locks				
Fixtures/lights				
Outlets/switches				
Other				
Bedrooms:				
Floors/carpets				
Walls/ceiling				
Doors/locks				
Fixtures/lights				
Outlets/switches				
Other				
Bathrooms:				
Faucets				
Toilet				
Sink/tub				
Floors/carpets				
Walls/ceiling				
Doors/locks				
Fixtures/lights				
Outlets/switches				
Other				
Kitchen:				
Refrigerator				
Range				
Oven				
Dishwasher				
Sink/disposal				
Cabinets/counters				
Floors/carpets				
Walls/ceiling				
Doors/locks				
Fixtures/lights				
Outlets/switches				
Other				
Kitchen:				
Closets/pantry				
Garage				
Keys				
Other				

This page intentionally left blank.

Pet Agreement

THIS AGREEMENT is made pursuant to that certain Lease dated _____, 20____
between _____ as Landlord
and _____as Tenant, for rental of the property
located at _____.

In consideration of $_____ as nonrefundable cleaning payment and $_____
as additional security deposit paid by Tenant to Landlord, Tenant is allowed to keep the
following pet(s): _____ on the premises
_____ under the following conditions:

1.   ☐   If the pet is a dog or cat, it is spayed or neutered.
     ☐   In the event the pet produces a litter, Tenant may keep them at the
         premises no longer than one month past weaning.

2.   Tenant shall not engage in any commercial pet-raising activities.

3.   No pets other than those listed above shall be kept on the premises without the
     further written permission of the Landlord.

4.   Tenant agrees at all times to keep the pet from becoming a nuisance to
     neighbors and/or other tenants. This includes controlling the barking of the pet, if
     necessary, and cleaning any animal waste on and about the premises.

5.   In the event the pet causes destruction of the property, becomes a nuisance, or
     Tenant otherwise violates this agreement, Landlord may terminate the Lease
     according to California law.

6.   An additional security deposit of $_____ shall be deposited with
     Landlord.

Date: _____

Landlord: Tenant:

_____   _____

_____   _____

This page intentionally left blank.

Agreement for Use of Waterbed

The property received a valid Certificate of Occupancy after January 1, 1973, and water-filled furniture (herein called bedding) is permitted as provided by California Civil Code 1940.5

Landlord and Tenant agree as follows:

1.   Tenant shall provide owner with a valid waterbed insurance policy or certificate or insurance for property damage in the amount of $_____ (not less than $100,000) prior to installation of the bedding. The policy shall remain in effect until the bedding is permanently removed from the rental property.

2.   The bedding must have been constructed after January 1, 1973, and must conform to the rules and regulations of the Bureau of Home Furnishings pursuant to Section 19155 of the Business and Professional Code and shall display a label declaring said compliance.

3.   The bedding must not exceed the pounds-per-square-foot limitation of the rental property.

4.   Tenant shall give Landlord at least 24 hours' written notice of installation, moving, or removal of the bedding and Landlord may be present at these times.

5.   Landlord may increase the security deposit by an additional one-half month's rent.

6.   All other provisions of Civil Code 1940.5 are incorporated into this agreement.

_____   _____
Landlord/Agent   Date

_____   _____
Tenant   Date

_____   _____
Tenant   Date

This page intentionally left blank.

Lease

LANDLORD: _____   TENANT: _____

_____   _____

PROPERTY: _____

IN CONSIDERATION of the mutual covenants and agreements herein contained, Landlord hereby leases to Tenant and Tenant hereby leases from Landlord the above-described property under the following terms:

    1. TERM. This lease shall be for a term of _____ beginning _____, _____ and ending _____, _____. If Tenant is in possession of the unit for one year or more, a sixty-day notice to vacate will be served by Landlord. Additional rent shall be charged on a daily basis if Tenant holds over, prorated as 1/30th of the monthly rent at that time, using a thirty-day month for proration.

    2. RENT. The rent shall be $_____ per month and shall be due on or before the _____ day of each month. If rent is received more than three days late, a late charge of $_____ shall be paid.

    3. PAYMENT. Payment must be received by Landlord on or before the due date at the following address: _____ or such place as designated by Landlord in writing. Tenant understands that this may require early mailing. If a check bounces, Tenant agrees to pay a late charge of $_____, and Landlord may require future payments in cash, money order, or certified funds. Tenant is hereby notified that default of financial obligations under this agreement may be reported to credit reporting companies and may result in derogatory information on Tenant's credit report. Payment in person may be made on □Monday □Tuesday □Wednesday □Thursday □Friday □Saturday □Sunday between the hours of _____(am) and _____(pm). Acceptable methods of payment are: □cash □personal check □cashier's check □money order □eft/credit (contact owner or agent to arrange).

    4. DEFAULT. In the event Tenant defaults under any terms of this agreement, Landlord may recover possession as provided by law and seek monetary damages.

    5. SECURITY. Landlord acknowledges receipt of the sum of $_____ as security deposit. This deposit may not be used as last month's rent. Landlord may withhold from the security deposit amounts necessary to cover unpaid rent, damages to the premises and/or Landlord's personal property caused by Tenant beyond ordinary wear and tear, and cleaning of the premises, if necessary.

    Within three weeks after Landlord retakes possession of the premises, Landlord shall furnish Tenant with a written statement itemizing the amounts withheld with explanation and returning any unused portion of the deposit to Tenant.

    6. UTILITIES. Tenant agrees to pay all utility charges on the property except: _____.

    7. MAINTENANCE. Tenant has examined the premises and has found them to be clean, safe, and in good repair and condition with the exception of the following: _____ _____.

    Tenant agrees to return the premises to Landlord at the termination of the tenancy in the same clean, safe, good repair and condition, except for normal wear and tear.

8. LOCKS. If Tenant adds or changes locks on the premises, Landlord shall be given copies of the keys. Landlord shall at all times have keys for access to the premises in case of emergencies.

9. ASSIGNMENT AND SUBLETTING. Tenant may not sublet the premises nor any portion of the premises, nor may Tenant assign this agreement without written permission of Landlord.

10. USE. Tenant shall not use the premises for any illegal purpose or any purpose which will increase the rate of insurance, and shall not cause a nuisance for Landlord or neighbors. Tenant shall not create any environmental hazards on the premises.

11. LAWN (CHECK AND INITIAL): Tenant agrees to maintain the lawn and other landscaping on the premises at Tenant's expense. Yes_____ No_____Initials _____

12. LIABILITY. Tenant shall be responsible for insurance on Tenant's own property and agrees not to hold Landlord liable for any damages to Tenant's property on the premises.

13. ACCESS. Landlord may enter the premises as allowed by Section 1954 of the California Civil Code. Refusal by the tenant to allow entry as permitted by the code will breach this contract and may result in eviction. The word "Landlord" includes owner(s), owner's agent(s), and employee(s).

14. PETS. No pets shall be allowed on the premises except: _____
_____.

15. WATERBEDS. No waterbeds or liquid-filled furniture shall be allowed on the premises without Landlord's written permission.

16. OCCUPANCY. The premises shall be occupied as a residence only, and shall be occupied only by the following persons: (List all occupants, both adults and minors) _____
_____.

17. TENANT'S APPLIANCES. Tenant agrees not to use any heaters, fixtures, or appliances drawing excessive current without consent of Landlord.

18. PARKING. Tenant agrees that no parking is allowed on the premises except: _____. No boats, recreation vehicles, or disassembled automobiles may be stored on the premises.

19. FURNISHINGS. Any articles provided to Tenant and listed on attached schedule are to be returned in good condition at the termination of this agreement.

20. ALTERATIONS AND IMPROVEMENTS. Tenant shall make no alterations to the property without the written consent of Landlord, and any such alterations or improvements shall become the property of Landlord.

21. SMOKE DETECTORS. Tenant shall be responsible for keeping smoke detectors operational and for changing batteries when needed.

22. LIENS. The estate of Landlord shall not be subject to any liens for improvements contracted by Tenant.

23. HARASSMENT. Tenant shall not do any acts to intentionally harass Landlord or other tenants.

24. ATTORNEY'S FEES. In the event of legal action, the prevailing party (shall) (shall not) recover reasonable attorney's fees in addition to any other recovery.

25. SEVERABILITY. In the event any section of this agreement shall be held to be invalid, all remaining provisions shall remain in full force and effect.

26. RECORDING. This agreement shall not be recorded in any public records.

27. WAIVER. Any failure by Landlord to exercise any rights under this agreement shall not constitute a waiver of Landlord's rights.

28. SUBORDINATION. Tenant's interest in the premises shall be subordinate to any encumbrances now or hereafter placed on the premises, to any advances made under such encumbrances, and to any extensions or renewals thereof. Tenant agrees to sign any documents indicating such subordination which may be required by lenders.

29. ATTACHMENTS: The following attachments are incorporated and made a part of this agreement. (Tenant should initial)

A. _____   B. _____

C. _____   D. _____

30. ENTIRE AGREEMENT. This rental agreement, including the above initialed attachments, constitutes the entire agreement between the parties and may not be modified except in writing signed by all parties.

31. OWNER OR MANAGER. The owner or manager for service of legal notices is: _____.

32. NOTICE: The California Department of Justice, sheriff's departments, police departments serving jurisdictions of 200,000 or more, and many other local law enforcement authorities maintain for public access a database of the locations of persons required to register pursuant to paragraph (1) of subdivision (a) of Section 290.4 of the Penal Code. The data base is updated on a quarterly basis and is a source of information about the presence of these individuals in any neighborhood. The Department of Justice also maintains a Sex Offender Identification Line through which inquiries about individuals may be made. This is a "900" telephone service. Callers must have specific information about individuals they are checking. Information regarding neighborhoods is not available through the "900" telephone service.

WITNESS the hands and seals of the parties hereto as of this _____ day of _____, _____.

LANDLORD: TENANT:

_____   _____

_____   _____

This page intentionally left blank.

Condominium Lease

LANDLORD: _____ TENANT: _____

_____ _____

PROPERTY: _____
IN CONSIDERATION of the mutual covenants and agreements herein contained,
Landlord hereby leases to Tenant and Tenant hereby leases from Landlord the above-
described property under the following terms:

     1. TERM. This lease shall be for a term of _____ beginning
_____, _____ and ending _____, _____. If Tenant
is in possession of the unit for one year or more, a sixty-day notice to vacate will be
served by Landlord. Additional rent shall be charged on a daily basis if Tenant holds
over, prorated as 1/30th of the monthly rent at that time, using a thirty-day month for
proration.

     2. RENT. The rent shall be $_____ per month and shall be
due on or before the _____ day of each month. If rent is received more than
three days late, a late charge of $_____ shall be paid.

     3. PAYMENT. Payment must be received by Landlord on or before the due date
at the following address: _____
or such place as designated by Landlord in writing. Tenant understands that this may
require early mailing. If a check bounces, Tenant agrees to pay a late charge of
$_____, and Landlord may require future payments in cash, money
order, or certified funds. Tenant is hereby notified that default of financial obligations
under this agreement may be reported to credit reporting companies and may result in
derogatory information on Tenant's credit report. Payment in person may be made on
☐Monday ☐Tuesday ☐Wednesday ☐Thursday ☐Friday ☐Saturday ☐Sunday between
the hours of _____(am) and _____(pm). Acceptable methods of payment are: ☐cash
☐personal check ☐cashier's check ☐money order ☐eft/credit (contact owner or agent
to arrange).

     4. DEFAULT. In the event Tenant defaults under any terms of this agreement,
Landlord may recover possession as provided by law and seek monetary damages.

     5. SECURITY. Landlord acknowledges receipt of the sum of $_____
as security deposit. This deposit may not be used as last month's rent. Landlord may
withhold from the security deposit amounts necessary to cover unpaid rent, damages to
the premises and/or Landlord's personal property caused by Tenant beyond ordinary
wear and tear, and cleaning of the premises, if necessary.

     Within three weeks after Landlord retakes possession of the premises, Landlord
shall furnish Tenant with a written statement itemizing the amounts withheld with
explanation and returning any unused portion of the deposit to Tenant.

     6. UTILITIES. Tenant agrees to pay all utility charges on the property except:
_____.

     7. MAINTENANCE. Tenant has examined the premises and has found them to
be clean, safe, and in good repair and condition with the exception of the following:
_____
_____.

     Tenant agrees to return the premises to Landlord at the termination of the
tenancy in the same clean, safe, good repair and condition, except for normal wear and
tear.

     8. LOCKS. If Tenant adds or changes locks on the premises, Landlord shall be
given copies of the keys. Landlord shall at all times have keys for access to the premises
in case of emergencies.

9. ASSIGNMENT AND SUBLETTING. Tenant may not sublet the premises nor any portion of the premises, nor may Tenant assign this agreement without written permission of Landlord.

10. COMMON INTEREST PROPERTY. Tenant acknowledges that the premises are subject to a Declaration of Covenants, Conditions, and Restrictions and Association Rules and Regulations. Copies of these documents are attached to and made part of this agreement. Tenant agrees to comply with the requirements of these documents and to reimburse Landlord for any fines or charges levied against Landlord for Tenant's failure to comply with these requirements.

11. USE. Tenant shall not use the premises for any illegal purpose or any purpose which will increase the rate of insurance, and shall not cause a nuisance for Landlord or neighbors. Tenant shall not create any environmental hazards on the premises.

12. LAWN (CHECK AND INITIAL). Tenant agrees to maintain the lawn and other landscaping on the premises at Tenant's expense. Yes _____ No _____ Initials _____

13. LIABILITY. Tenant shall be responsible for insurance on Tenant's own property and agrees not to hold Landlord liable for any damages to Tenant's property on the premises.

14. ACCESS. Landlord may enter the premises as allowed by Section 1954 of the California Civil Code. Refusal by the tenant to allow entry as permitted by the code will breach this contract and may result in eviction. The word "Landlord" includes owner(s), owner's agent(s), and employee(s).

15. PETS. No pets shall be allowed on the premises except: _____

_____.

16. WATERBEDS. No waterbeds or liquid-filled furniture shall be allowed on the premises without Landlord's written permission.

17. OCCUPANCY. The premises shall be occupied as a residence only, and shall be occupied only by the following persons: (List all occupants, both adults and minors)_____

_____.

18. TENANT'S APPLIANCES. Tenant agrees not to use any heaters, fixtures, or appliances drawing excessive current without consent of Landlord.

19. PARKING. Tenant agrees that no parking is allowed on the premises except: _____. No boats, recreation vehicles, or disassembled automobiles may be stored on the premises.

20. FURNISHINGS. Any articles provided to Tenant and listed on attached schedule are to be returned in good condition at the termination of this agreement.

21. ALTERATIONS AND IMPROVEMENTS. Tenant shall make no alterations to the property without the written consent of Landlord and any such alterations or improvements shall become the property of Landlord.

22. SMOKE DETECTORS. Tenant shall be responsible for keeping smoke detectors operational and for changing batteries when needed.

23. LIENS. The estate of Landlord shall not be subject to any liens for improvements contracted by Tenant.

24. HARASSMENT. Tenant shall not do any acts to intentionally harass Landlord or other tenants.

25. ATTORNEY'S FEES. In the event of legal action, the prevailing party (shall) (shall not) recover reasonable attorney's fees in addition to any other recovery.

26. SEVERABILITY. In the event any section of this agreement shall be held to be invalid, all remaining provisions shall remain in full force and effect.

27. RECORDING. This agreement shall not be recorded in any public records.

28. WAIVER. Any failure by Landlord to exercise any rights under this agreement shall not constitute a waiver of Landlord's rights.

29. SUBORDINATION. Tenant's interest in the premises shall be subordinate to any encumbrances now or hereafter placed on the premises, to any advances made under such encumbrances, and to any extensions or renewals thereof. Tenant agrees to sign any documents indicating such subordination which may be required by lenders.

30. ATTACHMENTS. The following attachments are incorporated and made a part of this agreement. (Tenant should initial)

A. _____   B. _____

C. _____   D. _____

32. ENTIRE AGREEMENT. This rental agreement, including the above initialed attachments, constitutes the entire agreement between the parties and may not be modified except in writing signed by all parties.

32. OWNER OR MANAGER. The owner or manager for service of legal notices is: _____ .

33. NOTICE: The California Department of Justice, sheriff's departments, police departments serving jurisdictions of 200,000 or more, and many other local law enforcement authorities maintain for public access a database of the locations of persons required to register pursuant to paragraph (1) of subdivision (a) of Section 290.4 of the Penal Code. The data base is updated on a quarterly basis and is a source of information about the presence of these individuals in any neighborhood. The Department of Justice also maintains a Sex Offender Identification Line through which inquiries about individuals may be made. This is a "900" telephone service. Callers must have specific information about individuals they are checking. Information regarding neighborhoods is not available through the "900" telephone service.

WITNESS the hands and seals of the parties hereto as of this _____ day of _____, _____ .

LANDLORD: TENANT:

_____   _____

_____   _____

This page intentionally left blank.

Rental Agreement

LANDLORD: _____   TENANT: _____

_____   _____

PROPERTY: _____

IN CONSIDERATION of the mutual covenants and agreements herein contained, Landlord hereby rents to Tenant and Tenant hereby rents from Landlord the above-described property under the following terms:

    1. TERM. This Rental Agreement shall be for a month-to-month tenancy. Unless prohibited by law, this agreement may be terminated by either party or modified by Landlord upon service of 30 days' written notice. If Tenant is in possession of the unit for one year or more, a sixty-day notice to vacate will be served by Landlord. Additional rent shall be charged on a daily basis if Tenant holds over, prorated as 1/30th of the monthly rent at that time, using a thirty-day month for proration.

    2. RENT. The rent shall be $_____ per month and shall be due on or before the _____ day of each month. If rent is received more than three days late, a late charge of $_____ shall be paid.

    3. PAYMENT. Payment must be received by Landlord on or before the due date at the following address: _____ or such place as designated by Landlord in writing. Tenant understands that this may require early mailing. If a check bounces, Tenant agrees to pay a late charge of $_____, and Landlord may require future payments in cash, money order, or certified funds. Tenant is hereby notified that default of financial obligations under this agreement may be reported to credit reporting companies and may result in derogatory information on Tenant's credit report. Payment in person may be made on □Monday □Tuesday □Wednesday □Thursday □Friday □Saturday □Sunday between the hours of _____(am) and _____(pm). Acceptable methods of payment are: □cash □personal check □cashier's check □money order □eft/credit (contact owner or agent to arrange).

    4. DEFAULT. In the event Tenant defaults under any terms of this agreement, Landlord may recover possession as provided by law and seek monetary damages.

    5. SECURITY. Landlord acknowledges receipt of the sum of $_____ as security deposit. This deposit may not be used as last month's rent. Landlord may withhold from the security deposit amounts necessary to cover unpaid rent, damages to the premises and/or landlord's personal property caused by the Tenant beyond ordinary wear and tear and cleaning of the premises, if necessary.

    Within three weeks after Landlord retakes possession of the premises, Landlord shall furnish Tenant with a written statement itemizing the amounts withheld with explanation and returning any unused portion of the deposit to Tenant.

    6. UTILITIES. Tenant agrees to pay all utility charges on the property except: _____.

    7. MAINTENANCE. Tenant has examined the premises and has found them to be clean, safe, and in good repair and condition with the exception of the following:_____   _____ _____.

    Tenant agrees to return the premises to Landlord at the termination of the tenancy in the same clean, safe, good repair and condition, except for normal wear and tear.

8. LOCKS. If Tenant adds or changes locks on the premises, Landlord shall be given copies of the keys. Landlord shall at all times have keys for access to the premises in case of emergencies.

9. ASSIGNMENT AND SUBLETTING. Tenant may not sublet the premises nor any portion of the premises, nor may Tenant assign this agreement without written permission of Landlord.

10. USE. Tenant shall not use the premises for any illegal purpose or any purpose which will increase the rate of insurance, and shall not cause a nuisance for Landlord or neighbors. Tenant shall not create any environmental hazards on the premises.

11. LAWN (CHECK AND INITIAL). Tenant agrees to maintain the lawn and other landscaping on the premises at Tenant's expense. Yes _____ No _____ Initials _____

12. LIABILITY. Tenant shall be responsible for insurance on Tenant's own property and agrees not to hold Landlord liable for any damages to Tenant's property on the premises.

13. Landlord may enter the premises as allowed by Section 1954 of the California Civil Code. Refusal by the tenant to allow entry as permitted by the code will breach this contract and may result in eviction. The word "Landlord" includes owner(s), owner's agent(s), and employee(s).

14. PETS. No pets shall be allowed on the premises except: _____
_____.

15. WATERBEDS. No waterbeds or liquid-filled furniture shall be allowed on the premises without Landlord's written permission.

16. OCCUPANCY. The premises shall be occupied as a residence only, and shall be occupied only by the following persons: (List all occupants, both adults and minors) _____
_____.

17. TENANT'S APPLIANCES. Tenant agrees not to use any heaters, fixtures, or appliances drawing excessive current without consent of Landlord.

18. PARKING. Tenant agrees that no parking is allowed on the premises except: _____. No boats, recreation vehicles, or disassembled automobiles may be stored on the premises.

19. FURNISHINGS. Any articles provided to tenant and listed on attached schedule are to be returned in good condition at the termination of this agreement.

20. ALTERATIONS AND IMPROVEMENTS. Tenant shall make no alterations to the property without the written consent of Landlord and any such alterations or improvements shall become the property of Landlord.

21. SMOKE DETECTORS. Tenant shall be responsible for keeping smoke detectors operational and for changing batteries when needed.

22. LIENS. The estate of Landlord shall not be subject to any liens for improvements contracted by Tenant.

23. HARASSMENT. Tenant shall not do any acts to intentionally harass Landlord or other tenants.

24. ATTORNEY'S FEES. In the event of legal action, the prevailing party (shall) (shall not) recover reasonable attorney's fees in addition to any other recovery.

25. SEVERABILITY. In the event any section of this agreement shall be held to be invalid, all remaining provisions shall remain in full force and effect.

26. RECORDING. This agreement shall not be recorded in any public records.

27. WAIVER. Any failure by Landlord to exercise any rights under this agreement shall not constitute a waiver of Landlord's rights.

28. SUBORDINATION. Tenant's interest in the premises shall be subordinate to any encumbrances now or hereafter placed on the premises, to any advances made under such encumbrances, and to any extensions or renewals thereof. Tenant agrees to sign any documents indicating such subordination which may be required by lenders.

29. ATTACHMENTS: The following attachments are incorporated and made a part of this agreement. (Tenant should initial)

A. _____   B. _____

C. _____   D. _____

30. ENTIRE AGREEMENT. This rental agreement, including the above initialed attachments, constitutes the entire agreement between the parties and may not be modified except in writing signed by all parties.

31. OWNER OR MANAGER. The owner or manager for service of legal notices is: _____.

32. NOTICE: The California Department of Justice, sheriff's departments, police departments serving jurisdictions of 200,000 or more, and many other local law enforcement authorities maintain for public access a data base of the locations of persons required to register pursuant to paragraph (1) of subdivision (a) of Section 290.4 of the Penal Code. The data base is updated on a quarterly basis and is a source of information about the presence of these individuals in any neighborhood. The Department of Justice also maintains a Sex Offender Identification Line through which inquiries about individuals may be made. This is a "900" telephone service. Callers must have specific information about individuals they are checking. Information regarding neighborhoods is not available through the "900" telephone service.

WITNESS the hands and seals of the parties hereto as of this _____ day of _____, _____.

LANDLORD: TENANT:

_____   _____

_____   _____

This page intentionally left blank.

Condominium Rental Agreement

LANDLORD: _____ TENANT: _____

_____ _____

PROPERTY: _____

IN CONSIDERATION of the mutual covenants and agreements herein contained, Landlord hereby rents to Tenant and Tenant hereby rents from Landlord the above-described property under the following terms:

1. TERM. This Rental Agreement shall be for a month-to-month tenancy. Unless prohibited by law, this agreement may be terminated by either party or modified by Landlord upon service of 30 days' written notice. If tenant is in possession of the unit for one year or more, a sixty-day notice to vacate will be served by Landlord. Additional rent shall be charged on a daily basis if Tenant holds over, prorated as 1/30th of the monthly rent at that time, using a thirty-day month for proration.

2. RENT. The rent shall be $_____ per month and shall be due on or before the _____ day of each month. If rent is received more than three days late, a late charge of $_____ shall be paid.

3. PAYMENT. Payment must be received by Landlord on or before the due date at the following address: _____ or such place as designated by Landlord in writing. Tenant understands that this may require early mailing. If a check bounces, Tenant agrees to pay a late charge of $_____, and Landlord may require future payments in cash, money order, or certified funds. Tenant is hereby notified that default of financial obligations under this agreement may be reported to credit reporting companies and may result in derogatory information on Tenant's credit report. Payment in person may be made on ☐Monday ☐Tuesday ☐Wednesday ☐Thursday ☐Friday ☐Saturday ☐Sunday between the hours of _____(am) and _____(pm). Acceptable methods of payment are: ☐cash ☐personal check ☐cashier's check ☐money order ☐eft/credit (contact owner or agent to arrange).

4. DEFAULT. In the event Tenant defaults under any terms of this agreement, Landlord may recover possession as provided by law and seek monetary damages.

5. SECURITY. Landlord acknowledges receipt of the sum of $_____ as security deposit. This deposit may not be used as last month's rent. Landlord may withhold from the security deposit amounts necessary to cover unpaid rent, damages to the premises and/or landlord's personal property caused by the Tenant beyond ordinary wear and tear, and cleaning of the premises, if necessary.

Within three weeks after Landlord retakes possession of the premises, Landlord shall furnish Tenant with a written statement itemizing the amounts withheld with explanation and returning any unused portion of the deposit to Tenant.

6. UTILITIES. Tenant agrees to pay all utility charges on the property except: _____.

7. MAINTENANCE. Tenant has examined the premises and has found them to be clean, safe, and in good repair and condition with the exception of the following: _____.

Tenant agrees to return the premises to Landlord at the termination of the tenancy in the same clean, safe, good repair and condition, except for normal wear and tear.

8. LOCKS. If Tenant adds or changes locks on the premises, Landlord shall be given copies of the keys. Landlord shall at all times have keys for access to the premises in case of emergencies.

9. ASSIGNMENT AND SUBLETTING. Tenant may not sublet the premises nor any portion of the premises, nor may Tenant assign this agreement without written permission of Landlord.

10. COMMON INTEREST PROPERTY. Tenant acknowledges that the premises are subject to a Declaration of Covenants, Conditions, and Restrictions and Association Rules and Regulations. Copies of these documents are attached to and made part of this agreement. Tenant agrees to comply with the requirements of these documents and to reimburse Landlord for any fines or charges levied against Landlord for Tenant's failure to comply with these requirements.

11. USE. Tenant shall not use the premises for any illegal purpose or any purpose which will increase the rate of insurance, and shall not cause a nuisance for Landlord or neighbors. Tenant shall not create any environmental hazards on the premises.

12. LAWN. (CHECK AND INITIAL): Tenant agrees to maintain the lawn and other landscaping on the premises at Tenant's expense. Yes ____ No ____ Initials _____

13. LIABILITY. Tenant shall be responsible for insurance on Tenant's own property and agrees not to hold Landlord liable for any damages to Tenant's property on the premises.

14. ACCESS. Landlord may enter the premises as allowed by Section 1954 of the California Civil Code. Refusal by the tenant to allow entry as permitted by the code will breach this contract and may result in eviction. The word "Landlord" includes owner(s), owner's agent(s), and employee(s).

15. PETS. No pets shall be allowed on the premise except: _____
_____.

16. WATERBEDS. No waterbeds or liquid-filled furniture shall be allowed on the premises without Landlord's written permission.

17. OCCUPANCY. The premises shall be occupied as a residence only, and shall be occupied only by the following persons: (List all occupants, both adults and minors)_____
_____.

18. TENANT'S APPLIANCES. Tenant agrees not to use any heaters, fixtures, or appliances drawing excessive current without consent of Landlord.

19. PARKING. Tenant agrees that no parking is allowed on the premises except: _____. No boats, recreation vehicles, or disassembled automobiles may be stored on the premises.

20. FURNISHINGS. Any articles provided to Tenant and listed on attached schedule are to be returned in good condition at the termination of this agreement.

21. ALTERATIONS AND IMPROVEMENTS. Tenant shall make no alterations to the property without the written consent of Landlord and any such alterations or improvements shall become the property of Landlord.

22. SMOKE DETECTORS. Tenant shall be responsible for keeping smoke detectors operational and for changing batteries when needed.

23. LIENS. The estate of Landlord shall not be subject to any liens for improvements contracted by Tenant.

24. HARASSMENT. Tenant shall not do any acts to intentionally harass Landlord or other tenants.

25. ATTORNEY'S FEES. In the event of legal action, the prevailing party (shall) (shall not) recover reasonable attorney's fees in addition to any other recovery.

Amendment to Lease/Rental Agreement

The undersigned parties to that certain agreement dated _____, _____
on the premises known as _____,
hereby agree to amend said agreement as follows:

WITNESS the hands and seals of the parties hereto this _____ day of _____, _____.

LANDLORD: TENANT:

_____   _____

_____   _____

This page intentionally left blank.

Guarantee of Lease/Rental Agreement

The undersigned Guarantor(s), in consideration of the Lease or Rental Agreement between _____ as Landlord and _____ as Tenant, dated _____, _____, and other good and valuable consideration, receipt whereof is hereby acknowledged, does/do hereby guarantee to Landlord and his/her/its successors and assigns, the faithful performance of the Lease or Rental Agreement and all sums due thereunder.

In the event of breach by Tenant of any of the terms of said Lease or Rental Agreement, including damage to the premises and attorney's fees paid in enforcement of said agreement, Guarantor(s) shall be liable, and Landlord and his/her/its successors and assigns may have recourse against Guarantor(s) without first taking action against Tenant.

It is understood between the parties that this Guarantee does not confer any right to possession of the premises, or to require any notices to be served upon Guarantor(s), but only serves as an inducement for Landlord to enter into a Lease or Rental Agreement with Tenant.

This Guarantee shall remain in effect until Tenant has fully complied with the Lease or Rental Agreement or until released in writing by Landlord or his/her/its successors or assigns.

Date: _____, _____.

Guarantor(s):

_____

_____

This page intentionally left blank.

Disclosure of Information on Lead-Based Paint and/or Lead-Based Paint Hazards

Lead Warning Statement

Housing built before 1978 may contain lead-based paint. Lead from paint, paint chips, and dust can pose health hazards if not managed properly. Lead exposure is especially harmful to young children and pregnant women. Before renting pre-1978 housing, lessors must disclose the presence of known lead-based paint and/or lead-based paint hazards in the dwelling. Lessees must also receive a federally approved pamphlet on lead poisoning prevention.

Lessor's Disclosure

(a) Presence of lead-based paint and/or lead-based paint hazards (check (i) or (ii) below):

    (i) _____ Known lead-based paint and/or lead-based paint hazards are present in the housing (explain).

    _____

    _____

    (ii) _____ Lessor has no knowledge of lead-based paint and/or lead-based paint hazards in the housing.

(b) Records and reports available to the lessor (check (i) or (ii) below):

    (i) _____ Lessor has provided the lessee with all available records and reports pertaining to lead-based paint and/or lead-based paint hazards in the housing (list documents below).

    _____

    _____

    (ii) _____ Lessor has no reports or records pertaining to lead-based paint and/or lead-based paint hazards in the housing.

Lessee's Acknowledgment (initial)

(c) _____ Lessee has received copies of all information listed above.

(d) _____ Lessee has received the pamphlet *Protect Your Family from Lead in Your Home.*

Agent's Acknowledgment (initial)

(e) _____ Agent has informed the lessor of the lessor's obligations under 42 U.S.C. 4852(d) and is aware of his/her responsibility to ensure compliance.

Certification of Accuracy

The following parties have reviewed the information above and certify, to the best of their knowledge, that the information they have provided is true and accurate.

Lessor	Date	Lessor	Date
Lessee	Date	Lessee	Date
Agent	Date	Agent	Date

This page intentionally left blank.

California Landlord Disclosures

Date: _____

To: _____

    The undersigned owner(s) of the property located at _____
_____ make the following
disclosures regarding this property:

1. The property ☐ is ☐ is not within one mile of a former military base where ammunition or explosives were kept.

2.   ☐ Your electric bill only includes electricity used in your unit.

    ☐ You electric bill includes electricity used outside your unit as follows: _____
_____.

    ☐ The owner has received or applied for a permit to demolish all or a portion of the premises.

3. Other _____
_____
_____
_____
_____
_____
_____

_____   _____
Owner   date   Owner   date

The undersigned tenant(s) acknowledge receipt and understanding of the above disclosures.

_____   _____
Tenant   date   Tenant   date

This page intentionally left blank.

Notice to Enter

Date: _____

To: _____

It will be necessary to enter your dwelling unit on (Date) _____
(Approximate Time) _____ or during normal business hours for the
following purpose(s).

1. _____

2. _____

3. _____

4. _____

5. _____

_____
Owner/Agent

_____
Address

_____
Phone

Proof of Service

I, the undersigned, being at least 18 years of age, served this notice, of which this is a true copy,
on _____, the person(s) named above. The
notice was served by:

☐   Mailing by U.S. mail a copy of the notice to each resident with proper postage and
      address to their place of residence.
☐   Personal delivery of a copy to the above named person(s).
☐   Delivery of a copy for each of the above named to a person of suitable age and discretion
      at the above named person(s)' residence/business after attempting to personally serve
      the above named person(s) at his/her/their residence and place of business (if known)
      and mailing by first-class mail a second copy to his/her/their residence.
☐   Posting a copy for each of the above named person(s) in a conspicuous place on the
      above identified property, being unable to personally serve a person of suitable age or
      discretion at the residence or known place(s) of business of the above named person(s)
      and mailing on the same date by first-class mail a second copy to each above named
      person(s) to the address of the above identified property.

I declare under penalty of perjury that the foregoing is true and correct and could testify
competently if called as a witness.

Name _____   Date _____

This page intentionally left blank.

Statement for Repairs

Date: _____

To: _____

It has been necessary to repair damage to the premises which you occupy which was caused by you or your guests. The costs for repairs were as follows:

This amount is your responsibility under the terms of the lease and California law and should be forwarded to us at the address below.

Sincerely,

_____

Name

Address:

Phone:

Proof of Service

I, the undersigned, being at least 18 years of age, served this notice, of which this is a true copy, on _____, the person(s) named above. The notice was served by:

☐   Personal delivery of a copy to the above named person(s).

☐   Delivery of a copy for each of the above named to a person of suitable age and discretion at the above named person(s)' residence/business after attempting to personally serve the above named person(s) at his/her/their residence and place of business (if known) and mailing by first-class mail a second copy to his/her/their residence.

☐   Posting a copy for each of the above named person(s) in a conspicuous place on the above identified property, being unable to personally serve a person of suitable age or discretion at the residence or known place(s) of business of the above named person(s) and mailing on the same date by first-class mail a second copy to each above named person(s) to the address of the above identified property.

I declare under penalty of perjury that the foregoing is true and correct and could testify competently if called as a witness.

Name _____   Date _____

This page intentionally left blank.

Notice of Change of Terms
Civil Code Section 827

Date: _____

To: _____

Dear _____:

You are hereby notified that effective _____, _____, the terms of your rental agreement will be changed as follows:

☐ Rent: From $_____ per _____ To: $_____ per _____.

☐ Other Changes:

Sincerely,

_____

Name

Address:

Phone:

Proof of Service

I, the undersigned, being at least 18 years of age, served this notice, of which this is a true copy, on _____, the person(s) named above. The notice was served by:

☐   Mailing by U.S. mail a copy of the notice to each resident with proper postage and address to their place of residence.

☐   Personal delivery of a copy to the above named person(s).

☐   Delivery of a copy for each of the above named to a person of suitable age and discretion at the above named person(s)' residence/business after attempting to personally serve the above named person(s) at his/her/their residence and place of business (if known) and mailing by first-class mail a second copy to his/her/their residence.

☐   Posting a copy for each of the above named person(s) in a conspicuous place on the above identified property, being unable to personally serve a person of suitable age or discretion at the residence or known place(s) of business of the above named person(s) and mailing on the same date by first-class mail a second copy to each above named person(s) to the address of the above identified property.

I declare under penalty of perjury that the foregoing is true and correct and could testify competently if called as a witness.

Name _____   Date _____

This page intentionally left blank.

Letter to Vacating Tenant

Date: _____

To: _____

Dear _____:

     This letter is to remind you that your lease will expire on _____, _____.
Please be advised that we do not intend to renew or extend the lease.

     The keys should be delivered to us at the address below on or before the end of the lease along with your forwarding address. You have the right to request an initial inspection of your residence. The form for this request is attached hereto and made a part hereof. Please fill out this form and return it to the owner or agent.

Sincerely,

_____
Name

Address:

Phone:

Proof of Service

I, the undersigned, being at least 18 years of age, served this notice, of which this is a true copy, on _____, the person(s) named above. The notice was served by:

❑   Personal delivery of a copy to the above named person(s).

❑   Delivery of a copy for each of the above named to a person of suitable age and discretion at the above named person(s)' residence/business after attempting to personally serve the above named person(s) at his/her/their residence and place of business (if known) and mailing by first-class mail a second copy to his/her/their residence.

❑   Posting a copy for each of the above named person(s) in a conspicuous place on the above identified property, being unable to personally serve a person of suitable age or discretion at the residence or known place(s) of business of the above named person(s) and mailing on the same date by first-class mail a second copy to each above named person(s) to the address of the above identified property.

I declare under penalty of perjury that the foregoing is true and correct and could testify competently if called as a witness.

Name _____   Date _____

This page intentionally left blank.

Annual Letter—Continuation of Tenancy

Date: _____

To: _____

Dear _____:

This letter is to remind you that your lease will expire on _____.
Please advise us within _____ days as to whether you intend to renew your lease.
If so, we will prepare a new lease for your signature(s).

If you do not intend to renew your lease, the keys should be delivered to us at the address below on or before the end of the lease along with your forwarding address. You have the right to request an initial inspection of your residence. The form for this request is attached hereto and made a part hereof. Please fill out this form and return it to the owner or agent.

If we have not heard from you as specified above we will assume that you will be vacating the premises and will arrange for a new tenant to move in at the end of your term.

Sincerely,

_____
Name

Address:

Phone:

Proof of Service

I, the undersigned, being at least 18 years of age, served this notice, of which this is a true copy, on _____, the person(s) named above. The notice was served by:

- ❏ Personal delivery of a copy to the above named person(s).
- ❏ Delivery of a copy for each of the above named to a person of suitable age and discretion at the above named person(s)' residence/business after attempting to personally serve the above named person(s) at his/her/their residence and place of business (if known) and mailing by first-class mail a second copy to his/her/their residence.
- ❏ Posting a copy for each of the above named person(s) in a conspicuous place on the above identified property, being unable to personally serve a person of suitable age or discretion at the residence or known place(s) of business of the above named person(s) and mailing on the same date by first-class mail a second copy to each above named person(s) to the address of the above identified property.

I declare under penalty of perjury that the foregoing is true and correct and could testify competently if called as a witness.

Name _____   Date _____

This page intentionally left blank.

Notice of Termination of Agent

Date: _____

To: _____

    You are hereby advised that _____
is no longer our agent effective _____, _____. On and after this date
he or she is no longer authorized to collect rent, accept notices, or to make any representations
or agreements regarding the property.

    Rent should thereafter be paid to us directly at _____
_____.

If you have any questions, you may contact us at the address or phone number below.

                                      Sincerely,

                                   _____

                                   Name

                                   Address:

                                   Phone:

This page intentionally left blank.

Notice of Appointment of Agent

Date: _____

To: _____

     You are hereby advised that effective _____, _____, our agent for collection of rent and other matters regarding the property will be_____
_____.

Rent should be paid at:

_____

_____

_____

However, no terms of the written lease may be modified or waived without our written signature(s).

     If you have any questions, you may contact us at the address or phone number below.

                        Sincerely,

                        _____

                        Name

                        Address:

                        Phone:

This page intentionally left blank.

Notice of Dishonored Check and Demand for Payment

Date: _____

To: _____

You are advised that your check number _____, dated _____, _____ in the amount of _____ dollars ($_____) was returned unpaid.

Unless this check is paid within thirty (30) days you may be liable for the amount of the check plus triple the amount of the check in damages, but in no case less that one hundred dollars ($100) or more than one thousand, five hundred dollars ($1,500).

Additionally, a report of your failure to pay this debt be made to a credit reporting agency. The applicable part of California Civil Code Section 1719 is as follows:

1719. (a) (1) Notwithstanding any penal sanctions that may apply, any person who passes a check on insufficient funds shall be liable to the payee for the amount of the check and a service charge payable to the payee for an amount not to exceed twenty-five dollars ($25) for the first check passed on insufficient funds and an amount not to exceed thirty-five dollars ($35) for each subsequent check to that payee passed on insufficient funds.

(2) Notwithstanding any penal sanctions that may apply, any person who passes a check on insufficient funds shall be liable to the payee for damages equal to treble the amount of the check if a written demand for payment is mailed by certified mail to the person who had passed a check on insufficient funds and the written demand informs this person of (A) the provisions of this section, (B) the amount of the check, and (C) the amount of the service charge payable to the payee. The person who had passed a check on insufficient funds shall have 30 days from the date the written demand was mailed to pay the amount of the check, the amount of the service charge payable to the payee, and the costs to mail the written demand for payment. If this person fails to pay in full the amount of the check, the service charge payable to the payee, and the costs to mail the written demand within this period, this person shall then be liable instead for the amount of the check, minus any partial payments made toward the amount of the check or the service charge within 30 days of the written demand, and damages equal to treble that amount, which shall not be less than one hundred dollars ($100) nor more than one thousand five hundred dollars ($1,500). When a person becomes liable for treble damages for a check that is the subject of a written demand, that person shall no longer be liable for any service charge for that check and any costs to mail the written demand.

_____

Payee

Address:

Phone:

This page intentionally left blank.

Itemized Security Deposit Disposition
(CIVIL CODE SECTION 1950.5)

Date: _____

To: _____

_____

_____

Property Address: _____

Amount held as security: $_____

Interest: $_____

Total: $_____

DEDUCTIONS

1. Unpaid Rent: $_____ for (Dates) _____

_____

2. Repairs: $_____ for (Explanation) _____

_____

3. Cleaning: $_____ for (Explanation) _____

_____

4. Judgment: $_____ for (Explanation) _____

_____

Total Deductions: $_____

Amount owed by Tenant $_____

Amount owed to Tenant $_____

Further comments or explanations: _____

_____

_____

From: _____

_____

_____

Phone: _____

This page intentionally left blank.

Three-Day Notice to Pay Rent or Quit

To: _____

Tenants' and Subtenants' Full Names and Names of all Other Residents

_____

Address   Unit #

_____

City, State, Zip Code

From: _____

Date: _____

You are hereby notified that you are indebted to me in the sum of $_____
for past due rent for occupancy of the premises located at the above address.

From _____ through _____ $_____

From _____ through _____ $_____

From _____ through _____ $_____

You are required to pay this amount on or before _____ at the address below
or quit and deliver possession of the premises.   (Date)

Payment in person may be made on ☐Monday ☐Tuesday ☐Wednesday ☐Thursday ☐Friday
☐Saturday ☐Sunday between the hours of _____(am) and _____ (pm).

Failure to comply will result in forfeiture of your lease/rental agreement and a lawsuit against you
for Unlawful Detainer. A judgment may result, which may include attorney's fees and court costs,
as well as possible punitive damages of $600. This may also result in a negative credit history.
This notice supercedes any and all previous Three-day Notices to Pay Rent or Quit.

_____

Signature

_____

Owner/Agent

_____

Address

_____

City, State, Zip Code

_____

Phone Number

Proof of Service

I, the undersigned, being at least 18 years of age, served this notice, of which this is a true copy, on _____, the person(s) named above. The notice was served by:

- ☐ Personal delivery of a copy to the above named person(s).
- ☐ Delivery of a copy for each of the above named to a person of suitable age and discretion at the above named person(s)' residence/business after attempting to personally serve the above named person(s) at his/her/their residence and place of business (if known) and mailing by first-class mail a second copy to his/her/their residence.
- ☐ Posting a copy for each of the above named person(s) in a conspicuous place on the above identified property, being unable to personally serve a person of suitable age or discretion at the residence or known place(s) of business of the above named person(s) and mailing on the same date by first-class mail a second copy to each above named person(s) to the address of the above identified property.

I clare under penalty of perjury that the foregoing is true and correct and could testify co etently if called as a witness.

Nar _____   Date _____

Three-Day Notice to Comply or Quit

To: _____

Tenants' and Subtenants' Full Names and Names of all Other Residents

_____

Address   Unit #

_____

City, State, Zip Code

From: _____

Date: _____

You are hereby notified that you are not complying with your lease/rental agreement. The specific covenants or conditions violated are:

_____
_____
_____
_____
_____

You have breached the above covenants or conditions as follows (specific facts):

_____
_____
_____
_____
_____

A copy of your lease/rental agreement is attached.

Demand is hereby made that you comply within three days of service of this notice or quit and deliver up the premises.

Failure to comply will result in forfeiture of your lease/rental agreement and a lawsuit against you for Unlawful Detainer. A judgment may result which may include attorney's fees and court costs, as well as possible punitive damages of $600. This may also result in a negative credit history. This notice supercedes any and all previous Three-Day Notices to Comply or Quit.

_____

Signature

Owner/Agent _____

Address _____

_____

Phone Number _____

Proof of Service

I, the undersigned, being at least 18 years of age, served this notice, of which this is a true copy, on _____, the person(s) named above. The notice was served by:

Personal delivery of a copy to the above named person(s).

Delivery of a copy for each of the above named to a person of suitable age and discretion at the above named person(s)' residence/business after attempting to personally serve the above named person(s) at his/her/their residence and place of business (if known) and mailing by first-class mail a second copy to his/her/their residence.

Posting a copy for each of the above named person(s) in a conspicuous place on the above identified property, being unable to personally serve a person of suitable age or discretion at the residence or known place(s) of business of the above named person(s) and mailing on the same date by first-class mail a second copy to each above named person(s) to the address of the above identified property.

I declare under penalty of perjury that the foregoing is true and correct and could testify competently if called as a witness.

Name _____   Date _____

Three-Day Notice to Quit For Breach of Covenant(s) or Condition(s)

To: _____

Tenants' and Subtenants' Full Names and Names of all Other Residents

_____
Address   Unit #

_____
City, State, Zip Code

From: _____

Date: _____

The covenants or conditions breached are:

_____
_____
_____
_____
_____
_____
_____

You have breached the above covenants or conditions as follows (specific facts):

_____
_____
_____
_____
_____
_____
_____

A copy of your lease/rental agreement is attached.

_____
Signature

Owner/Agent _____

Address _____

_____

Phone Number _____

242

Proof of Service

I, the undersigned, being at least 18 years of age, served this notice, of which this is a true copy, on _____, the person(s) named above. The notice was served by:

☐   Personal delivery of a copy to the above named person(s).

☐   Delivery of a copy for each of the above named to a person of suitable age and discretion at the above named person(s)' residence/business after attempting to personally serve the above named person(s) at his/her/their residence and place of business (if known) and mailing by first-class mail a second copy to his/her/their residence.

☐   Posting a copy for each of the above named person(s) in a conspicuous place on the above identified property, being unable to personally serve a person of suitable age or discretion at the residence or known place(s) of business of the above named person(s) and mailing on the same date by first-class mail a second copy to each above named person(s) to the address of the above identified property.

I declare under penalty of perjury that the foregoing is true and correct and could testify competently if called as a witness.

Name _____   Date _____

Thirty-Day Notice of Termination of Tenancy

To: _____
(Full names of tenants, subtenants, and all others in possession)

Rental Property: _____ Unit _____
(Street address, City, County, Zip)

You are notified that your tenancy of the above property is terminated effective 30 days from service of this notice or _____, _____,
(Date)
whichever is later. At that time you must surrender possession of the premises. If you do not, an action for unlawful detainer will be filed. This may result in eviction as well as a judgment against you for payment of court costs.

You are obligated to continue to pay rent on the property until the date of termination.

You have the right to request an initial inspection of your residence. The form for this request is attached hereto and made a part of. Please fill out this form and return it to the owner or agent.

_____
Date

_____
Landlord/Agent

Proof of Service

I, the undersigned, being at least 18 years of age, served this notice, of which this is a true copy, on _____, the person(s) named above. The notice was served by:

☐   Personal delivery of a copy to the above named person(s).

☐   Delivery of a copy for each of the above named to a person of suitable age and discretion at the above named person(s)' residence/business after attempting to personally serve the above named person(s) at his/her/their residence and place of business (if known) and mailing by first-class mail a second copy to his/her/their residence.

☐   Posting a copy for each of the above named person(s) in a conspicuous place on the above identified property, being unable to personally serve a person of suitable age or discretion at the residence or known place(s) of business of the above named person(s) and mailing on the same date by first-class mail a second copy to each above named person(s) to the address of the above identified property.

I declare under penalty of perjury that the foregoing is true and correct and could testify competently if called as a witness.

Name _____   Date _____

This page intentionally left blank.

Notice of Belief of Abandonment

To: _____

(Name of lessee/tenant)

_____

(Address of lessee/tenant)

This notice is given pursuant to Section 1951.3 of the Civil Code concerning the real property leased by you at _____ (state location of the property by address or other sufficient description). The rent on this property has been due and unpaid for 14 consecutive days and the lessor/landlord believes that you have abandoned the property.

The real property will be deemed abandoned within the meaning of Section 1951.2 of the Civil Code and your lease will terminate on _____, _____ (here insert a date not less than 15 days after this notice is served personally or, if mailed, not less than 18 days after this notice is deposited in the mail) unless before such date the undersigned receives at the address indicated below a written notice from you stating both of the following:

(1)   Your intent not to abandon the real property.

(2)   An address at which you may be served by certified mail in any action for unlawful detainer of the real property.

You are required to pay the rent due and unpaid on this real property as required by the lease, and your failure to do so can lead to a court proceeding against you.

Dated: _____

_____

(Signature of lessor/landlord)

_____

(Type or print name of lessor/landlord)

_____

(Address to which lessee/tenant is to send notice)

Proof of Service

I, the undersigned, being at least 18 years of age, served this notice, of which this is a true copy, on _____, the person(s) named above. The notice was served by:

☐   Personal delivery of a copy to the above named person(s).

☐   Delivery of a copy for each of the above named to a person of suitable age and discretion at the above named person(s)' residence/business after attempting to personally serve the above named person(s) at his/her/their residence and place of business (if known) and mailing by first-class mail a second copy to his/her/their residence.

☐   Posting a copy for each of the above named person(s) in a conspicuous place on the above identified property, being unable to personally serve a person of suitable age or discretion at the residence or known place(s) of business of the above named person(s) and mailing on the same date by first-class mail a second copy to each above named person(s) to the address of the above identified property.

I declare under penalty of perjury that the foregoing is true and correct and could testify competently if called as a witness.

Name _____   Date _____

Notice to Resident for Request of Initial Inspection of Your Rental Unit

You have the right to request an initial inspection of your residence. The purpose of this inspection is to allow you to repair any damage or do any cleaning necessary in order to avoid deductions from your security deposit.

No repairs may be made which are not permitted in your lease or rental agreement.

After the inspection, you will receive an itemized statement of any repairs and/or cleaning that would cause a deduction from your security deposit. This is not a final statement.

You will receive a final itemized statement within 21 days after you vacate the premises, showing any deductions from your security deposit and the reasons for any such deductions.

If you request an initial inspection, it will be conducted within two weeks of the termination of your lease or rental agreement.

You have the right to a 48-hour notice before the inspection but may waive this right.

You may choose to be present at the inspection but are not required to be present.

Please return this form to the owner/agent at: _____

Address

_____

Owner/Agent

_____

Date

Please check the appropriate box or boxes below.

☐   I do not want an initial inspection.
☐   I want an initial inspection and will be present.
☐   I want an initial inspection but will not be present.

My phone number to arrange a time for the inspection is _____.
The best time to reach me is between _____ and _____.

☐   I waive my right to a 48-hour notice before the initial inspection.
☐   I require a 48-hour notice before the initial inspection.

_____   _____

       Date   Resident

_____   _____

       Date   Resident

Proof of Service

I, the undersigned, being at least 18 years of age, declare that I served this notice, of which this is a true copy, on the _____ day of _____, 20_____, in the city of _____, California, as follows:

☐ I personally delivered the notice to the resident or person of suitable age and discretion at the premises or resident's place of business at least 24 or 48 hours, as required, before the intended entry.

☐ I left a copy of the notice at or near or under the usual entry door of the premises at least 24 or 48 hours, as required, before the intended entry.

☐ I mailed a copy of the notice with proper postage and address to the resident at least 6 days prior to the intended entry.

I declare under penalty of perjury that the foregoing is true and correct and could testify competently if called as a witness.

_____
Signature of Declarant

CM-01

ATTORNEY OR PARTY WITHOUT ATTORNEY *(Name, State Bar number, and address):*	*FOR COURT USE ONLY*
TELEPHONE NO.: FAX NO.:	
ATTORNEY FOR *(Name):*	

SUPERIOR COURT OF CALIFORNIA, COUNTY OF
STREET ADDRESS:
MAILING ADDRESS:
CITY AND ZIP CODE:
BRANCH NAME:

CASE NAME:

CIVIL CASE COVER SHEET ☐ **Unlimited** ☐ **Limited** (Amount (Amount demanded demanded is exceeds $25,000) $25,000 or less)	**Complex Case Designation** ☐ **Counter** ☐ **Joinder** Filed with first appearance by defendant (Cal. Rules of Court, rule 1811)	CASE NUMBER: JUDGE: DEPT:

Items 1–5 below must be completed (see instructions on page 2).

1. Check **one** box below for the case type that best describes this case:

Auto Tort
☐ Auto (22)
☐ Uninsured motorist (46)
Other PI/PD/WD (Personal Injury/Property Damage/Wrongful Death) Tort
☐ Asbestos (04)
☐ Product liability (24)
☐ Medical malpractice (45)
☐ Other PI/PD/WD (23)
Non-PI/PD/WD (Other) Tort
☐ Business tort/unfair business practice (07)
☐ Civil rights (08)
☐ Defamation (13)
☐ Fraud (16)
☐ Intellectual property (19)
☐ Professional negligence (25)
☐ Other non-PI/PD/WD tort (35)
Employment
☐ Wrongful termination (36)
☐ Other employment (15)

Contract
☐ Breach of contract/warranty (06)
☐ Collections (09)
☐ Insurance coverage (18)
☐ Other contract (37)
Real Property
☐ Eminent domain/Inverse condemnation (14)
☐ Wrongful eviction (33)
☐ Other real property (26)
Unlawful Detainer
☐ Commercial (31)
☐ Residential (32)
☐ Drugs (38)
Judicial Review
☐ Asset forfeiture (05)
☐ Petition re: arbitration award (11)
☐ Writ of mandate (02)
☐ Other judicial review (39)

Provisionally Complex Civil Litigation (Cal. Rules of Court, rules 1800–1812)
☐ Antitrust/Trade regulation (03)
☐ Construction defect (10)
☐ Mass tort (40)
☐ Securities litigation (28)
☐ Environmental/Toxic tort (30)
☐ Insurance coverage claims arising from the above listed provisionally complex case types (41)
Enforcement of Judgment
☐ Enforcement of judgment (20)
Miscellaneous Civil Complaint
☐ RICO (27)
☐ Other complaint (not specified above) (42)
Miscellaneous Civil Petition
☐ Partnership and corporate governance (21)
☐ Other petition (not specified above) (43)

2. This case ☐ is ☐ is not complex under rule 1800 of the California Rules of Court. If the case is complex, mark the factors requiring exceptional judicial management:
   a. ☐ Large number of separately represented parties   d. ☐ Large number of witnesses
   b. ☐ Extensive motion practice raising difficult or novel issues that will be time-consuming to resolve   e. ☐ Coordination with related actions pending in one or more courts in other counties, states, or countries, or in a federal court
   c. ☐ Substantial amount of documentary evidence   f. ☐ Substantial postjudgment judicial supervision
3. Type of remedies sought *(check all that apply):*
   a. ☐ monetary   b. ☐ nonmonetary; declaratory or injunctive relief   c. ☐ punitive
4. Number of causes of action *(specify):*
5. This case ☐ is ☐ is not a class action suit.
6. If there are any known related cases, file and serve a notice of related case. *(You may use form CM-015.)*
Date: ▶

_____   _____
(TYPE OR PRINT NAME)   (SIGNATURE OF PARTY OR ATTORNEY FOR PARTY)

NOTICE
- Plaintiff must file this cover sheet with the first paper filed in the action or proceeding (except small claims cases or cases filed under the Probate Code, Family Code, or Welfare and Institutions Code). (Cal. Rules of Court, rule 201.8.) Failure to file may result in sanctions.
- File this cover sheet in addition to any cover sheet required by local court rule.
- If this case is complex under rule 1800 et seq. of the California Rules of Court, you must serve a copy of this cover sheet on **all** other parties to the action or proceeding.
- Unless this is a complex case, this cover sheet will be used for statistical purposes only.

Page 1 of 2

INSTRUCTIONS ON HOW TO COMPLETE THE COVER SHEET

To Plaintiffs and Others Filing First Papers

If you are filing a first paper (for example, a complaint) in a civil case, you **must** complete and file, along with your first paper, the *Civil Case Cover Sheet* contained on page 1. This information will be used to compile statistics about the types and numbers of cases filed. You must complete items 1 through 5 on the sheet. In item 1, you must check **one** box for the case type that best describes the case. If the case fits both a general and a more specific type of case listed in item 1, check the more specific one. If the case has multiple causes of action, check the box that best indicates the **primary** cause of action. To assist you in completing the sheet, examples of the cases that belong under each case type in item 1 are provided below. A cover sheet must be filed only with your initial paper. You do not need to submit a cover sheet with amended papers. Failure to file a cover sheet with the first paper filed in a civil case may subject a party, its counsel, or both to sanctions under rules 201.8(c) and 227 of the California Rules of Court.

To Parties in Complex Cases

In complex cases only, parties must also use the *Civil Case Cover Sheet* to designate whether the case is complex. If a plaintiff believes the case is complex under rule 1800 of the California Rules of Court, this must be indicated by completing the appropriate boxes in items 1 and 2. If a plaintiff designates a case as complex, the cover sheet must be served with the complaint on all parties to the action. A defendant may file and serve no later than the time of its first appearance a joinder in the plaintiff's designation, a counter-designation that the case is not complex, or, if the plaintiff has made no designation, a designation that the case is complex.

CASE TYPES AND EXAMPLES

Auto Tort
Auto (22)–Personal Injury/Property
    Damage/Wrongful Death
Uninsured Motorist (46) *(if the
    case involves an uninsured
    motorist claim subject to
    arbitration, check this item
    instead of Auto)*

**Other PI/PD/WD (Personal Injury/
Property Damage/Wrongful Death)
Tort**
Asbestos (04)
    Asbestos Property Damage
    Asbestos Personal Injury/
        Wrongful Death
Product Liability *(not asbestos or
    toxic/environmental)* (24)
Medical Malpractice (45)
    Medical Malpractice–
        Physicians & Surgeons
    Other Professional Health Care
        Malpractice
Other PI/PD/WD (23)
    Premises Liability (e.g., slip
        and fall)
    Intentional Bodily Injury/PD/WD
        (e.g., assault, vandalism)
    Intentional Infliction of
        Emotional Distress
    Negligent Infliction of
        Emotional Distress
    Other PI/PD/WD

Non-PI/PD/WD (Other) Tort
Business Tort/Unfair Business
    Practice (07)
Civil Rights (e.g., discrimination,
    false arrest) *(not civil
    harassment)* (08)
Defamation (e.g., slander, libel)
    (13)
Fraud (16)
Intellectual Property (19)
Professional Negligence (25)
    Legal Malpractice
    Other Professional Malpractice
        (not medical or legal)
Other Non-PI/PD/WD Tort (35)

Employment
Wrongful Termination (36)
Other Employment (15)

Contract
Breach of Contract/Warranty (06)
    Breach of Rental/Lease
        Contract *(not unlawful detainer
        or wrongful eviction)*
    Contract/Warranty Breach–Seller
        Plaintiff *(not fraud or negligence)*
    Negligent Breach of Contract/
        Warranty
    Other Breach of Contract/Warranty
Collections (e.g., money owed, open
    book accounts) (09)
    Collection Case–Seller Plaintiff
    Other Promissory Note/Collections
        Case
Insurance Coverage *(not provisionally
    complex)* (18)
    Auto Subrogation
    Other Coverage
Other Contract (37)
    Contractual Fraud
    Other Contract Dispute

Real Property
Eminent Domain/Inverse
    Condemnation (14)
Wrongful Eviction (33)
Other Real Property (e.g., quiet title) (26)
    Writ of Possession of Real Property
    Mortgage Foreclosure
    Quiet Title
    Other Real Property *(not eminent
        domain, landlord/tenant, or
        foreclosure)*

Unlawful Detainer
Commercial (31)
Residential (32)
Drugs (38) *(if the case involves illegal
    drugs, check this item; otherwise,
    report as Commercial or
    Residential)*

Judicial Review
Asset Forfeiture (05)
Petition Re: Arbitration Award (11)
Writ of Mandate (02)
    Writ–Administrative Mandamus
    Writ–Mandamus on Limited Court
        Case Matter
    Writ–Other Limited Court Case
        Review
Other Judicial Review (39)
    Review of Health Officer Order
    Notice of Appeal–Labor
        Commissioner Appeals

**Provisionally Complex Civil Litigation
(Cal. Rules of Court Rules 1800–1812)**
Antitrust/Trade Regulation (03)
Construction Defect (10)
Claims Involving Mass Tort (40)
Securities Litigation (28)
Environmental/Toxic Tort (30)
Insurance Coverage Claims
    *(arising from provisionally
    complex case type listed above)*
    (41)

Enforcement of Judgment
Enforcement of Judgment (20)
    Abstract of Judgment (Out of
        County)
    Confession of Judgment *(non-
        domestic relations)*
    Sister State Judgment
    Administrative Agency Award
        (not unpaid taxes)
    Petition/Certification of Entry of
        Judgment on Unpaid Taxes
    Other Enforcement of Judgment
        Case

Miscellaneous Civil Complaint
RICO (27)
Other Complaint *(not specified
    above)* (42)
    Declaratory Relief Only
    Injunctive Relief Only *(non-
        harassment)*
    Mechanics Lien
    Other Commercial Complaint
        Case *(non-tort/non-complex)*
    Other Civil Complaint
        (non-tort/non-complex)

Miscellaneous Civil Petition
Partnership and Corporate
    Governance (21)
Other Petition *(not specified above)*
    (43)
    Civil Harassment
    Workplace Violence
    Elder/Dependent Adult
        Abuse
    Election Contest
    Petition for Name Change
    Petition for Relief from Late
        Claim
    Other Civil Petition

CIVIL CASE COVER SHEET

UD-100

ATTORNEY OR PARTY WITHOUT ATTORNEY *(Name, State Bar number, and address):*	*FOR COURT USE ONLY*
TELEPHONE NO.: FAX NO. *(Optional):*	
E-MAIL ADDRESS *(Optional):*	
ATTORNEY FOR *(Name):*	

SUPERIOR COURT OF CALIFORNIA, COUNTY OF
   STREET ADDRESS:
   MAILING ADDRESS:
   CITY AND ZIP CODE:
   BRANCH NAME:

PLAINTIFF:

DEFENDANT:

☐ DOES 1 TO _____

COMPLAINT — UNLAWFUL DETAINER* ☐ **COMPLAINT** ☐ **AMENDED COMPLAINT** *(Amendment Number):* _____	CASE NUMBER:

Jurisdiction *(check all that apply):*
☐ **ACTION IS A LIMITED CIVIL CASE**
  Amount demanded ☐ **does not exceed $10,000**
              ☐ **exceeds $10,000 but does not exceed $25,000**
☐ **ACTION IS AN UNLIMITED CIVIL CASE (amount demanded exceeds $25,000)**
☐ **ACTION IS RECLASSIFIED by this amended complaint or cross-complaint** *(check all that apply):*
  ☐ from unlawful detainer to general unlimited civil (possession not in issue) ☐ from limited to unlimited
  ☐ from unlawful detainer to general limited civil (possession not in issue) ☐ from unlimited to limited

1. PLAINTIFF *(name each):*

  alleges causes of action against DEFENDANT *(name each):*

2. a. Plaintiff is (1) ☐ an individual over the age of 18 years. (4) ☐ a partnership.
           (2) ☐ a public agency.   (5) ☐ a corporation.
           (3) ☐ other *(specify):*

  b. ☐ Plaintiff has complied with the fictitious business name laws and is doing business under the fictitious name of *(specify):*

3. Defendant named above is in possession of the premises located at *(street address, apt. no., city, zip code, and county):*

4. Plaintiff's interest in the premises is ☐ as owner ☐ other *(specify):*
5. The true names and capacities of defendants sued as Does are unknown to plaintiff.
6. a. On or about *(date):*   defendant *(name each):*

    (1) agreed to rent the premises as a ☐ month-to-month tenancy ☐ other tenancy *(specify):*
    (2) agreed to pay rent of $ payable ☐ monthly ☐ other *(specify frequency):*
    (3) agreed to pay rent on the ☐ first of the month ☐ other day *(specify):*
  b. This ☐ written ☐ oral agreement was made with
    (1) ☐ plaintiff.   (3) ☐ plaintiff's predecessor in interest.
    (2) ☐ plaintiff's agent.   (4) ☐ other *(specify):*

* NOTE: Do not use this form for evictions after sale (Code Civ. Proc., § 1161a).

Page 1 of 3

Form Approved for Optional Use
Judicial Council of California
UD–100 [Rev. July 1, 2005]

COMPLAINT—UNLAWFUL DETAINER

Civil Code, § 1940 et seq.
Code of Civil Procedure §§ 425.12, 1166
www.courtinfo.ca.gov

PLAINTIFF *(Name):*	CASE NUMBER:
DEFENDANT*(Name):*	

6. c. ☐ The defendants not named in item 6a are

    (1) ☐ subtenants.

    (2) ☐ assignees.

    (3) ☐ other *(specify):*

  d. ☐ The agreement was later changed as follows *(specify):*

  e. ☐ A copy of the written agreement, including any addenda or attachments that form the basis of this complaint, is attached and labeled Exhibit 1. *(Required for residential property, unless item 6f is checked. See Code Civ. Proc., § 1166.)*

  f. ☐ *(For residential property)* A copy of the written agreement is **not** attached because *(specify reason):*

    (1) ☐ the written agreement is not in the possession of the landlord or the landlord's employees or agents.

    (2) ☐ this action is solely for nonpayment of rent (Code Civ. Proc., § 1161(2)).

7. ☐ a. Defendant *(name each):*

was served the following notice on the same date and in the same manner:

    (1) ☐ 3-day notice to pay rent or quit   (4) ☐ 3-day notice to perform covenants or quit

    (2) ☐ 30-day notice to quit   (5) ☐ 3-day notice to quit

    (3) ☐ 60-day notice to quit   (6) ☐ Other *(specify):*

  b. (1) On *(date):*   the period stated in the notice expired at the end of the day.

    (2) Defendants failed to comply with the requirements of the notice by that date.

  c. All facts stated in the notice are true.

  d. ☐ The notice included an election of forfeiture.

  e. ☐ A copy of the notice is attached and labeled Exhibit 2. *(Required for residential property. See Code Civ. Proc., § 1166.)*

  f. ☐ One or more defendants were served (1) with a different notice, (2) on a different date, or (3) in a different manner, as stated in Attachment 8c. *(Check item 8c and attach a statement providing the information required by items 7a–e and 8 for each defendant.)*

8. a. ☐ The notice in item 7a was served on the defendant named in item 7a as follows:

    (1) ☐ by personally handing a copy to defendant on *(date):*

    (2) ☐ by leaving a copy with *(name or description):*   ,

    a person of suitable age and discretion, on *(date):*   at defendant's

    ☐ residence ☐ business   AND mailing a copy to defendant at defendant's place of residence on

    (date):   because defendant cannot be found at defendant's residence or usual

    place of business.

    (3) ☐ by posting a copy on the premises on *(date):*   ☐ AND giving a copy to a

    person found residing at the premises AND mailing a copy to defendant at the premises on

    (date):

        (a) ☐ because defendant's residence and usual place of business cannot be ascertained OR

        (b) ☐ because no person of suitable age or discretion can be found there.

    (4) ☐ *(Not for 3-day notice; see Civil Code, § 1946 before using)* by sending a copy by certified or registered mail addressed to defendant on *(date):*

    (5) ☐ *(Not for residential tenancies; see Civil Code, § 1953 before using)* in the manner specified in a written commercial lease between the parties.

  b. ☐ *(Name):*

  was served on behalf of all defendants who signed a joint written rental agreement.

  c. ☐ Information about service of notice on the defendants alleged in item 7f is stated in Attachment 8c.

  d. ☐ Proof of service of the notice in item 7a is attached and labeled Exhibit 3.

    COMPLAINT—UNLAWFUL DETAINER

PLAINTIFF *(Name):*	CASE NUMBER:
DEFENDANT*(Name):*	

9. ☐ Plaintiff demands possession from each defendant because of expiration of a fixed-term lease.

10. ☐ At the time the 3-day notice to pay rent or quit was served, the amount of **rent due** was $

11. ☐ The fair rental value of the premises is $ per day.

12. ☐ Defendant's continued possession is malicious, and plaintiff is entitled to statutory damages under Code of Civil Procedure section 1174(b). *(State specific facts supporting a claim up to $600 in Attachment 12.)*

13. ☐ A written agreement between the parties provides for attorney fees.

14. ☐ Defendant's tenancy is subject to the local rent control or eviction control ordinance of *(city or county, title of ordinance, and date of passage):*

      Plaintiff has met all applicable requirements of the ordinances.

15. ☐ Other allegations are stated in Attachment 15.

16. Plaintiff accepts the jurisdictional limit, if any, of the court.

17. **PLAINTIFF REQUESTS**
   a. possession of the premises.
   b. costs incurred in this proceeding:
   c. ☐ past-due rent of $
   d. ☐ reasonable attorney fees.
   e. ☐ forfeiture of the agreement.
   f. ☐ damages at the rate stated in item 11 from *(date):*   for each day that defendants remain in possession through entry of judgment.
   g. ☐ statutory damages up to $600 for the conduct alleged in item 12.
   h. ☐ other *(specify):*

18. ☐ Number of pages attached *(specify):* _____

UNLAWFUL DETAINER ASSISTANT (Bus. & Prof. Code, §§ 6400–6415)

19. *(Complete in all cases.)* An unlawful detainer assistant ☐ did **not** ☐ did for compensation give advice or assistance with this form. *(If plaintiff has received **any** help or advice for pay from an unlawful detainer assistant, state:)*

   a. Assistant's name:
   b. Street address, city, and zip code:
   c. Telephone No.:
   d. County of registration:
   e. Registration No.:
   f. Expires on *(date):*

Date:

_____
(TYPE OR PRINT NAME)

▶ _____
(SIGNATURE OF PLAINTIFF OR ATTORNEY)

VERIFICATION

(Use a different verification form if the verification is by an attorney or for a corporation or partnership.)

I am the plaintiff in this proceeding and have read this complaint. I declare under penalty of perjury under the laws of the State of California that the foregoing is true and correct.

Date:

_____
(TYPE OR PRINT NAME)

▶ _____
(SIGNATURE OF PLAINTIFF)

COMPLAINT—UNLAWFUL DETAINER

This page intentionally left blank.

SUM-130

SUMMONS
(CITACION JUDICIAL)
UNLAWFUL DETAINER—EVICTION
(RETENCIÓN ILÍCITA DE UN INMUEBLE—DESALOJO)

NOTICE TO DEFENDANT:
(AVISO AL DEMANDADO):

YOU ARE BEING SUED BY PLAINTIFF:
(LO ESTÁ DEMANDANDO EL DEMANDANTE):

FOR COURT USE ONLY
(SOLO PARA USO DE LA COR')

You have **5 CALENDAR DAYS** after this summons and legal papers are served on you to file a written response ِ this court and have a copy served on the plaintiff. (To calculate the five days, count Saturday and Sunday, but do not count other court ؟olidays. If the last day falls on a Saturday, Sunday, or a court holiday then you have the next court day to file a written response.) A le' er or phone call will not protect you. Your written response must be in proper legal form if you want the court to hear your case. There r ay be a court form that you can use for your response. You can find these court forms and more information at the California Courts ِnline Self-Help Center (www.courtinfo.ca.gov/selfhelp), your county law library, or the courthouse nearest you. If you cannot pay th ؟ filing fee, ask the court clerk for a fee waiver form. If you do not file your response on time, you may lose the case by default, and yِ ِr wages, money, and property may be taken without further warning from the court.

There are other legal requirements. You may want to call an attorney right away. If you do not know anِ ِtorney, you may want to call an attorney referral service. If you cannot afford an attorney, you may be eligible for free legal services frِ n a nonprofit legal services program. You can locate these nonprofit groups at the California Legal Services Web site (www.lawhelp ِ ِlifornia.org), the California Courts Online Self-Help Center (www.courtinfo.ca.gov/selfhelp), or by contacting your local court or coِ nty bar association.

Tiene 5 DÍAS DE CALENDARIO después de que le entreguen esta citación y papeles legales para prِ sentar una respuesta por escrito en esta corte y hacer que se entregue una copia al demandante. (Para calcular los cinco días, cuente losِ sábados y los domingos pero no los otros días feriados de la corte. Si el último día cae en sábado o domingo, o en un día en que la corteِ esté cerrada, tiene hasta el próximo día de corte para presentar una respuesta por escrito). Una carta o una llamada telefónica no lo prِ tegen. Su respuesta por escrito tiene que estar en formato legal correcto si desea que procesen su caso en la corte. Es posible que haِ a un formulario que usted pueda usar para su respuesta. Puede encontrar estos formularios de la corte y más información en el Centِ ِo de Ayuda de las Cortes de California (www.courtinfo.ca.gov/selfhelp/espanol/), en la biblioteca de leyes de su condado o en la corteِ ؟ue le quede más cerca. Si no puede pagar la cuota de presentación, pida al secretario de la corte que le dé un formulario de exención deِ ِago de cuotas. Si no presenta su respuesta a tiempo, puede perder el caso por incumplimiento y la corte le podrá quitar su sueldo, dinerِ y bienes sin más advertencia.

Hay otros requisitos legales. Es recomendable que llame a un abogado inmediatamente. Si no conoce a un abogado, puede llamar a un servicio de remisión a abogados. Si no puede pagar a un abogado, es posible que cumplaِ ِon los requisitos para obtener servicios legales gratuitos de un programa de servicios legales sin fines de lucro. Puede encontrar ؟stos grupos sin fines de lucro en el sitio web de California Legal Services, (www.lawhelpcalifornia.org), en el Centro de Ayuda de las Cortِ ِs de California, (www.courtinfo.ca.gov/selfhelp/espanol/) o poniéndose en contacto con la corte o el colِ gio de abogados locales.

1. The name and address of the court is:
   (El nombre y dirección de la corte es):

CASE NUMBER:
(Número del caso):

2. The name, address, and telephone number of plaintiff's attorney, or plaintif' without an attorney, is:
   (El nombre, la dirección y el número de teléfono del abogado del demandante, o del demandante que no tiene abogado, es):

3. *(Must be answered in all cases)* An **unlawful detainer assistant (Bus. & Prof. Code, §§ 6400–6415)** ☐ did **not** ☐ did for compensation give advice or assistance with this form. *(If plaintiff has received **any** help or advice for pay from an unlawful detainer assistant, complete item 6 on the next page.)*

Date: _____   Clerk, by _____, Deputy
(Fecha)   *(Secretario)*   *(Adjunto)*

(For proof of service of this summons, use Proof of Service of Summons *(form POS-010).)*
(Para prueba de entrega de esta citación use el formulario Proof of Service of Summons, *(POS-010)).*

[SEAL]

4. **NOTICE TO THE PERSON SERVED:** You are served
   a. ☐ as an individual defendant.
   b. ☐ as the person sued under the fictitious name of *(specify):*
   c. ☐ as an occupant
   d. ☐ on behalf of *(specify):*
      under: ☐ CCP 416.10 (corporation)   ☐ CCP 416.60 (minor)
             ☐ CCP 416.20 (defunct corporation)   ☐ CCP 416.70 (conservatee)
             ☐ CCP 416.40 (association or partnership) ☐ CCP 416.90 (authorized person)
             ☐ CCP 415.46 (occupant)   ☐ other *(specify):*
5. ☐ by personal delivery on *(date):*

Page 1 of 2

PLAINTIFF *(Name):*	CASE NUMBER:
DEFENDANT *(Name):*	

6. **Unlawful detainer assistant** *(complete if plaintiff has received any help or advice for pay from an unlawful detainer assistant):*

   a. Assistant's name:

   b. Telephone no.:

   c. Street address, city, and ZIP:

   d. County of registration:

   e. Registration no.:

   f. Registration expires on *(date):*

POS-010

ATTORNEY OR PARTY WITHOUT ATTORNEY *(Name, State Bar number, and address):*	*FOR COURT USE ONLY*
TELEPHONE NO.: FAX NO. *(Optional):* E–MAIL ADDRESS *(Optional):* ATTORNEY FOR *(Name):*	

SUPERIOR COURT OF CALIFORNIA, COUNTY OF
    STREET ADDRESS:
    MAILING ADDRESS:
    CITY AND ZIP CODE:
    BRANCH NAME:

PLAINTIFF/PETITIONER: DEFENDANT/RESPONDENT:	CASE NUMBER:

PROOF OF SERVICE OF SUMMONS	Ref. No. or File No.:

(Separate proof of service is required for each party served.)

1. At the time of service I was at least 18 years of age and not a party to this action.

2. I served copies of:

    a. ☐ summons

    b. ☐ complaint

    c. ☐ Alternative Dispute Resolution (ADR) package

    d. ☐ Civil Case Cover Sheet *(served in complex cases only)*

    e. ☐ cross-complaint

    f. ☐ other *(specify documents):*

3. a. Party served *(specify name of party as shown on documents served):*

    b. Person served: ☐ party in item 3a   ☐ other *(specify name and relationship to the party named in item 3a):*

4. Address where the party was served:

5. I served the party *(check proper box)*

    a. ☐ **by personal service.** I personally delivered the documents listed in item 2 to the party or person authorized to receive service of process for the party (1) on *(date):*   (2) at *(time):*

    b. ☐ **by substituted service.** On *(date):*   at *(time):*   I left the documents listed in item 2 with or in the presence of *(name and title or relationship to person indicated in item 3b):*

        (1) ☐ **(business)** a person at least 18 years of age apparently in charge at the office or usual place of business of the person to be served. I informed him or her of the general nature of the papers.

        (2) ☐ **(home)** a competent member of the household (at least 18 years of age) at the dwelling house or usual place of abode of the party. I informed him or her of the general nature of the papers.

        (3) ☐ **(physical address unknown)** a person at least 18 years of age apparently in charge at the usual mailing address of the person to be served, other than a United States Postal Service post office box. I informed him or her of the general nature of the papers.

        (4) ☐ I thereafter mailed (by first-class, postage prepaid) copies of the documents to the person to be served at the place where the copies were left (Code Civ. Proc., § 415.20). I mailed the documents on *(date):*   from *(city):*   **or** ☐ a declaration of mailing is attached.

        (5) ☐ I attach a **declaration of diligence** stating actions taken first to attempt personal service.

Page 1 of 2

258

c. ☐ **by mail and acknowledgment of receipt of service.** I mailed the documents listed in item 2 to the party, to the address shown in item 4, by first-class mail, postage prepaid,

    (1) on *(date):*   (2) from *(city):*

    (3) ☐ with two copies of the *Notice and Acknowledgment of Receipt* and a postage-paid return envelope addressed to me. *(Attach completed* Notice and Acknowledgement of Receipt.*) (Code Civ. Proc., § 415.30.)*

    (4) ☐ to an address outside California with return receipt requested. (Code Civ. Proc., § 415.40.)

d. ☐ **by other means** *(specify means of service and authorizing code section):*

☐ Additional page describing service is attached.

6. The "Notice to the Person Served" (on the summons) was completed as follows:
    a. ☐ as an individual defendant.
    b. ☐ as the person sued under the fictitious name of *(specify):*
    c. ☐ as occupant.
    d. ☐ On behalf of *(specify):*
        under the following Code of Civil Procedure section:

        ☐ 416.10 (corporation)   ☐ 415.95 (business organization, form unknown)
        ☐ 416.20 (defunct corporation)   ☐ 416.60 (minor)
        ☐ 416.30 (joint stock company/association)   ☐ 416.70 (ward or conservatee)
        ☐ 416.40 (association or partnership)   ☐ 416.90 (authorized person)
        ☐ 416.50 (public entity)   ☐ 415.46 (occupant)
                            ☐ other:

7. **Person who served papers**
    a. Name:
    b. Address:
    c. Telephone number:
    d. **The fee** for service was: $
    e. I am:
        (1) ☐ not a registered California process server.
        (2) ☐ exempt from registration under Business and Professions Code section 22350(b).
        (3) ☐ registered California process server:
            (i) ☐ owner ☐ employee ☐ independent contractor.
            (ii) Registration No.:
            (iii) County:

8. ☐ **I declare** under penalty of perjury under the laws of the State of California that the foregoing is true and correct.

    or

9. ☐ **I am a California sheriff or marshal and** I certify that the foregoing is true and correct.

Date:

▶

_____   _____
(NAME OF PERSON WHO SERVED PAPERS/SHERIFF OR MARSHAL)   (SIGNATURE)

NOTICE: **EVERYONE WHO LIVES IN THIS RENTAL UNIT MAY BE EVICTED BY COURT ORDER. READ THIS FORM IF YOU LIVE HERE AND IF YOUR NAME IS NOT ON THE ATTACHED SUMMONS AND COMPLAINT.**

1. If you live here and you do not complete and submit this form within 10 days of the date of service shown on this form, you will be evicted without further hearing by the court along with the persons named in the Summons and Complaint.
2. If you file this form, your claim will be determined in the eviction action against the persons named in the Complaint.
3. If you do not file this form, you will be evicted without further hearing.

CLAIMANT OR CLAIMANT'S ATTORNEY *(Name and Address)*:	TELEPHONE NO.:	*FOR COURT USE ONLY*
ATTORNEY FOR *(Name)*:		

NAME OF COURT:

STREET ADDRESS:

MAILING ADDRESS:

CITY AND ZIP CODE:

BRANCH NAME:

PLAINTIFF:

DEFENDANT:

PREJUDGMENT CLAIM OF RIGHT TO POSSESSION

CASE NUMBER:

Complete this form only if ALL of these statements are true: **1. You are NOT named in the accompanying Summons and Complaint.** **2. You occupied the premises on or before the date the unlawful detainer (eviction) Complaint was filed.** **3. You still occupy the premises.**	*(To be completed by the process server)* DATE OF SERVICE: *(Date that this form is served or delivered, and posted, and mailed by the officer or process server)*

I DECLARE THE FOLLOWING UNDER PENALTY OF PERJURY:

1. My name is *(specify)*:

2. I reside at *(street address, unit No., city and ZIP code)*:

3. The address of "the premises" subject to this claim is *(address)*:

4. On *(insert date)*: _____ , the landlord or the landlord's authorized agent filed a complaint to recover possession of the premises. *(This date is the court filing date on the accompanying Summons and Complaint.*

5. I occupied the premises on the date the complaint was filed *(the date in item 4)*. I have continued to occupy the premises ever since.

6. I was at least 18 years of age on the date the complaint was filed *(the date in item 4)*.

7. I claim a right to possession of the premises because I occupied the premises on the date the complaint was filed *(the date in item 4)*.

8. I was not named in the Summons and Complaint.

9. I understand that if I make this claim of right to possession, I will be added as a defendant to the unlawful detainer (eviction) action.

10. *(Filing fee)* I understand that I must go to the court and pay a filing fee of $ _____ or file with the court the form "Application for Waiver of Court Fees and Costs." I understand that if I don't pay the filing fee or file with the court the form for waiver of court fees within 10 days from the date of service on this form (excluding court holidays), I will not be entitled to make a claim of right to possession.

(Continued on reverse)

PREJUDGMENT CLAIM OF RIGHT TO POSSESSION

Code of Civil Procedure §§ 415.46, 715.010, 715.020, 1174.25

PLAINTIFF (Name):	CASE NUMBER:
DEFENDANT (Name):	

NOTICE: If you fail to file this claim, you will be evicted without further hearing.

11. *(Response required within five days after you file this form)* I understand that I will have *five days* (excluding court holidays) to file a response to the Summons and Complaint after I file this Prejudgment Claim of Right to Possession form.

12. **Rental agreement.** I have *(check all that apply to you)*:
   a. ☐ an oral rental agreement with the landlord.
   b. ☐ a written rental agreement with the landlord.
   c. ☐ an oral rental agreement with a person other than the landlord.
   d. ☐ a written rental agreement with a person other than the landlord.
   e. ☐ other *(explain)*:

I declare under penalty of perjury under the laws of the State of California that the foregoing is true and correct.

WARNING: Perjury is a felony punishable by imprisonment in the state prison.

Date:

. . . . ▶ _____
(TYPE OR PRINT NAME)   (SIGNATURE OF CLAIMANT)

NOTICE: If you file this claim of right to possession, the unlawful detainer (eviction) action against you will be determined at trial. At trial, you may be found liable for rent, costs, and, in some cases, treble damages.

— NOTICE TO OCCUPANTS —

YOU MUST ACT AT ONCE if all the following are true:
   1. You are NOT named in the accompanying Summons and Complaint.
   2. You occupied the premises on or before the date the unlawful detainer (eviction) complaint was filed. *(The date is the court filing date on the accompanying Summons and Complaint.)*
   3. You still occupy the premises.

(Where to file this form) You can complete and SUBMIT THIS CLAIM FORM WITHIN 10 DAYS from the date of service (on the reverse of this form) at the court where the unlawful detainer (eviction) complaint was filed.

(What will happen if you do not file this form) If you do not complete and submit this form and pay a filing fee or file the form for proceeding in forma pauperis if you cannot pay the fee), YOU WILL BE EVICTED.

After this form is properly filed, you will be added as a defendant in the unlawful detainer (eviction) action and your right to occupy the premises will be decided by the court. *If you do not file this claim, you will be evicted without a hearing.*

982(a)(6)

ATTORNEY OR PARTY WITHOUT ATTORNEY *(Name, State Bar number, and address):*	*FOR COURT USE ONLY*
TELEPHONE NO.: FAX NO. *(Optional):* E-MAIL ADDRESS *(Optional):* ATTORNEY FOR *(Name):*	

SUPERIOR COURT OF CALIFORNIA, COUNTY OF

STREET ADDRESS:
MAILING ADDRESS:
CITY AND ZIP CODE:
BRANCH NAME:

PLAINTIFF/PETITIONER:

DEFENDANT/RESPONDENT:

REQUEST FOR (Application) ☐ **Entry of Default** ☐ **Clerk's Judgment** ☐ **Court Judgment**	CASE NUMBER:

1. TO THE CLERK: On the complaint or cross-complaint filed
   a. on *(date):*

   b. by *(name):*

   c. ☐ Enter default of defendant *(names):*

   d. ☐ I request a court judgment under Code of Civil Procedure sections 585(b), 585(c), 989, etc., against defendant *(names):*

   (Testimony required. Apply to the clerk for a hearing date, unless the court will enter a judgment on an affidavit under Code Civ. Proc., § 585(d).)

   e. ☐ Enter clerk's judgment
        (1) ☐ for restitution of the premises only and issue a writ of execution on the judgment. Code of Civil Procedure section 1174(c) does not apply. (Code Civ. Proc., § 1169.)
            ☐ Include in the judgment all tenants, subtenants, named claimants, and other occupants of the premises. The *Prejudgment Claim of Right to Possession* was served in compliance with Code of Civil Procedure section 415.46.
        (2) ☐ under Code of Civil Procedure section 585(a). *(Complete the declaration under Code Civ. Proc., § 585.5 on the reverse (item 5).)*
        (3) ☐ for default previously entered on *(date):*

2. **Judgment to be entered.**

	Amount	Credits acknowledged	Balance
a. Demand of complaint	$	$	$
b. Statement of damages *			
(1) Special	$	$	$
(2) General	$	$	$
c. Interest	$	$	$
d. Costs *(see reverse)*	$	$	$
e. Attorney fees	$	$	$
f. **TOTALS**	$	$	$

   g. **Daily damages** were demanded in complaint at the rate of: $ per day beginning *(date):*
   (Personal injury or wrongful death actions; Code Civ. Proc., § 425.11.)*

3. ☐ *(Check if filed in an unlawful detainer case)* **Legal document assistant or unlawful detainer assistant** information is on the reverse *(complete item 4).*

Date:

▶

_____   _____
(TYPE OR PRINT NAME)   (SIGNATURE OF PLAINTIFF OR ATTORNEY FOR PLAINTIFF)

FOR COURT USE ONLY	(1) ☐ Default entered as requested on *(date):* (2) ☐ Default NOT entered as requested *(state reason):* Clerk, by _____ , Deputy

Page 1 of 2

Form Adopted for Mandatory Use
Judicial Council of California
982(a)(6) [Rev. February 18, 2005]

REQUEST FOR ENTRY OF DEFAULT
(Application to Enter Default)

Code of Civil Procedure,
§§ 585–587, 1169
www.courtinfo.ca.gov

PLAINTIFF/PETITIONER:	CASE NUMBER:
DEFENDANT/RESPONDENT:	

4. **Legal document assistant or unlawful detainer assistant (Bus. & Prof. Code, § 6400 et seq.).** A legal document assistant or unlawful detainer assistant ☐ did ☐ did **not** for compensation give advice or assistance with this form. *(If declarant has received **any** help or advice for pay from a legal document assistant or unlawful detainer assistant, state):*

   a. Assistant's name:
   b. Street address, city, and zip code:

   c. Telephone no.:
   d. County of registration:
   e. Registration no.:
   f. Expires on *(date):*

5. ☐ **Declaration under Code of Civil Procedure Section 585.5** *(required for entry of default under Code Civ. Proc., § 585(a)).*
   This action

   a. ☐ is ☐ is not   on a contract or installment sale for goods or services subject to Civ. Code, § 1801 et seq. (Unruh Act).
   b. ☐ is ☐ is not   on a conditional sales contract subject to Civ. Code, § 2981 et seq. (Rees-Levering Motor Vehicle Sales and Finance Act).
   c. ☐ is ☐ is not   on an obligation for goods, services, loans, or extensions of credit subject to Code Civ. Proc., § 395(b).

6. **Declaration of mailing (Code Civ. Proc., § 587).** A copy of this *Request for Entry of Default* was

   a. ☐ **not mailed** to the following defendants, whose addresses are **unknown** to plaintiff or plaintiff's attorney *(names):*

   b. ☐ **mailed** first-class, postage prepaid, in a sealed envelope addressed to each defendant's attorney of record or, if none, to each defendant's last known address as follows:
      (1) Mailed on *(date):*   (2) To *(specify names and addresses shown on the envelopes):*

I declare under penalty of perjury under the laws of the State of California that the foregoing items 4, 5, and 6 are true and correct.
Date:

▶

_____   _____
(TYPE OR PRINT NAME)   (SIGNATURE OF DECLARANT)

7. **Memorandum of costs** *(required if money judgment requested).* Costs and disbursements are as follows (Code Civ. Proc., § 1033.5):

   a. Clerk's filing fees .... $
   b. Process server's fees .... $
   c. Other *(specify):* .... $
   d. .... $
   e. **TOTAL** .... $ _____
   f. ☐ Costs and disbursements are waived.
   g. I am the attorney, agent, or party who claims these costs. To the best of my knowledge and belief this memorandum of costs is correct and these costs were necessarily incurred in this case.

I declare under penalty of perjury under the laws of the State of California that the foregoing is true and correct.
Date:

▶

_____   _____
(TYPE OR PRINT NAME)   (SIGNATURE OF DECLARANT)

8. ☐ **Declaration of nonmilitary status** *(required for a judgment).* No defendant named in item 1c of the application is in the military service so as to be entitled to the benefits of the Servicemembers Civil Relief Act (50 U.S.C. App. § 501 et seq.).

I declare under penalty of perjury under the laws of the State of California that the foregoing is true and correct.
Date:

▶

_____   _____
(TYPE OR PRINT NAME)   (SIGNATURE OF DECLARANT)

REQUEST FOR ENTRY OF DEFAULT
(Application to Enter Default)

ATTORNEY OR PARTY WITHOUT ATTORNEY *(Name and Address):*	FOR COURT USE ONLY
ATTORNEY FOR *(Name):*	
Insert name of court and name of judicial district and branch court, if any:	
PLAINTIFF: DEFENDANT:	

CLERK'S JUDGMENT FOR POSSESSION **UNLAWFUL DETAINER**	CASE NUMBER

The defendant(s) in this cause having been served with a summons and complaint, having failed to appear and answer the complaint within the time allowed by law, and default having been entered against them, upon application having been filed pursuant to Code of Civil procedure §1169, the Clerk hereby enters the following judgment:

ADJUDGED that plaintiff(s) _____ _____

☐ Tenant(s) _____ _____

☐ Subtenant (s) _____ _____

☐ Named Claimant(s) _____ _____

☐ Other Occupant(s) _____ _____

the restitution and possession of those premises situated in the county of _____, state of California, more particularly described as follows: _____

_____

This judgment was entered on

_____
in _____ Book _____
at Page _____

_____
                             Clerk
By:

_____
                      Deputy Clerk

This page intentionally left blank.

ATTORNEY OR PARTY WITHOUT ATTORNEY *(Name and Address)*:	FOR COURT USE ONLY
ATTORNEY FOR *(Name)*:	
Insert name of court and name of judicial district and branch court, if any:	
PLAINTIFF:	
DEFENDANT:	

DEFAULT JUDGMENT **UNLAWFUL DETAINER**	CASE NUMBER

The defendant(s) in this cause having been served with a summons and complaint, having failed to appear and answer the complaint within the time allowed by law, and default having been entered against them, upon application having been filed by plaintiff(s), and the Court having ☐ heard the testimony and considered the evidence
      ☐ received the declaration submitted by plaintiff(s)   it is,

ORDERED AND ADJUDGED that plaintiff(s) _____
_____ have and recover from defendant(s) _____
_____ the restitution and possession of those premises situated in the county of
_____, state of California, more particularly described as follows: _____
_____

for costs in the amount of $_____ and rent/damages in the amount of $_____
for a total of $_____.

Date:_____

_____
                                                              Judge

This judgment was entered on

_____
in _____ Book _____
at Page _____

_____
                                         Clerk
By:

_____
                        Deputy Clerk

DEFAULT JUDGMENT
UNLAWFUL DETAINER   Code of Civil Procedure §1169 § 1174

This page intentionally left blank.

UD-116

ATTORNEY OR PARTY WITHOUT ATTORNEY *(Name, state bar number, and address):*	FOR COURT USE ONLY
TELEPHONE NO.: FAX NO. *(Optional):*	
E-MAIL ADDRESS *(Optional):*	
ATTORNEY FOR *(Name):*	

SUPERIOR COURT OF CALIFORNIA, COUNTY OF
STREET ADDRESS:
MAILING ADDRESS:
CITY AND ZIP CODE:
BRANCH NAME:

PLAINTIFF *(Name):*

DEFENDANT *(Name):*

DECLARATION FOR DEFAULT JUDGMENT BY COURT (Unlawful Detainer—Code Civil Proc., § 585(d))	CASE NUMBER:

1. My name is *(specify):*
   a. ☐ I am the plaintiff in this action.
   b. I am
      (1) ☐ an owner of the property   (3) ☐ an agent of the owner
      (2) ☐ a manager of the property   (4) ☐ other *(specify):*

2. The property concerning this action is located at *(street address, apartment number, city, and county):*

3. **Personal knowledge.** I personally know the facts stated in this declaration and, if sworn as a witness, could testify competently thereto. I am personally familiar with the rental or lease agreement, defendant's payment record, the condition of the property, and defendant's conduct.

4. Agreement was ☐ written ☐ oral as follows:
   a. On or about *(date):*   defendant *(name each):*

      (1) agreed to rent the property for a ☐ month-to-month tenancy ☐ other tenancy *(specify):*
      (2) agreed to pay rent of $ payable ☐ monthly ☐ other *(specify frequency):*
          with rent due on the ☐ first of the month ☐ other day *(specify):*

   b. ☐ Original agreement is attached *(specify):* ☐ to the original complaint.
      ☐ to the *Application for Immediate Writ of Possession.* ☐ to this declaration, labeled Exhibit 4b.
   c. ☐ Copy of agreement with a declaration and order to admit the copy is attached *(specify):*
      ☐ to the *Application for Immediate Writ of Possession.* ☐ to this declaration, labeled Exhibit 4c.

5. ☐ Agreement changed.
   a. ☐ More than one change in rent amount *(specify history of all rent changes and effective dates up to the last rent change)* on *Attachment 5a (form MC-025).*

   b. ☐ Change in rent amount *(specify last rent change).* The rent was changed from $ to $, which became effective on *(date):*   and was made
      (1) ☐ by agreement of the parties and subsequent payment of such rent.
      (2) ☐ by service on defendant of a notice of change in terms pursuant to Civil Code section 827 *(check item 5d).*
      (3) ☐ pursuant to a written agreement of the parties for change in terms *(check item 5e or 5f).*

   c. ☐ Change in rent due date. Rent was changed, payable in advance, due on *(specify day):*   .
   d. ☐ A copy of the notice of change in terms is attached to this declaration, labeled Exhibit 5d.
   e. ☐ Original agreement for change in terms is attached *(specify):* ☐ to the original complaint.
      ☐ to the *Application for Immediate Writ of Possession.* ☐ to this declaration, labeled Exhibit 5e.
   f. ☐ Copy of agreement for change in terms with a declaration and order to admit the copy is attached *(specify):*
      ☐ to the *Application for Immediate Writ of Possession.* ☐ to this declaration, labeled Exhibit 5f.

Page 1 of 3

Form Approved for Optional Use
Judicial Council of California
UD–116 [Rev. July 1, 2003]

DECLARATION FOR DEFAULT JUDGMENT BY COURT
(Unlawful Detainer—Code Civ. Proc., § 585(d))

Code of Civil Procedure, § 585(d)
www.courtinfo.ca.gov

PLAINTIFF (Name):	CASE NUMBER:
DEFENDANT (Name):	

6. Notice to quit.
   a. ☐ Defendant was served with a
   - (1) ☐ 3-day notice to pay rent or quit
   - (2) ☐ 3-day notice to perform covenants or quit
   - (3) ☐ Other (specify):
   - (4) ☐ 3-day notice to quit
   - (5) ☐ 30-day notice to quit
   - (6) ☐ 60-day notice to quit

   b. ☐ The 3-day notice to pay rent or quit demanded rent due in the amount of (specify): $ for the rental period beginning on (date)   and ending on (date)   .

   c. ☐ The total rent demanded in the 3-day notice under item 6b is different from the agreed rent in item 4a(2) (specify history of dates covered by the 3-day notice and any partial payments received to arrive at the balance) on Attachment 6c (form MC-025).

   d. ☐ The original or copy of the notice specified in item 6a is attached to (specify): ☐ the original complaint.
   ☐ this declaration, labeled Exhibit 6d. (The original or a copy of the notice MUST be attached to this declaration if not attached to the original complaint.)

7. Service of notice.
   a. The notice was served on defendant (name each):
   - (1) ☐ personally on (date):
   - (2) ☐ by substituted service, including a copy mailed to the defendant, on (date):
   - (3) ☐ by posting and mailing on (date mailed):

   b. ☐ A prejudgment claim of right to possession was served on the occupants pursuant to Code of Civil Procedure section 415.46.

8. Proof of service of notice. The original or copy of the proof of service of the notice in item 6a is attached to (specify):
   a. ☐ the original complaint.
   b. ☐ this declaration, labeled Exhibit 8b. (The original or copy of the proof of service MUST be attached to this declaration if not attached to the original complaint.)

9. Notice expired. On (date):   the notice in item 6 expired at the end of the day and defendant failed to comply with the requirements of the notice by that date. No money has been received and accepted after the notice expired.

10. The fair rental value of the property is $ per day, calculated as follows:
   a. ☐ (rent per month) x (0.03288) (12 months divided by 365 days)
   b. ☐ rent per month divided by 30
   c. ☐ other valuation (specify):

11. Possession. The defendant
   a. ☐ vacated the premises on (date):
   b. ☐ continues to occupy the property on (date of this declaration):

12. ☐ Holdover damages. Declarant has calculated the holdover damages as follows:
   a. Damages demanded in the complaint began on (date):
   b. Damages accrued through (date specified in item 11):
   c. Number of days that damages accrued (count days using the dates in items 12a and 12b):
   d. Total holdover damages ((daily rental value in item 10) x (number of days in item 12c)): $

13. ☐ Reasonable attorney fees are authorized in the lease or rental agreement pursuant to paragraph (specify): and reasonable attorney fees for plaintiff's attorney (name):   are $.

14. ☐ Court costs in this case, including the filing fee, are $

DECLARATION FOR DEFAULT JUDGMENT BY COURT
(Unlawful Detainer—Code Civ. Proc., § 585(d))

PLAINTIFF (Name):	CASE NUMBER:
DEFENDANT (Name):	

15. ☐ Declarant requests a judgment on behalf of plaintiff for:
    a. ☐ A money judgment as follows:

(1) ☐	Past-due rent (item 6b)	$	
(2) ☐	Holdover damages (item 12d)	$	
(3) ☐	Attorney fees (item 13)*	$	
(4) ☐	Costs (item 14)	$	
(5) ☐	Other (specify):	$	
(6)	**TOTAL JUDGMENT**	$	

* ☐ Attorney fees are to be paid by (name)   only.

    b. ☐ Possession of the premises in item 2 (check only if a clerk's judgment for possession was **not** entered).
    c. ☐ Cancellation of the rental agreement. ☐ Forfeiture of the lease.

I declare under penalty of perjury under the laws of the State of California that the foregoing is true and correct.

Date:

_____
(TYPE OR PRINT NAME)

} _____
(SIGNATURE OF DECLARANT)

Summary of Exhibits

16. ☐ Exhibit 4b: Original rental agreement.

17. ☐ Exhibit 4c: Copy of rental agreement with declaration and order to admit the copy.

18. ☐ Exhibit 5d: Copy of notice of change in terms.

19. ☐ Exhibit 5e: Original agreement for change of terms.

20. ☐ Exhibit 5f: Copy of agreement for change in terms with declaration and order to admit copy.

21. ☐ Exhibit 6d: Original or copy of the notice to quit under item 6a (MUST be attached to this declaration if it is not attached to original complaint).

22. ☐ Exhibit 8b: Original or copy of proof of service of notice in item 6a (MUST be attached to this declaration if it is not attached to original complaint).

23. ☐ Other exhibits (specify number and describe):

This page intentionally left blank.

UD-110

ATTORNEY OR PARTY WITHOUT ATTORNEY *(Name, state bar number, and address):*	FOR COURT USE ONLY

TELEPHONE NO.:   FAX NO. *(Optional):*

E-MAIL ADDRESS *(Optional):*

ATTORNEY FOR *(Name):*

SUPERIOR COURT OF CALIFORNIA, COUNTY OF

STREET ADDRESS:

MAILING ADDRESS:

CITY AND ZIP CODE:

BRANCH NAME:

PLAINTIFF:

DEFENDANT:

JUDGMENT—UNLAWFUL DETAINER	CASE NUMBER:
☐ By Clerk ☐ By Default ☐ After Court Trial ☐ By Court ☐ Possession Only ☐ Defendant Did Not Appear at Trial	

JUDGMENT

1. ☐ **BY DEFAULT**

    a. Defendant was properly served with a copy of the summons and complaint.

    b. Defendant failed to answer the complaint or appear and defend the action within the time allowed by law.

    c. Defendant's default was entered by the clerk upon plaintiff's application.

    d. ☐ **Clerk's Judgment** (Code Civ. Proc., § 1169). For possession only of the premises described on page 2 (item 4).

    e. ☐ **Court Judgment** (Code Civ. Proc., § 585(b)). The court considered

        (1) ☐ plaintiff's testimony and other evidence.

        (2) ☐ plaintiff's or others' written declaration and evidence (Code Civ. Proc., § 585(d)).

2. ☐ **AFTER COURT TRIAL.** The jury was waived. The court considered the evidence.

    a. The case was tried on *(date and time):*

    before *(name of judicial officer):*

    b. Appearances by:

    ☐ Plaintiff *(name each):*   ☐ Plaintiff's attorney *(name each):*

                                                     (1)

                                                     (2)

    ☐ Continued on *Attachment* 2b (form MC-025).

    ☐ Defendant *(name each):*   ☐ Defendant's attorney *(name each):*

                                                     (1)

                                                     (2)

    ☐ Continued on *Attachment* 2b (form MC-025).

    c. ☐ Defendant did not appear at trial. Defendant was properly served with notice of trial.

    d. ☐ A statement of decision (Code Civ. Proc., § 632) ☐ was not ☐ was requested.

Form Approved for Optional Use
Judicial Council of California
UD-110 [New January 1, 2003]

JUDGMENT—UNLAWFUL DETAINER

Code of Civil Procedure, §§ 415.46,
585(d), 664.6, 1169

PLAINTIFF:	CASE NUMBER:
DEFENDANT:	

JUDGMENT IS ENTERED AS FOLLOWS BY: ☐ **THE COURT** ☐ **THE CLERK**

3. **Parties.** Judgment is

   a. ☐ for plaintiff *(name each):*

      and against defendant *(name each):*

      ☐ Continued on *Attachment* 3a (form MC-025).

   b. ☐ for defendant *(name each):*

4. ☐ Plaintiff ☐ Defendant is entitled to possession of the premises located at *(street address, apartment, city, and county):*

5. ☐ Judgment applies to all occupants of the premises including tenants, subtenants if any, and named claimants if any (Code Civ. Proc., §§ 715.010, 1169, and 1174.3).

6. **Amount and terms of judgment**

   a. ☐ Defendant named in item 3a above must pay plaintiff on the complaint:

   b. ☐ Plaintiff is to receive nothing from defendant named in item 3b.

      ☐ Defendant named in item 3b is to recover costs: $

      ☐ and attorney fees: $.

(1) ☐	Past-due rent	$
(2) ☐	Holdover damages	$
(3) ☐	Attorney fees	$
(4) ☐	Costs	$
(5) ☐	Other *(specify):*	$
(6)	**TOTAL JUDGMENT**	$

   c. ☐ The rental agreement is canceled. ☐ The lease is forfeited.

7. ☐ **Conditional judgment.** Plaintiff has breached the agreement to provide habitable premises to defendant as stated in *Judgment—Unlawful Detainer Attachment* (form UD–110S), which is attached.

8. ☐ **Other** *(specify):*

   ☐ Continued on *Attachment* 8 (form MC-025).

Date: ☐ _____
                            JUDICIAL OFFICER

Date: ☐ Clerk, by _____ , Deputy

(SEAL)	**CLERK'S CERTIFICATE** *(Optional)*
	I certify that this is a true copy of the original judgment on file in the court.
	Date:
	Clerk, by _____ , Deputy

    JUDGMENT—UNLAWFUL DETAINER

UD–115

ATTORNEY OR PARTY WITHOUT ATTORNEY *(Name and state bar number, and address):*	FOR COURT USE ONLY
TELEPHONE NO.: FAX NO. *(Optional):*	
E–MAIL ADDRESS *(Optional):*	
ATTORNEY FOR *(Name):*	

SUPERIOR COURT OF CALIFORNIA, COUNTY OF
STREET ADDRESS:
MAILING ADDRESS:
CITY AND ZIP CODE:
BRANCH NAME:

PLAINTIFF:

DEFENDANT:

STIPULATION FOR ENTRY OF JUDGMENT **(Unlawful Detainer)**	CASE NUMBER:

1. IT IS STIPULATED by plaintiff *(name each):*   and
   defendant *(name each):*

2. ☐ Plaintiff ☐ Defendant *(specify name):*   is awarded
   a. ☐ possession of the premises located at *(street address, apartment number, city, and county):*

   b. ☐ cancellation of the rental agreement.   ☐ forfeiture of the lease.
   c. ☐ past due rent $
   d. ☐ total holdover damages $
   e. ☐ attorney fees $
   f. ☐ costs $
   g. ☐ deposit of $ ☐ See item 3.
   h. ☐ other *(specify):*
   i. Total $ to be paid by ☐ *(date):*   ☐ installment payments (see item 5)

3. ☐ Deposit. If not awarded under item 2g, then plaintiff must
   a. ☐ return deposit of $ to defendant by *(date):*
   b. ☐ give an itemized deposit statement to defendant within three weeks after defendant vacates the premises
      (Civ. Code, § 1950.5).
   c. ☐ mail the ☐ deposit ☐ itemized statement   to the defendant at *(mailing address):*

4. ☐ A writ of possession will issue immediately, but there will be no lockout before *(date):*

5. ☐ AGREEMENT FOR INSTALLMENT PAYMENTS
   a. Defendant agrees to pay $ on the *(specify day)*   day of each month beginning
      on *(specify date)*   until paid in full.

   b. If any payment is more than *(specify)*   days late, the entire amount in item 2i will become immediately due and
      payable plus interest at the legal rate.

6. a. ☐ Judgment will be entered now.
   b. ☐ Judgment will be entered only upon default of payment of the amount in item 2i or the payment arrangement in item 5a.
      The case is calendared for dismissal on *(date and time)*   in
      department *(specify)*   unless plaintiff or defendant otherwise notifies the court.
   c. ☐ Judgment will be entered as stated in *Judgment —Unlawful Detainer Attachment* (form UD-110S), which is attached.
   d. ☐ Judgment will be entered as stated in item 7.

Page 1 of 2

STIPULATION FOR ENTRY OF JUDGMENT
(Unlawful Detainer)
Code of Civil Procedure, § 664.6

PLAINTIFF:	CASE NUMBER:
DEFENDANT:	

7. ☐ Plaintiff and defendant further stipulate as follows *(specify)*:

8. a. **The parties named in item 1 understand that they have the right to (1) have an attorney present and (2) receive notice of and have a court hearing about any default in the terms of this stipulation.**

   b. Date:

   _____
   (TYPE OR PRINT NAME)

   ▶ _____
   (SIGNATURE OF PLAINTIFF OR ATTORNEY)

   _____
   (TYPE OR PRINT NAME)

   ▶ _____
   (SIGNATURE OF PLAINTIFF OR ATTORNEY)

   ☐ Continued on *Attachment* 8b (form MC-025).

   c. Date:

   _____
   (TYPE OR PRINT NAME)

   ▶ _____
   (SIGNATURE OF DEFENDANT OR ATTORNEY)

   _____
   (TYPE OR PRINT NAME)

   ▶ _____
   (SIGNATURE OF DEFENDANT OR ATTORNEY)

   _____
   (TYPE OR PRINT NAME)

   ▶ _____
   (SIGNATURE OF DEFENDANT OR ATTORNEY)

   ☐ Continued on *Attachment* 8c (form MC-025).

9. IT IS SO ORDERED.

Date:

_____
JUDICIAL OFFICER

STIPULATION FOR ENTRY OF JUDGMENT
(Unlawful Detainer)

ATTORNEY OR PARTY WITHOUT ATTORNEY *(Name and Address)*:

ATTORNEY FOR *(Name)*:

Insert name of court and name of judicial district and branch court, if any:

FOR COURT USE ONLY

PLAINTIFF:

DEFENDANT:

JUDGMENT PURSUANT TO STIPULATION

CASE NUMBER

Pursuant to the stipulation entered into between the plaintiff(s) and defendant(s) in this cause, it is

ORDERED AND ADJUDGED that plaintiff(s) _____
have and recover from defendant(s) _____
the restitution and possession of those premises situated in the county of _____,
state of California, more particularly described as follows: _____
_____,

costs in the amount of $_____ and damages in the amount of $_____.

Date:_____

_____
Judge

This judgment was entered on

_____
in _____ Book _____
at Page _____

_____
                                        Clerk
By:

_____
                                Deputy Clerk

This page intentionally left blank.

AT-138, EJ-125

ATTORNEY OR PARTY WITHOUT ATTORNEY *(Name, state bar number, and address):*	FOR COURT USE ONLY
TELEPHONE NO.: FAX NO.:	
ATTORNEY FOR *(Name)*:	

NAME OF COURT:
STREET ADDRESS:
MAILING ADDRESS:
CITY AND ZIP CODE:
BRANCH NAME:

PLAINTIFF:

DEFENDANT:

APPLICATION AND ORDER FOR APPEARANCE AND EXAMINATION	CASE NUMBER:
☐ **ENFORCEMENT OF JUDGMENT** ☐ **ATTACHMENT (Third Person)** ☐ **Judgment Debtor** ☐ **Third Person**	

ORDER TO APPEAR FOR EXAMINATION

1. TO *(name)*:

2. YOU ARE ORDERED TO APPEAR personally before this court, or before a referee appointed by the court, to

   a. ☐ furnish information to aid in enforcement of a money judgment against you.

   b. ☐ answer concerning property of the judgment debtor in your possession or control or concerning a debt you owe the judgment debtor.

   c. ☐ answer concerning property of the defendant in your possession or control or concerning a debt you owe the defendant that is subject to attachment.

Date: Time: Dept. or Div.:   Rm.:
Address of court ☐ shown above ☐ is:

3. This order may be served by a sheriff, marshal, registered process server, **or** the following specially appointed person *(name)*:

Date: _____

                                               _____
                                               JUDGE OR REFEREE

This order must be served not less than 10 days before the date set for the examination.

IMPORTANT NOTICES ON REVERSE

APPLICATION FOR ORDER TO APPEAR FOR EXAMINATION

4. ☐ Judgment creditor   ☐ Assignee of record   ☐ Plaintiff who has a right to attach order
   applies for an order requiring *(name)*:   to appear and furnish information
   to aid in enforcement of the money judgment or to answer concerning property or debt.

5. The person to be examined is

   a. ☐ the judgment debtor.

   b. ☐ a third person (1) who has possession or control of property belonging to the judgment debtor or the defendant or (2) who owes the judgment debtor or the defendant more than $250. An affidavit supporting this application under Code of Civil Procedure section 491.110 or 708.120 is attached.

6. The person to be examined resides or has a place of business in this county or within 150 miles of the place of examination.

7. ☐ This court is **not** the court in which the money judgment is entered or *(attachment only)* the court that issued the writ of attachment. An affidavit supporting an application under Code of Civil Procedure section 491.150 or 708.160 is attached.

8. ☐ The judgment debtor has been examined within the past 120 days. An affidavit showing good cause for another examination is attached.

I declare under penalty of perjury under the laws of the State of California that the foregoing is true and correct.

Date:

▶

_____
(TYPE OR PRINT NAME)

_____
(SIGNATURE OF DECLARANT)

(Continued on reverse)

Form Adopted for Mandatory Use Judicial Council of California AT-138, EJ-125 [Rev. July 1, 2000]	**APPLICATION AND ORDER FOR APPEARANCE AND EXAMINATION** (Attachment—Enforcement of Judgment)	Code of Civil Procedure, §§ 491.110, 708.110, 708.120

278

APPEARANCE OF JUDGMENT DEBTOR (ENFORCEMENT OF JUDGMENT)

NOTICE TO JUDGMENT DEBTOR If you fail to appear at the time and place specified in this order, you may be subject to arrest and punishment for contempt of court, and the court may make an order requiring you to pay the reasonable attorney fees incurred by the judgment creditor in this proceeding.

APPEARANCE OF A THIRD PERSON
(ENFORCEMENT OF JUDGMENT)

(1) NOTICE TO PERSON SERVED If you fail to appear at the time and place specified in this order, you may be subject to arrest and punishment for contempt of court, and the court may make an order requiring you to pay the reasonable attorney fees incurred by the judgment creditor in this proceeding.

(2) NOTICE TO JUDGMENT DEBTOR The person in whose favor the judgment was entered in this action claims that the person to be examined pursuant to this order has possession or control of property which is yours or owes you a debt. This property or debt is as follows *(Describe the property or debt using typewritten capital letters)*:

If you claim that all or any portion of this property or debt is exempt from enforcement of the money judgment, you must file your exemption claim in writing with the court and have a copy personally served on the judgment creditor not later than three days before the date set for the examination. You must appear at the time and place set for the examination to establish your claim of exemption or your exemption may be waived.

APPEARANCE OF A THIRD PERSON (ATTACHMENT)

NOTICE TO PERSON SERVED If you fail to appear at the time and place specified in this order, you may be subject to arrest and punishment for contempt of court, and the court may make an order requiring you to pay the reasonable attorney fees incurred by the plaintiff in this proceeding.

APPEARANCE OF A CORPORATION, PARTNERSHIP,
ASSOCIATION, TRUST, OR OTHER ORGANIZATION

It is your duty to designate one or more of the following to appear and be examined: officers, directors, managing agents, or other persons who are familiar with your property and debts.

**APPLICATION AND ORDER
FOR APPEARANCE AND EXAMINATION**
(Attachment—Enforcement of Judgment)

Judgment Debtor Questionnaire

Full name: _____

Driver's license number: _____

List any other names used by you: _____

Are you married? Yes_____ No_____

If yes, complete the following:

Spouse's full name: _____

Spouse's driver's license number: _____

List any other names used by your spouse: _____

EMPLOYMENT

Your occupation: _____ Employed _____ Self-Employed _____

Name of your business or employer: _____

Address: _____ City: _____

County: _____ State: _____ Zip code: _____

Gross monthly income: _____ Take home pay: _____

How often are you paid? Weekly___ Every two weeks ____ Twice monthly ____ Monthly ____

How long at this business or job? _____

If less than two years, previous business or employer:

Name of your business or employer: _____

Address: _____ City: _____

County: _____ State: _____ Zip code: _____

Job Title: _____

Gross monthly income: _____

Spouse's Occupation: _____ Employed _____ Self-Employed _____

Name of spouse's business or employer: _____

Address: _____ City: _____

County: _____ State: _____ Zip code: _____

Gross monthly income: _____ Take home pay: _____

How often paid? Weekly_____ Every two weeks _____ Twice monthly _____ Monthly _____

How long at this business or job? _____

If less than two years, previous business or employer:

Name of spouse's business or employer: _____

Address: _____ City: _____

County: _____ State: _____ Zip code: _____

Job Title: _____

Gross monthly income: _____

FINANCIAL ASSETS

How much money do you have with you now? _____

How much money do you or your spouse have in banks, savings and loans, credit unions, and other financial institutions, either in your name or jointly? List:

Names and Addresses Financial institution	Account Number	Type of Account (Checking/Savings)	Balance
1. _____	_____	_____	_____
2. _____	_____	_____	_____
3. _____	_____	_____	_____
4. _____	_____	_____	_____

Do you have any credit cards? Yes _____ No _____

If yes, list all credit cards:

Credit Card Name	Account Number	Maximum Credit	Amount Owed
1._____	_____	_____	_____
2._____	_____	_____	_____
3._____	_____	_____	_____

Do you have any checkbooks with you? Yes _____ No _____
Do you have any credit cards with you? Yes _____ No _____
Do you or your spouse have a safe-deposit box? Yes _____ No _____
Name of institution and address where the box is located: _____
List of all persons allowed into the box: _____
List what is kept in the box: _____
_____
_____

Do you or your spouse own any stocks, bonds, or other securities? Yes _____ No _____
Where are these securities kept? _____
If with a broker, name and address: _____
_____

Approximate total value: _____
Do you or your spouse have a life insurance policy? Yes _____ No _____
Can you borrow against the policy? Yes _____ No _____
If yes, how much can you borrow? _____

Do you or your spouse own any notes, mortgages, trust deeds, or any other financial instruments on which you are owed money and/or receiving payments? Yes _____ No _____

If yes, list these instruments, the total amount owing to you, and the amount of payments you are receiving: _____
_____

OTHER PERSONAL PROPERTY

Do you or your spouse own any automobiles, trucks, recreational vehicles, boats, or any other vehicles, either separately or jointly? Yes _____ No _____

If yes, list all of these items:

Make and Year	License Number	Value	Owner	Amount Owed
1. _____	_____	_____	_____	_____
2. _____	_____	_____	_____	_____
3. _____	_____	_____	_____	_____

Where are these items located?
1. _____
2. _____
3. _____

REAL PROPERTY

Do you or your spouse own any real estate? Yes _____ No _____

If yes, list all such property

Address or Location	Market Value	Amount Owing and to Whom
1. _____	_____	_____
2. _____	_____	_____

Which of these properties is your home? 1. _____ 2. _____ None _____
Do you receive any income from any of these properties? Yes _____ No _____

If yes, list all sources of income and the amounts: _____
_____
_____

Do you rent your residence? Yes _____ No _____
If yes, complete the following:
Do you rent month-to-month or lease? _____
If you lease, how long is your lease? _____
Amount of monthly rent? _____ Is your payment current? Yes _____ No _____
If no, amount in arrears: _____
Name and address of landlord: _____
_____

Do you receive any income from roommates or tenant? Yes _____ No _____
If yes, amount received and from whom: _____

OTHER ASSETS AND INCOME

List all property not yet listed that you own, except household furniture, which has a value of $100 or more (include jewelry, machinery, business inventory, and any other items): _____
_____
_____
_____

List all income not yet listed which you are receiving or expect to receive (include judgments, settlements, bequests, inheritances or any other income), the amount and source of the income, and when you expect it.
_____
_____
_____

_____	_____
Signature	Date

This page intentionally left blank.

ATTORNEY OR PARTY WITHOUT ATTORNEY *(Name and Address)*:	TELEPHONE NO.:	LEVYING OFFICER *(Name and Address)*:

ATTORNEY FOR *(Name)*:

NAME OF COURT, JUDICIAL DISTRICT OR BRANCH COURT, IF ANY:

PLAINTIFF:

DEFENDANT:

APPLICATION FOR EARNINGS WITHHOLDING ORDER **(Wage Garnishment)**	LEVYING OFFICER FILE NO.:	COURT CASE NO.:

TO THE SHERIFF OR ANY MARSHAL OR CONSTABLE OF THE COUNTY OF
OR ANY REGISTERED PROCESS SERVER

1. The judgment creditor *(name)*:

   requests issuance of an Earnings Withholding Order directing the employer to withhold the earnings of the judgment debtor (employee).

   Name and address of employer   Name and address of employee

   Social Security Number *(if known)*:

2. The amounts withheld are to be paid to
   a. ☐ The attorney (or party without an attorney)   b. ☐ Other *(name, address, and telephone)*:
   named at the top of this page.

3. a. Judgment was entered on *(date)*:
   b. Collect the amount directed by the Writ of Execution unless a lesser amount is specified here:
      $

4. ☐ The Writ of Execution was issued to collect delinquent amounts payable for the **support** of a child, former spouse, or spouse of the employee.

5. ☐ Special instructions *(specify)*:

6. *(Check a or b)*
   a. ☐ I have not previously obtained an order directing this employer to withhold the earnings of this employee.
      —OR—
   b. ☐ I have previously obtained such an order, but that order *(check one)*:
      ☐ was terminated by a court order, but I am entitled to apply for another Earnings Withholding Order under the provisions of Code of Civil Procedure section 706.105(h).
      ☐ was ineffective.

▶

....
(TYPE OR PRINT NAME)   *(SIGNATURE OF ATTORNEY OR PARTY WITHOUT ATTORNEY)*

I declare under penalty of perjury under the laws of the State of California that the foregoing is true and correct.

Date:

▶

....
(TYPE OR PRINT NAME)   *(SIGNATURE OF DECLARANT)*

Form Adopted by the Judicial Council of California 982.5(1) [Rev. January 1, 1993]	**APPLICATION FOR EARNINGS WITHHOLDING ORDER** **(Wage Garnishment)**	CCP 706.121

This page intentionally left blank.

EJ-100

ATTORNEY OR PARTY WITHOUT ATTORNEY *(Name, State Bar number, and address):*
After recording return to:

TELEPHONE NO.:
FAX NO. *(Optional):*
E-MAIL ADDRESS *(Optional):*
ATTORNEY FOR *(Name):*

SUPERIOR COURT OF CALIFORNIA, COUNTY OF
STREET ADDRESS:
MAILING ADDRESS:
CITY AND ZIP CODE:
BRANCH NAME:

FOR RECORDER'S OR SECRETARY OF STATE'S USE ONLY

PLAINTIFF:

DEFENDANT:

CASE NUMBER:

ACKNOWLEDGMENT OF SATISFACTION OF JUDGMENT	*FOR COURT USE ONLY*

◻ **FULL** ◻ **PARTIAL** ◻ **MATURED INSTALLMENT**

1. Satisfaction of the judgment is acknowledged as follows:
   a. ◻ Full satisfaction
      (1) ◻ Judgment is satisfied in full.
      (2) ◻ The judgment creditor has accepted payment or performance other than that specified in the judgment in full satisfaction of the judgment.
   b. ◻ Partial satisfaction
      The amount received in partial satisfaction of the judgment is $
   c. ◻ Matured installment
      All matured installments under the installment judgment have been satisfied as of *(date):*

2. Full name and address of judgment creditor:*

3. Full name and address of assignee of record, if any:

4. Full name and address of judgment debtor being fully or partially released:*

5. a. Judgment entered on *(date):*
   b. ◻ Renewal entered on *(date):*

6. ◻ An ◻ abstract of judgment ◻ certified copy of the judgment has been recorded as follows *(complete all information for each county where recorded):*

COUNTY	DATE OF RECORDING	INSTRUMENT NUMBER

7. ◻ A notice of judgment lien has been filed in the office of the Secretary of State as file number *(specify):*

NOTICE TO JUDGMENT DEBTOR: If this is an acknowledgment of full satisfaction of judgment, it will have to be recorded in each county shown in item 6 above, if any, in order to release the judgment lien, and will have to be filed in the office of the Secretary of State to terminate any judgment lien on personal property.

Date: ▶

_____
*(SIGNATURE OF JUDGMENT CREDITOR OR ASSIGNEE OF CREDITOR OR ATTORNEY**)*

Page 1 of 1

*The names of the judgment creditor and judgment debtor must be stated as shown in any Abstract of Judgment which was recorded and is being released by this satisfaction. ** **A separate notary acknowledgment must be attached for each signature.**

Form Approved for Optional Use
Judicial Council of California
EJ-100 [Rev. January 1, 2005]

ACKNOWLEDGMENT OF SATISFACTION OF JUDGMENT

Code of Civil Procedure, §§ 724.060, 724.120, 724.250

This page intentionally left blank.

Notice of Right to Reclaim Abandoned Property
(UNDER $300)
(Personal Property — Civil Code Sec. 1984)

To: _____
(Full names of tenants, subtenants, and all others in possession)

Rental Property: _____ _____ Unit _____
(Street address, City, County, Zip)

When the above-identified premises was vacated by you, the personal property described below remained.

Unless you pay reasonable storage costs and take possession of the property not later than 18 days after the mailing of this notice, the property may be disposed of pursuant to Civil Code section 1988.

Because the property is believed to be worth less than $300, it may be kept, sold, or destroyed without further notice to you if you fail to reclaim it within the above indicated time limit.

Address where you may claim the property:

_____
(Street Address)   (City)   (County)   (State)   (Zip)

The personal property is described as follows: _____

_____

_____

_____

Mailing Date _____

Landlord/Agent _____

Address _____

_____

This page intentionally left blank.

Notice of Right to Reclaim Abandoned Property
($300 OR MORE)
(Personal Property — Civil Code Sec. 1984)

To: _____
(Full names of tenants, subtenants, and all others in possession)

Rental Property: _____ Unit _____
(Street address, City, County, Zip)

When the above-identified premises was vacated by you, the personal property described below remained.

Unless you pay reasonable storage costs and take possession of the property not later than 18 days after the mailing of this notice, the property may be disposed of pursuant to Civil Code section 1988.

The property is believed to be worth more than $300. It will be sold at public sale after notice by publication if you fail to reclaim it within the time indicated above. You have the right to bid on the property at the sale. After the costs of storage, advertising, and sale are deducted from the sale proceeds, the remaining balance will be paid to the county. You may claim this money within one year of its receipt by the county.

Address where you may claim the property:

_____

| (Street Address) | (City) | (County) | (State) | (Zip) |

The personal property is described as follows: _____
_____
_____
_____
_____

Mailing Date _____

Landlord/Agent _____

Address _____

_____

This page intentionally left blank.

EJ-001

ATTORNEY OR PARTY WITHOUT ATTORNEY *(Name, address, State Bar number, and telephone number):*

Recording requested by and return to:

☐ ATTORNEY FOR   ☐ JUDGMENT CREDITOR   ☐ ASSIGNEE OF RECORD

SUPERIOR COURT OF CALIFORNIA, COUNTY OF

STREET ADDRESS:

MAILING ADDRESS:

CITY AND ZIP CODE:

BRANCH NAME:

FOR RECORDER'S USE ONLY

PLAINTIFF:

DEFENDANT:

CASE NUMBER:

| **ABSTRACT OF JUDGMENT—CIVIL AND SMALL CLAIMS**   ☐ **Amended** | *FOR COURT USE ONLY* |

1. The ☐ judgment creditor ☐ assignee of record applies for an abstract of judgment and represents the following:
   a. Judgment debtor's

   ⌐   Name and last known address   ¬

   L   ⌐

   b. Driver's license No. and state: ☐ Unknown
   c. Social security No.:   ☐ Unknown
   d. Summons or notice of entry of sister-state judgment was personally served or mailed to *(name and address):*

2. ☐ Information on additional judgment debtors is shown on page 2.

3. Judgment creditor *(name and address):*

4. ☐ Information on additional judgment creditors is shown on page 2.

5. ☐ Original abstract recorded in this county:
   a. Date:
   b. Instrument No.:

Date:

▶

_____
(TYPE OR PRINT NAME)

_____
(SIGNATURE OF APPLICANT OR ATTORNEY)

6. Total amount of judgment as entered or last renewed:
   $

7. All judgment creditors and debtors are listed on this abstract.

8. a. Judgment entered on *(date):*
   b. Renewal entered on *(date):*

9. ☐ This judgment is an installment judgment.

[SEAL]

This abstract issued on *(date):*

10. ☐ An ☐ execution lien ☐ attachment lien is endorsed on the judgment as follows:
    a. Amount: $
    b. In favor of *(name and address):*

11. A stay of enforcement has
    a. ☐ not been ordered by the court.
    b. ☐ been ordered by the court effective until *(date):*

12. a. ☐ I certify that this is a true and correct abstract of the judgment entered in this action.
    b. ☐ A certified copy of the judgment is attached.

Clerk, by _____ , Deputy

Form Adopted for Mandatory Use
Judicial Council of California
EJ-001 [Rev. January 1, 2006]

ABSTRACT OF JUDGMENT—CIVIL AND SMALL CLAIMS

Code of Civil Procedure, §§ 488.480, 674, 700.190

292

<table>
<tr><td>PLAINTIFF:</td><td rowspan="2">CASE NUMBER:</td></tr>
<tr><td>DEFENDANT:</td></tr>
</table>

NAMES AND ADDRESSES OF ADDITIONAL JUDGMENT CREDITORS:

13. Judgment creditor *(name and address):*   14. Judgment creditor *(name and address):*

15. ☐ Continued on Attachment 15.

INFORMATION ON ADDITIONAL JUDGMENT DEBTORS:

16.　　　　Name and last known address

Driver's license No. & state: ☐ Unknown
Social security No.: ☐ Unknown
Summons was personally served at or mailed to *(address):*

17.　　　　Name and last known address

Driver's license No. & state: ☐ Unknown
Social security No.: ☐ Unknown
Summons was personally served at or mailed to *(address):*

18.　　　　Name and last known address

Driver's license No. & state: ☐ Unknown
Social security No.: ☐ Unknown
Summons was personally served at or mailed to *(address):*

19.　　　　Name and last known address

Driver's license No. & state: ☐ Unknown
Social security No.: ☐ Unknown
Summons was personally served at or mailed to *(address):*

20.　　　　Name and last known address

Driver's license No. & state: ☐ Unknown
Social security No.: ☐ Unknown
Summons was personally served at or mailed to *(address):*

21.　　　　Name and last known address

Driver's license No. & state: ☐ Unknown
Social security No.: ☐ Unknown
Summons was personally served at or mailed to *(address):*

22. ☐ Continued on Attachment 22.

Preliminary Lien Notice

TO _____
(occupant)

_____
(address)

_____
(state)

You owe and have not paid rent and/or other charges for the use of storage _____
(space number) at _____
(name and address of storage facility). These charges total $ _____ (amount)
and have been due for more than 14 days. They are itemized as follows:

Due Date	Description	Amount

TOTAL: $ _____

If this sum is not paid in full before _____, _____ (date at least 14 days from
mailing), your right to use the storage space will terminate, you will be denied access, and an
owner's lien on any stored property will be imposed.
You may pay this sum and may contact the owner at:

_____
(name)

_____
(address)

_____
(state)

_____
(telephone)

_____
(date)

_____
(owner's signature)

This page intentionally left blank.

Three-Day/Sixty-Day Notice
Notice to Pay Rent or Quit

TO _____

And all other tenants, subtenants, and others in possession of the property located at:

Address: _____ Space number _____

City of _____ County of _____

State of California

Rent on the above described property is due and owing from _____, _____

(date) in the amount of $ _____.

You are required to pay the amount owing in full within three (3) days after the service of this notice to _____ (Owner/Agent/Park Manager) or quit and deliver possession of the premises to the above party.

Failure to deliver up the premises will result in legal action against you to recover all monies owed as well as the premises and all other damages allowed by law. Failure to pay the money owed will also result in the termination of your lease/rental agreement.

You are also notified that negative information may be submitted to a credit reporting agency which may result in a negative credit report if you fail to meet your financial obligations.

_____   _____
Owner/Agent   Date

Proof of Service

I, the undersigned, being at least 18 years of age, served this notice, of which this is a true copy, on _____, the person(s) named above. The notice was served by:

☐   Personal delivery of a copy to the above named person(s).

☐   Delivery of a copy for each of the above named to a person of suitable age and discretion at the above named person(s)' residence/business after attempting to personally serve the above named person(s) at his/her/their residence and place of business (if known) and mailing by first-class mail a second copy to his/her/their residence.

☐   Posting a copy for each of the above named person(s) in a conspicuous place on the above identified property, being unable to personally serve a person of suitable age or discretion at the residence or known place(s) of business of the above named person(s) and mailing on the same date by first-class mail a second copy to each above named person(s) to the address of the above identified property.

I declare under penalty of perjury that the foregoing is true and correct and could testify competently if called as a witness.

Name _____   Date _____

WARNING

CALIFORNIA HEALTH AND SAFETY GODE SECTION 25249.6

CHEMICALS DECLARED BY THE STATE OF CALIFORNIA AS KNOWN TO CAUSE CANCER, BIRTH DEFECTS OR OTHER REPRODUCTIVE HARM ARE PRESENT IN THIS AREA.

Proposition 65 Fact Sheet for Tenants

Office of Environmental Health Hazard Assessment
California Environmental Protection Agency

This fact sheet was prepared by the Office of Environmental Health Hazard Assessment (OEHHA), which administers the Proposition 65 program. It provides information to tenants whose apartment managers and owners have posted or distributed Proposition 65 warnings.

What is Proposition 65?

In 1986, California voters approved an initiative to address their growing concerns about exposure to toxic chemicals. That initiative became the Safe Drinking Water and Toxic Enforcement Act of 1986, better known by its original name of Proposition 65. Proposition 65 requires the State to publish a list of chemicals known to cause cancer, birth defects, or other reproductive harm. The list has grown to include over 750 chemicals since it was first published in 1987.

What chemicals are on the Proposition 65 list?

The Proposition 65 list contains two types of chemicals: *carcinogens*, which can cause cancer, and *reproductive toxicants*, which cause birth defects or other reproductive harm, such as sterility or miscarriages. Some chemicals may be additives or ingredients in pesticides, common household products, food, or drugs. Others may be industrial chemicals, dyes, or solvents used in dry cleaning, manufacturing, and construction. Still others may be byproducts of chemical processes; for example, motor vehicle exhaust.

What does a Proposition 65 warning mean?

Under Proposition 65, businesses are required to give a "clear and reasonable" warning before knowingly exposing anyone to a listed chemical above a specified level. This warning can be included on the label of a consumer product or published in a newspaper. An equally common practice is for businesses to provide a warning at the workplace or in a public area affected by the chemical.

In recent months, many apartment owners and managers have posted or distributed warnings to notify tenants that they may be exposed to one or more chemicals on the Proposition 65 list. For example, a warning may be given because tenants are exposed to chemicals in pesticides applied to landscaping or structures or chemicals in housing construction materials, such as lead in paint or asbestos in ceiling coatings.

A growing trend among rental property owners and other businesses is to provide warnings for chemicals on the list, such as tobacco smoke or motor vehicle exhaust, which are regularly released into the environment in or near rental housing. In some cases, however, owners and managers are providing warnings to avoid potential violations and lawsuits, even though exposure to chemicals on the Proposition 65 list has not been verified. You should discuss the warning with the owner or manager to learn why it was provided so that you and your family can make informed decisions about exposure to any of these chemicals and your health.

Is my family's health at risk from exposure to these chemicals?

Warnings must be provided for chemicals listed under Proposition 65 if exposure to them may present a significant risk of cancer or reproductive harm. For *carcinogens*, the chemical must be present at or above a level that could cause one additional case of cancer in a population of 100,000 people exposed to the chemical over a lifetime. For *reproductive toxicants*, the chemical must be present at or above $1/1000^{th}$ of the level at which the chemical is determined to have no negative health risks (the "no-observable-effect level").

Proposition 65 generally does not prohibit a business from exposing people to listed chemicals nor does exposure to these chemicals necessarily create an immediate health risk. Also, as stated above, a warning may have been provided in some cases even though the level at which the chemical is present is actually too low to pose a significant health risk. It is important to find out why you have received the warning so that you can discover which chemicals you are exposed to, and at what levels, to determine how best to protect your family's health.

Where can I get more information?

Speak with the housing owner or manager directly to learn why you received a Proposition 65 warning. Property owners and managers are not required to notify OEHHA when they provide tenants with a warning. However, to obtain general information on the Proposition 65 list of chemicals, you may contact OEHHA at (916) 445-6900, or visit *http://www.oehha.ca.gov/prop65*. Following is a list of contacts for more information on Proposition 65 as well as chemicals that may be found in your home.

Type of Information	Contact
Proposition 65: Enforcement	California Attorney General (510) 622-2160, *prop65@doj.ca.gov*
Toxics Directory: Agency list	OEHHA (510) 622-3170 *http://www.oehha.ca.gov/public_info/TDHOMSC1a.html*
Asbestos Indoor air quality	Indoor Exposure Assessment Unit, Air Resources Board (916) 445-0753, *http://www.arb.ca.gov/html/fslist.htm*
Lead	o Lead Coordinator in your county government office o Childhood Lead Poisoning Prevention Program (510) 622-5000, *http://www.dhs.ca.gov/childlead/*
Tenant issues	o Department of Consumer Affairs (800) 952-5210, *http://dca.ca.gov* o Department of Housing and Community Development (916) 445-4782 or *http://www.hcd.ca.gov*
Basis for Warning Signs	o California Apartment Association (916) 447-7881, (800) 967-4222 or *http://www.prop65apt.org*

Index

About the Authors

John J. Talamo is a graduate of the University of Notre Dame and Detroit College of Law at Michigan State University. He is the author of *The Real Estate Dictionary*, which has sold over two million copies and is used nationally by government agencies, title companies, escrow companies, and real estate agents. In addition, he has written or co-authored several other self-help law titles, including the bestselling *The Mortgage Answer Book* and *Tenants' Rights in California*.

Mr. Talamo has taught real estate courses on a part-time basis for many years. He was also an adjunct professor at DeVry Institute of Technology in Ponoma, California, and taught law for thirty years at various colleges on the West Coast. He did all of this while maintaining his legal practice.

Mr. Talamo, while semi-retired, continues to writes from his home in the Las Vegas area.

Mark Warda received his law degree from the University of Illinois at Urbana-Champaign. He has written or co-authored over seventy self-help law books, including *The Complete Book of Real Estate Contracts* and *Essential Guide to Real Estate Leases*. He is also a licensed real estate broker and has taught numerous seminars on real estate law.

Mr. Warda maintains a busy legal practice, continues to write and currently resides in Winter Haven, Florida.